TALKING TICO
(Mis)adventures of a Gringo in and Around Costa Rica

ISBN-13: 978-1548607647
ISBN-10: 1548607649

www.JoeBaur.com

For Melanie, who constantly supports me (and my insufferably itchy feet).

Introduction

These stories are the result of notes taken over various trips throughout Costa Rica and around Central America. A selection of the stories featured were originally written as standalone articles for *The Tico Times* and other publications, but have been rewritten to some extent for the novel format. Everything has been recounted here to my best recollection.

I wrote this book, because this is the kind of book I like to read whenever I travel or begin to dream of living in a new country. You get travel stories all around Costa Rica with dips into Central America, a bit of history as I come across monuments or destinations with a backstory that I found interesting, and of course the opportunity to laugh at my expense for being the proverbial fish out of water. Plus there's not a ton out there in the realm of English literature that covers travel and life in Costa Rica outside of the guidebook format and blanketed takes on Costa Rica being an utopia where days begin and end at the beach. (Some days did, but not many.) With this book I hope you, dear Reader, will walk away with a better understanding of life and travel in Costa Rica and Central America.

Perhaps it will also be of some comfort to know that a small portion of proceeds will be donated to Centro Arte para La Paz and El Niño y la Bola, Salvadoran and Costa Rican non-profits I visit later on in the book. There exist so many works of art in the world that benefit from a country, a culture, or a people that don't see a dime in return. I'm trying to change that in my own *very* small way.

I don't say this to guilt others (well, a little) or pat myself on the back (well, a little), but rather so *you* can pat yourself on the back. By purchasing this book, you just donated to charity! See? Doesn't that feel nice? Yay, you! Worst comes to worst, those Lonely Planet guides aren't going anywhere.

Now talking about myself generally leaves me feeling a bit queasy, but it feels necessary before we set off to Costa Rica. Some things you'll learn about me are that I loathe cars and have a broadly unfavorable view of humanity. (We'll get into the details later.) Poop jokes amuse me (I get that from my mom) and I curse occasionally, but only when it comes out naturally. I share this now because the purpose of a travel book at its simplest level is to go on a trip with the author. Wouldn't you rather know from the beginning if we are going to get along or not? I mean, you wouldn't plan a camping trip with someone who makes you feel stab-y.

That said, I hope we do get along. Hey, maybe you'll even be one of those people I like! Whatever the case may be, I do very much appreciate your picking this book up and (potentially) joining me in Central America.

Let's Get Married and Move to Costa Rica

Moving abroad is an exciting prospect. It was something that intrigued me after my first overseas trip to Thailand and India in the summer of 2008 where I started to appreciate that a world exists beyond our political borders. I even pursued living abroad to some degree, foolheartedly so, sending my résumé to anyone who would look at it in Switzerland—a country I became enamored with during some genealogical research. Obviously that didn't pan out, because there are many strict requirements for hiring a foreigner in Switzerland and I was far from impressive enough to warrant such a hire.

Numbers are tricky on precisely how many U.S. citizens make the leap. The Association of Americans Resident Overseas uses some government info to make a broad estimate of four to seven million nongovernment-employed Americans living abroad. More interesting, a series of Zogby polls found that 1.6 million U.S. households have already determined to relocate overseas; 1.8 million were seriously contemplating a move; and a whopping 7.7 million were "somewhat seriously" considering it. These numbers have led to estimates of some three million U.S. citizens moving abroad a year.

I wanted to be one them.

So where could I go? I knew I wanted a country that felt foreign, but still relatively easy for a move. And what about my newlywed wife, Melanie? She's certainly no 1950s housewife, meaning she'd need a job. Seeing as work visas aren't easy to come by, we'd also need a country generally disinterested in going after foreigners without the proper paperwork.

The answer became clear: Costa Rica.

My brother studied abroad in Costa Rica and loved it. Plus you always see it high on those happiness index polls. Surely I would find happiness if we moved to the place that people dream of vacationing just once in their lives! The carefree, jovial spirit of the Costa Rican people within their natural, utopic surroundings would provide the international experience I sought. Of course in retrospect, anyone could smell that pile of trite bullshit a mile away.

It was settled. We were going to make Costa Rica happen.

While I can't pretend I was looking for some higher calling in life, waiting for "the universe" (barf) to give me answers, I can admit that part of me hoped to find some direction in where I was going in my career. Freelance writing was my primary gig at the time and hardly paying the bills. If some grand plan presented itself by the end of this little adventure, like Moses and the burning bush sans plague, I wasn't about to look the other way.

Feeling like I needed an academic motive to up the ante, I also applied to graduate school in Costa Rica at the United Nations-mandated University For Peace or UPEACE. Something told me that moving abroad for the sake of moving abroad would be frowned upon. By whom, I could never say. Perhaps it's cultural in nature. After all, as Americans we are taught from the moment that we can comprehend full sentences that we are citizens of the greatest country on Earth (despite lagging internationally on things that are kind of important, like math, science, early-childhood education, and infant mortality. We'll get you, Serbia!). This is the Almighty's chosen parcel of land where freedom, apple pie, and the right to a McMansion reign supreme.

Though I had already abandoned this coked-up, nationalistic ideology—thanks in part to previous travels and a heavy dose of Charlie Chaplin's satirical takes on trumped up nationalism that I studied in college—these things are bred into an American's DNA and can control you subconsciously. More often than not, we remain completely ignorant to this phenomenon as we continue to fear what we're told to fear, collectively nodding our heads to the popular consensus in order to keep the rat running with hopes of reaching the American Dream cheese prize at the end of the maze.

I was accepted to UPEACE, but had to postpone a year. Apparently they wanted money for this education I would be pursuing. Ridiculous, I know. (Europeans might not get that joke.)

Ultimately this worked with our timeline. Melanie and I wanted to get married before moving to Costa Rica to make it all easier from a legal standpoint. Plus, I guess we were kind of into each other.

The silver lining was that it gave us both time to mentally and linguistically prepare for our new home. I dusted off and improved upon my grade-school Spanish, and started following the news in Costa Rica. There was an exciting presidential election going on in which the incumbent and historical favorite Partido Liberación Nacional stood to lose to the more progressive Partido Acción Ciudadana. I took a strong interest in Nuestro Nombre Es Costa Rica's grassroots efforts to fight mainstream politics using social media, interviewing one of their members for one of my final articles before leaving. I learned that, like in the States, young Costa Ricans had become disenchanted with traditional political parties, income inequality, crumbling infrastructure and struggling schools. Most of all I appreciated their non-partisan efforts to get Costa Ricans to vote critically rather than along party lines.

Thanks to some familial connections, I was able to get a ring for Melanie that, I was told, would get the job done. I proposed on Christmas Eve, 2013, tricking her into a voting booth with a custom-made ballot asking her to marry me. (She loves voting and you should, too.) With her "yes," Melanie and her mother threw a wedding together in record time. We were married in July and had our tickets to Costa Rica less than a month later.

My cards were coming up aces. I had a beautiful wife, the kind where any objective person can tell who's the one settling in the relationship, and a new adventure ahead of me. On August 14, 2014, we were off to Costa Rica.

tico/a (*tee*·ko/a)
noun

1. The nickname of Costa Ricans, stemming from their tendency to add the diminutive "tico" or "tica" to denote that something is particularly small. It can also be used to denote emotion, such as a term of endearment.
2. "Los Ticos" can refer to the Costa Rican men's soccer team, popularized globally during their Cinderella run in the 2014 FIFA World Cup.

Example: "A Gringo visits Costa Rica and is instantly jealous of all the Ticos."

What the Hell is an Apostille?

When most people think of living abroad, they conjure up images of luxury and constant adventure: sipping a *cerveza* along the Caribbean coast, having an espresso outside the train station in Europe, and morning yoga at the ashram before another day of shopping. It's all just perfectly divine, right Sweetums?

Rarely does anyone imagine the bureaucratic nightmare involved with committing oneself to a significant amount of time abroad. It certainly wasn't at the forefront of my mind, nor Melanie's.

Me: Wanna move to Costa Rica?

Melanie: Sure! But let's check out the immigration procedure first, then we can Google Image some beaches.

Yeah, it didn't exactly go down like that, which I almost find surprising in retrospect. Melanie is someone who takes planning *very seriously*, proudly living by the motto of "Prior Planning Prevents Poor Performance," even for the more mundane aspects of life.

Me: Crap, I need to go to the bathroom.

Melanie: Why didn't you just go at the apartment?

Me: I didn't need to until we started walking.

Melanie: Well, you know what they say! Prior Planning Prevents Poor Performance.

Any destination with a significant immigrant or expatriate population will have relatively strict measures in place to ensure nobody overstays their welcome. Costa Rica, with its sandy beaches, preferable climate, and stable democracy is no different.

United States travel organizations strongly recommend having a return ticket purchased before making the flight down to San José for fear that either airline staff or immigration will expect you to have a way out of the country within ninety days, especially if you're from a country with a high emigrant population. For instance, any native of a Central American nation traveling to the United States needs a pre-approved visa due to the influx of immigrants from Mexico, Guatemala and El Salvador. Despite over a half-century of stability and the fact that most Ticos are more than happy to stay in their home country, Costa Ricans, too, must follow suit. Guilty by geographic proximity, I suppose.

Many U.S. travelers have also chanced it with just a one-way ticket. ("Chancing it" didn't fit into Melanie's *prior planning* framework, so that was out.) These are usually the backpacking types who don't know what hotel they're staying at once they land, much less where they'll be in ninety days. But for every dismissive story of carefree travel, there's a horror story of an American sent home—stories of being denied at the gate and being forced to purchase another ticket if they wish to continue to their destination. Others have reported back that immigration officials suspicious of a traveler's intentions will grant less than the typical ninety days.

Naturally these horror stories dominate the Facebook threads and TripAdvisor message boards, because life is basically an ongoing Yelp review. You only talk about it publicly if you have something to complain about.

To avoid any extra hassle, I intended to secure a student visa before our arrival. Doing so included receiving an FBI background check. Turns out having a criminal record before crossing political boundaries is frowned upon.

Unfortunately background checks are only good for so long. So instead of getting my background check as soon as I was notified of needing one back in early May of 2014, I was told to wait until early June after Melanie and I returned from two weeks of travel in Switzerland. This was to ensure my paperwork would still be valid by the time I finished all the required steps for receiving a student visa. Upon our return from Switzerland, I followed up with my university and was assured it was a good time to move forward with the background check. I diligently scheduled an appointment to copy my fingerprints and off they went to FBI offices in West Virginia.

I was not aware, however, that this process would take approximately six weeks. I recalled hearing three weeks—not a solid two months. So there we were in July, our wedding fast approaching, when I finally received my background check. As I suspected (and hoped), all was well. But I found myself in a bit of a time crunch to send my background check and visa application off to the Costa Rica consulate in Chicago so they could do whatever it was they had to do and schedule my appointment to approve my student visa.

Shortly after sending my background check, I received a call from Illinois. It was the consulate with some bad news regarding my documents.

"You need to get an apostille on your background check and birth certificate," a woman told me over the phone.

It's worth noting that before all this, I had no idea what an apostille was. The Internet told me it's "a form of authentication issued to documents for use in countries that participate in the Hague Convention of 1961." Well, that was the problem right there. I'm useless on Hague Convention knowledge post 1958 concerning the recognition and enforcement of decisions relating to maintenance obligations towards children. (Of course I looked that up.)

I assumed (incorrectly) that this would be taken care of by the FBI seeing as they're, y'know, the FBI.

Wrong.

"You need to get an apostille from either the federal secretary of state or at the secretary of state in Columbus," she explained.

Swell. More work. But it would all be worth it, I told myself ad nauseam, because the road led to Costa Rica.

We allowed for some time for the consulate to send my background check back to Cleveland. As soon as it arrived, I packaged it up with my birth certificate and shipped it off to Columbus via FedEx. I even included a paid envelope inside so Columbus could forward the documents straightaway to Chicago. Prior planning!

The package went out on a Monday and arrived early Wednesday. I then received a call from Columbus.

"We can put an apostille on your birth certificate, but we can't on your background check," I was told.

And why in the name of Lucifer's probing pitchfork is that? I thought to myself, replying with a far tamer version aloud.

"You need to take your background check to your bank to get it notarized. Then you need to take it to the Clerk of Courts in your county to get it county certified."

County certified? I said to myself. *Through how many hoops must I jump?*

Alas, my hands were tied. But at least Columbus could send my birth certificate on to Chicago while I finished up the background check. Since it took two days to get down to Columbus, I assumed I would get the documents by Friday morning—plenty of time to take care of bureaucratic nonsense and ship it again to Columbus.

Still, we were cutting it close. Our flight was in fifteen days from the morning I received that phone call from Columbus. I mostly kept my cool, but this was certainly pushing it past Melanie's liking. This is someone who the night before any trip will envision every possible scenario in which we'll miss our flight.

Melanie: What if two hours isn't enough?

Me: It's plenty.

Melanie: What if the train isn't running?

Me: There haven't been any notices.

Melanie: What if they can tell I'm nervous? They'll think I'm hiding something AND WON'T LET US ON THE PLANE!

Friday arrived and nothing was in the mail.

Surely Saturday, I told myself.

Nothing.

Okay, no problem. Definitely Monday.

Still, nothing. I decided I would give it until Tuesday afternoon before calling in. When nothing came in the mail that day, I called Columbus back. No answer, of course. So I left a voice message, explaining the need to get things moving along, ideally in a progressive fashion that would bring relief to the sudden throbbing pain I was experiencing in my brain.

There was no call the following day, so I tried again in the afternoon—now a week after my package first arrived in Columbus, for those keeping score.

I got ahold of the gentleman I had spoken with a week prior. In trying to figure out what could have happened, I asked what address he sent to.

"Whatever was written on the package," he told me, unwilling or uninterested in performing any kind of extra work to track it down. I persisted for more information and he finally relented to doing a search on his computer.

"668 Euclid Avenue," he replied.

Not good. See, Melanie and I had left our downtown address at the end of July, moving in with her parents for two weeks—the dream of all newlyweds and in-laws—before heading down to Costa Rica.

"Why did you send it there?" I asked. "I had our new address on the envelope."

The rest of the conversation boiled down to the gentleman on the other line vocally shrugging his shoulders.

At best, the package had been waiting for me at our old apartment. At worst, it was lost in forwarding limbo.

You can probably guess which one happened.

Talking with Melanie, we decided Chicago was out of the question. But this turned out to be a blessing in disguise. Traveling to Chicago at the last minute would cost more than the $200 fee I could instead pay in Costa Rica to change my visa status while abroad. Still, I needed my background check with all the necessary stamps, signatures, and God knows whatever else before leaving for Costa Rica in just over a week.

All we could do was wait and hope. As we waited, the consulate reached back out to remind me that I had a birth certificate just sitting there.

Oh, yeah. That.

I had to open a FedEx account so they could duly charge me in order to hurry the package back home to Cleveland. This was a Friday and they told me it would arrive by Monday. As long as it was before Thursday, our date with Costa Rica, we were happy.

Monday came and I received a call from our former apartment.

"We have a FedEx package for you," she said. "I think it's from Costa Rica or something."

Why this too was sent to our old address I'll never understand. My FedEx account gave the new address. I even explicitly followed up with the consulate to ensure they had the right address.

Ultimately it wasn't a huge ordeal. We could easily pick it up the next time we were downtown before Thursday.

I returned home, and what did we find in the mail? My background check, of course, with a generous three days to spare before our flight.

I double-checked my responsibilities with the Clerk of Courts. Contrary to what Columbus told me, I could simply get my notarization in their offices instead of wasting even more time at the bank. It was three-thirty at this point with an hour until government closed for the day. We hurried downtown in my father-in-law Patrick's hatchback.

I hadn't owned or regularly driven a vehicle in several years by design after experiencing in Chicago the marvels of life without a 4,000-pound polluting financial albatross. Plus they kill a lot of people, more than 30,000 Americans annually. Cars kill as many people in the States as guns. GUNS! When considering the world, cars end far more lives than terrorism or weapons specifically designed to kill people. (2015 saw 28,328 deaths worldwide due to terror attacks according to the United States State Department, and twenty-four percent of those deaths were the perpetrators of terrorist attacks.) Then add to that heaping pile of sadness the segregation caused by vehicular infrastructure and slew of health issues they either cause or exacerbate, like asthma and obesity.

Since graduating college, I never have nor ever will live in a place where I can't access everything I need by foot, public transit or bike. But in a race against the clock out in suburban Cleveland, this was the rare instance in which I actually preferred hopping in those metal bringers of death over transit or cycling. Seeing me in a car by choice is the equivalent of seeing a platypus in the wild—rare and like something went wrong.

On the way downtown, I called to ensure people would still be around. First, I tried a number I found online for the notary.

"Hi, my name's Joe Baur and I need a notary."

"You want to become a notary?" the woman asked. "You'll need to…"

"No, no," I interrupted. "I need something notarized."

"Oh, okay! I'll forward you to the right department."

After a quick hold, there was an answer. I again stated the purpose of my call. And again:

"You want to become a notary? You'll need to…"

"No!" I snapped. "I need something notarized."

Why in God's name was the assumption that my calling was in relation to wanting a new job? Do doctors assume you want information on how to get an M.D. when you call the office for an appointment? Methinks not.

Luckily we were able to get on the same page. Melanie dropped me off in front of the county courthouse. I ran in, emptied my pockets for security, and went on a hunt for room 101. In my haste I neglected to ask security for directions, prompting me to do a solid lap of the first floor, and a brief side-quest upstairs, running around like an anxious puppy trying desperately to latch onto a scent. Finally I took a breath and was able to find the notary's office quite literally next to security.

In the end, all was settled. My FBI background check, now a few months in the making, returned to my hands with all the necessary scribbles less than a day before our flight. All that was left was packing, which went by relatively smoothly considering we had to stuff our lives into two fifty-pound bags, two carry-ons and two personal items. Challenging stuff, even for someone like myself who considers himself a bit of a minimalist—by American standards, of course. But it did require several test weightings. What a sight it would have been if Melanie's parents walked in on us during that final weighing: me naked after a shower, slowly hoisting a bag to my shoulders like an Olympic Squat as Melanie looked closely at the measurement wrapped around the bag's handle.

Thankfully for all parties potentially involved, nobody came in.

Just before bed, we went ahead and bought a return ticket from San José to Cleveland for a random date in October. We had been working on plans for a border crossing to renew Melanie's tourist visa in early November but couldn't quite confirm everything in time for our departure. Rather than risk having to explain this to immigration in our evolving Spanish, we opted to purchase the safety flight with plans to cancel it upon our arrival and within the twenty-four-hour window airlines are required to give you for cancelling with a full refund. Plus it helped Melanie, who was certain immigration wouldn't let her into the country, sleep soundly on her final night in Ohio.

The morning of our flight was the kind of Cleveland morning I would actually miss: sunny skies and a cool breeze more like mid-autumn than August. We said our goodbyes, Melanie with tight hugs and tears as I refrained from showing emotion like a good Baur, and we made our way to the airport with plenty of time to spare. In fact, we arrived so early that we didn't even flinch when Melanie's carry-on had to be hand-inspected by the TSA. Turned out a Greek Orthodox religious icon of hers came up in the monitor looking like a weapon.

A Drummer Boy Slays A Gringo

I had some mixed feelings about starting our journey, our new life at an airport named after Juan Santamaría. This is nothing against Ticos. They have a perfectly reasonable reason for naming the airport after him. After all, Mr. Santamaría is recognized as the national hero of Costa Rica and was born in the city where the airport sits. He served in the military and died for his country in a valiant manner worthy of a Hollywood production (please, cast a Tico and not Jake Gyllenhaal with a tan).

Santamaría's heroism came on April 11, 1856 when facing a foreign invader attempting to overthrow the Costa Rican government. This contemptuous conqueror had already taken over Nicaragua in an attempt to turn the whole of Central America into a slave state. Take a wild guess as to where this foreign invader, with aspirations of empire and profiting off of slave labor, came from.

That's right, folks. One Mr. William Walker of Nashville, Tennessee is the villain in the story of Costa Rica's most prolific national hero. It seemed Mr. Walker had the idea of establishing English-speaking colonies in Central America for the sole purpose of committing all sorts of morally reprehensible deeds.

Luckily for the sake of the collective U.S. American conscience, Walker committed his atrocious conquest with private military expeditions. This wasn't the Union general trotting around on a horse through Central America.

As Walker swept through Nicaragua, Costa Rican president Juan Rafael Mora Porras called upon the populace to take up arms against the "filibusteros" or filibusters—then a term for anyone who underwent unauthorized military expeditions (rather than today's use for U.S. senators with the uncanny ability to hold their urine while reading the dictionary or a cookbook for an ungodly amount of time).

The Ticos met Walker on March 20, 1856 at La Casona ranch in Guanacaste and routed his army in about the span of a Super Bowl commercial break. They continued to chase him to Rivas, Nicaragua for another battle on April 11, 1856. Does that date look familiar? It does for a Costa Rican, because it was Santamaría's day for immortality.

Santamaría, a twenty-four-year-old soldier who joined the army as a drummer boy, volunteered to set fire to a wooden hostel where Walker and his men took refuge. The Second Battle of Rivas was bloody and the Ticos were unable to force Walker's band out of the hostel, which was an advantageous firing position. Soldiers, under the command of Salvadoran General José María Cañas, lit a torch and stormed the building. But again, Walker's men were set up nicely for picking off attacking soldiers.

Despite the likelihood of death, Santamaría volunteered to attack under the condition that someone would look after his mother should he, indeed, perish. Sadly, Santamaría was mortally wounded during his advance, the third attempt after two other soldiers had failed. But before passing, he was able to set fire to the hostel, drive Walker's men out, and give Costa Rica a decisive victory.

Of course, as with most things ripe for legend, historians argue over the veracity of the details in Santamaría's story.

Unfortunately there were no iPhones around to capture the shaky vertical footage, upload it to YouTube, and tweet out the heroism (#UnaAntorcha), but the larger point still stands. Many Costa Ricans continue to celebrate the story of a young Juan Santamaría rising from the rank of a poor campesino and the stigma of an illegitimate son to become a national hero. His story inspired a level of nationalism previously unseen in a nation of loosely connected provinces.

Today, El Erizo (or "the Porcupine" as soldiers called him on account of his spiky hair) is commemorated during the national holiday of Juan Santamaría Day on April 11 in Costa Rica. Walker, on the other hand, fell to the custody of Commander Nowell Salmon of the British Royal Navy, who had his own nefarious interests in Central America. Rather than return him to the United States, he gave Walker over to Honduran authorities who promptly executed him by firing squad.

Considering Walker's well-documented excursions in Latin America, there are still negative connotations associated with the United States and anyone holding a U.S. passport for some Ticos. Truth be told, Walker is hardly the only reason a Tico would be justified in holding a skeptical eye toward the United States. After all, Uncle Sam had a pretty reprehensible twentieth century in Latin America, especially with Costa Rica's Central American neighbors of Nicaragua, Panama, El Salvador, Honduras and Guatemala. History shows that the U.S. casts a large shadow over the region (the ominous kind that comes before something terrible happens in almost any film), tampering with local politics, contributing to genocide, and even injecting Guatemalans with syphilis. Yes, that happened, but more on all that later.

Regardless of the legend's accuracy, I still found a lovely touch of ironic humor in the fact that countless relocating and vacationing Gringos—myself included—must begin their journey through the gates of an airport named after a man whose legend exists thanks to his heroic efforts of dispelling a nefarious Gringo. I, however, was traveling with noble intentions, so thankfully the Ticos did not greet me at the airport gates with a flaming torch.

soda (*so*·da)
noun

1. Sodas are the lifeblood of Costa Rican society. The heartbeat of Costa Rican cuisine. It's where most everyone goes or drops by for lunch. They can range from a small shack with a couple of tables to a sit-down restaurant.

Example: "If you're ever hungry in Costa Rica, close your eyes, spin around and point. Then, open your eyes and you'll be looking at a soda."

Bienvenidos

After the pilot came over the loudspeaker to announce our initial descent, I made Melanie switch seats with me so I could stare out the window like a puppy. Wherever we were, it was immediately clear that we weren't in the proverbial Kansas anymore. All I could see was what appeared to be a perfectly combed beachside stretching along the western coast of the land beneath us. I had no idea if this was even Costa Rica or Nicaragua. Whatever it was, I felt an incredible sense of calm looking out the window over our new home full of lush green landscapes, rolling hills and serene coastline.

Further ahead, clouds began to form like a million pillows floating about in the sky. I had never seen so many clouds stretched together in such large formations. This was my vision of Heaven as a kid: angels bouncing from cloud to cloud with the same ease and normalcy as a morning walk on a city sidewalk.

We landed with a noticeable bump as the wheels hit the tarmac. I hoped it wasn't a metaphorical sign of our upcoming conversation with immigration. After pouring through dire Facebook warnings, we would finally find out just how strict Costa Rican immigration truly was.

An elderly woman who appeared to speak no English called us up. Unlike other border agents surrounding us who asked travelers basic questions, like the purpose of travel and how long said travelers planned to stay, our immigration officer asked nothing. She swiped our passports, stamped a page, and jotted down the maximum number of days allowed under a tourist visa —ninety—without even a glance.

All that preparation for crossing the border—getting our story straight like a couple of amateur bank robbers from the thirties and coming up with backup plan after backup plan should the worst happen—was suddenly moot. We were officially and legally in Costa Rica.

Outside of the airport, taxi operators hollered at us and tour guides offered their services as if we were walking through an auction.

"Where you going? Need a ride? What do you want to do? Are you going to the beach, my friend?'

The sun was strong and glaring through the clear blue sky, but the heat was hardly the sauna we had imagined. Straight ahead was Ramiro, maybe in his seventies with gray hair, glasses and a wide smile, holding a sign that read "Joe UPEACE" in blue marker on a dry erase board. He had been recommended to us as a local driver who regularly offers transportation to UPEACE students for a prearranged price that always comes out at a bargain compared to the official red taxis that have a reputation of ripping off passengers. Unbeknownst to us at the time, Ramiro was a pirate taxi—the very sort the guidebooks strongly warn against. Our first clue should have been that he picked us up in what was clearly a personal vehicle. He drove a light blue sedan comprised of a hodgepodge of parts from other cars. His phone was always buzzing with new ride requests he'd scribble down in a pocket-sized notebook.

We felt like we were in good hands with Ramiro. It was grandpa picking us up at the airport. No big deal.

Though the airport is outside of San José, we still got a taste of its notorious traffic. We were bumper to bumper, inching along like an elderly gentleman supported by a rolling walker. Finally Ramiro opted for a shortcut. This shortcut happened to be along a five kilometer, bumpy road running adjacent to the largest prison in Costa Rica.

"This is where the bad people go," Ramiro noted as he rolled up our windows.

The prison, indeed, stretched for miles. Barbed wire and security towers were ubiquitous. I could imagine what our parents might have been thinking if we were broadcasting a live feed of our travels.

"This is it. This is when they die!" horror film junkies would delight.

Carolina, our landlady who we had been in contact with via email, met us outside our new home as Ramiro dropped us off. She had a short, dark brown bob and was wearing a tank top and shorts—afternoon casual wear.

"Bienvenidos!" she exclaimed with a smile that immediately put to rest any leftover international moving jitters.

"This is Doggie and Blackie," she said, pointing to the small pair of mutts wagging their tails by her side.

Carolina then led us up the stairs to our new apartment. A note was in our door handle from our neighbor Andrea, a fellow UPEACE student from Canada, welcoming us and offering help should we need anything.

Melanie and I loved our apartment following the initial tour. The front door entered right into a living room furnished with a two-person couch, two chairs, and an old box television. This blended right into the kitchen, similar to our old apartment in Cleveland, so it was a natural fit. The kitchen connected to the backdoor and a shared patio with our new neighbor. The wooden floors of our living room and kitchen turned to white tiles overlooking the steep thoroughfare we just drove in on. To our left, we could see windmills spinning several miles in the distance atop the nearby mountains—so long as imminent rain clouds weren't blocking the view. The overhanging steel roof offered shade along with the help of some surrounding trees. In the hottest days, this would become our refuge. Nearly every morning started on this patio with a cup of coffee. Neither Melanie nor myself expected an ounce of luxury in our move, but this certainly made us feel spoiled.

Our bedroom was a bit smaller than back in Cleveland and Melanie noticed immediately the lack of closet space for her clothes—as in no closet whatsoever. I know, I know. Boo-freaking-hoo. With nothing but tee shirts and jeans, the transition was a tad easier for me. Plus I never had an issue with leaving my clothes out in plain view rather than "putting them away," as first my mother and now my patient wife have pleaded. It's a convenient system, I think.

What shall I wear today? How about that shirt at the top of the pile!

The system succeeds in its simplicity, but it's a system Melanie had never allowed me to embrace—until Costa Rica.

After settling in for a bit, we went for our first walk around Ciudad Colón. All we had to go by before was a Google Maps aerial that presented a grid-like street system and a couple of Google Streetview photospheres that displayed the center of town.

There was a bit more motorized traffic than either of us anticipated. It seemed similar to Puerto Rico, which we had visited eighteen months prior. Costa Ricans clearly valued their cars and noisy motorbikes, farting thick plumes of poisonous exhaust into the air. The constant drum of motors trying to get up the next hill could be heard invariably throughout town.

Sidewalks, also like in Puerto Rico, were a bit of a luxury. You definitely must watch your step, lest you stumble across a missing piece of concrete or plummet into an adjacent ditch. Never mind that the motorists themselves, guarded behind those thousands of pounds of steel, were the ones who had the final say in what would be a safe passing distance. I always preferred walking against traffic, especially without any sidewalks around. Melanie, on the other hand, always walked confidently, like a Tico, from day one. She never looked back even as the rumbling sound of a barely functioning vehicle neared. I, meanwhile, constantly peeked over my shoulder like a teenager in a nineties scare flick waiting to get stabbed.

Thankfully we were able to find the relative safety of some sidewalks within a couple of blocks of our apartment. In just one block, we had a Super Mora—a grocery store chain any North American would feel right at home in. Super Mora took up the majority of that block with a small church on the western corner that would fill our Sunday mornings with the cheerful hum of choral music as we sipped our coffee on the balcony (though we always felt bad for those who felt obligated to be in church on a beautiful Sunday morning while we foreign heathens enjoyed the great outdoors of Costa Rica).

After Super Mora was the town park of Parque Rafael, basically broken up into four quadrants: a basketball court that doubled as a concrete soccer field surrounded by a roller blade track, a playground for children, an open space anchored by a small splash pad, and a four-court sand volleyball pitch. The latter would prove to be our most frequented spot in town with many a weekend morning and evening spent embarrassing ourselves in front of a more highly-skilled Tico audience. Occasionally said court would be the host for regional tournaments featuring a variety of divisions broken up by age and gender. The last thing my ego needed was to challenge any one of those teenagers I saw on the court.

Continuing our tour of Ciudad Colón, we noticed the houses themselves were exceptionally well protected. Our modest abode alone would have required some welding to break into. I could only imagine the amount of programming required when entering and leaving some of the flashier homes in the cul-de-sac blocks of town.

The attention to security was a constant throughout Colón— regardless of the size of the house or state of repair. There were metal bars across the windows and gates protecting cars from an unknown yet imminent threat from an outsider. Melanie was initially alarmed, but supposedly the insistence on multiple layers of security has to do with an old belief that it speaks to how well a man takes care of his family.

Do you need a small army to breach your home? Then you're a man who cares for his wife and kids!

Something like that, I suppose.

We loved our walk around Ciudad Colón. As much as we could complain about the car-culture, it couldn't spoil the generally upbeat atmosphere of the town, the smell of fried empanadas emanating from the sodas that filled the central market, the busy green space and animated town center surrounding La Casa Cultural whose art screamed, *This is Latin America*. And this all was decided in just one walk.

There's the assumption that Central America is ubiquitously and always without exception unbearably hot. At least I was expecting to routinely sweat through my shirt, leaving unpleasant stains on my chest, back and armpits. To the contrary, I felt just fine in jeans and a tee shirt. Melanie was even more comfortable in a flowing dress (something I'm not so sure I could get away with). Being in the Central Valley meant some protection for the truly hostile heat and humidity that are staples of the Caribbean and Pacific coasts.

After wandering around a bit more in the evening, we settled on a seafood joint just south of the town center for dinner. I went with a plate of arroz con pollo and Melanie a chicken steak. We had later heard underwhelming reviews of the food, but that was hardly our experience, though I'm sure it didn't hurt that we had spent all day traveling and would have been thrilled with just about anything resembling edible food. A cold mug of Imperial (the beer of Costa Rica easily identified by its Germanic, black eagle logo) made it that much sweeter.

Our Spanish held up just fine, too, in our first experience dining in a foreign language. That is, until I asked for the receipt with an overly confident, "La receta, por favor."

The waiter, a smirk on his face, replied "La cuenta" and hurried off. A moment later I realized, I had asked for the recipe.

We took a detour back to our apartment through the center of town where Carolina had said there would be dancing. Underneath a large pavilion, which also served as the heart of the Saturday morning farmer's market, a small band performed a set list even Gringos can identify as Latino. A well-attended crowd of onlookers danced the night away.

On the walk back through Parque Rafael, we passed by the splash pad and basketball court that had since been taken over by skateboarders. We then made a quick stop at Super Mora to pick up the essentials of our new diet—breakfast cereal, milk, and a six pack of Imperial.

Though just a two-hour difference from home, the leap smacked us in the face as soon as we returned to our apartment. Suddenly that extra cerveza wasn't too appealing. But we weren't overrun with traveler's guilt, where we felt the need to force ourselves into our surroundings during a trip simply because we were there. After all, we knew we would be there for months to come. Ciudad Colón and that six pack would still be there when we woke up.

Our Tico Home

A closer look at our Tico home, I think, provides a more insightful analysis of the average Tico lifestyle than any Costa Rican guidebook or narrative can offer. You can read about border crossings, beaches and cities until your eyes dry out, but nothing beats a simple walkthrough of an actual living situation. It's necessary and something I wish more writers living abroad would discuss. These details matters. Not for practical replication, necessarily, but the home says something about a culture and the people living there. Looking Stateside, I'm sure an individual living in a McMansion with sprinklers shooting away throughout a California drought brings to mind a different person or feeling than someone living in a modest neighborhood home that has survived generations. To me, that same logic applies the world over.

How do you enter the house or apartment? Where and how do you prepare dinner? How do you clean dishes or do the laundry? I'm not entirely sure what that says about me—that I want to know how you, citizen of the world, salvage your dirty undies— but I do. It provides another level of understanding regarding life abroad. How one reacts to these changes says something about the individual. Suffice it to say, there were no shortage of scoffs from a handful of whiny North Americans when it came to, for example, doing laundry the Tico way. Meeting with recently transplanted travelers or following the various "expat" Facebook threads was a sure way to spot, to put it bluntly, a Gringo asshole.

Of course there's no right or wrong way to do laundry. The goal, as far as I understand, remains the same from Costa Rica to Russia. Looking at these details merely provides another layer to life abroad.

THE ENTRANCE

We entered through two metal gates. The first one was only about chest high—not exactly the greatest deterrent against criminals, but it gave the illusion of security. On that tiny gate, a tiny lock. We would have been fine leaving it unlocked, but our instructions from Carolina, typed out in broken English, asked us to lock everything anytime we left and throughout the night. Those instructions were laminated, so I assumed she was super serious about it. Like good guests, we complied.

Just past the first gate, to the right, was Carolina's home with her jovial husband Esteban (basically a Tico Santa Claus with a booming laugh to match). Though they have a gate themselves, a large sliding one that served as a garage door for their two cars, what little barrier there was between our two properties was minimal. Esteban and Carolina, in fact, frequently hopped over when it was time to feed the plants or they wanted to get our attention. This added to my theory that the first gates were not necessarily about protection.

The second gate, however, certainly must have been about protection. It blocked the way from wall to wall, ground to ceiling. We had to reach through one of the fence holes, same as the first gate, in order to access the lock. Just beyond there was the laundry machine, hose, and an industrial-style sink.

LAUNDRY

The laundry machine was shared between our neighbor, Andrea and ourselves. Nothing out of the ordinary. Instructions on how to use the machine, different than back home, intimidated us at first. Over time, it became second nature.

To begin, you had to fill up the washing end with water from the *manguera* (hose). Add two scoops of laundry soap, put the clothes in, and turn it on for about fifteen minutes. Then click over to *desagüe* (drain) to release the water, back over to the normal setting to fill it up again with just water, and repeat for three minutes. Drain it again and put some of the load into the adjacent centrifuge, which by my best estimation was a tiny clothes dryer that did its job by spinning around really fast, occasionally shaking the entire setup from side to side as if it were trying to come to life. Because no heat was involved, most clothes—athletic wear being the exception—had to be hung afterward to completely dry. We were later informed that the dryers we North Americans were accustomed to are cost prohibitive in Costa Rica. They drain power and suck up electricity.

UP THE STAIRS

Continuing on the tour, our washing machine was set next to a staircase of brown wooden steps that led up to a small, shared space between the two apartments for Melanie, myself and Andrea. The bookcase was filled with books on Costa Rica and Central America. A broom and its attached scoop leaned against the bookcase and an ironing board conquered the remaining space. More practically this was a small platform connecting our door to Andrea's. What's interesting is that we were still technically outside at that point. This wasn't a hallway between two neighbors or roommates. The fact that it was outside—though the tin roof did cover this area—made the units feel separate. But if you viewed the entire property from the front, you might think it was all for one family when in reality it's the Tico equivalent of the American duplex.

From this shared space, we entered our apartment. The door locked automatically, so we always had to be sure to bring keys along. Once while doing laundry, we forgot our keys, so we were left locked out between our apartment and the gate at the street entrance. Thankfully we only had to call out "Carolina!" a couple of times.

"Forgot your keys?" she said with a knowing smirk.

"Forgot our keys..." we replied, embarrassed at our predicament.

THE LIVING ROOM

Just through the main door, we walked into the living room with two chairs and a matching couch. All three had a soft green seat and wooden backing. For comfort's sake, we would sometimes throw a pillow behind us, but it was certainly doable for short sittings without. Admittedly, we did not love this couch when it came to watching something on TV or our computer. Staying positive, we decided the discomfort forced us to go be social and get out for the evening rather than remaining holed up as we so often would do with the comforts of our pillowy couch and Netflix account back home that have sucked countless hours out of our lives. (To be fair, those queues don't watch themselves.)

Separating the living room and kitchen straight ahead was a long, half-oval wooden isle where we would make a buffet line for tacos or keep a few books. Next to that was the "office," a simple computer desk and chair. This happened to be next to the fridge. Not a bad idea to have that within arm's reach, I always thought.

THE KITCHEN

The kitchen was, perhaps, most different than what I was accustomed to, but not in a bad way by any means. I actually preferred it in many ways.

First you would notice the sink area, which was the same height as anywhere else I've been in the world. The difference was that instead of cabinets, everything was open. Underneath the sink were two levels with all the plates, glasses and whatnot. I never had a period where I was feverishly searching for something, opening and slamming doors like a bad game show. Everything was there for us to see. No learning curve necessary.

What I didn't care much for were the ants. Specifically, hundreds of tiny ants the size of a needlepoint that would swarm any crumb or piece of food left out of for more than an hour—sometimes even less. Those bastards crawled out of everywhere —even the seemingly microscopic cracks between the wall and an electrical outlet. Melanie and I were stupefied the first time they invaded, marching in military fashion across the wall to whatever it was we left out. Probably cheese. Oh, they *loved* cheese. The best we could do was spray dabs of Raid over their path in hopes it would make others think twice. Those unfortunate ones left on the battlefield got swept up by a paper towel and unceremoniously discarded. That'd usually do the job, but it took just one scrap—*one freaking scrap*—of sustenance to draw them out again.

BED, BATH AND FRANKENSTEIN SHOWERS

Backtracking a bit, our bathroom and bedroom were to the left of the living room just before the kitchen. Our bedroom was simple with green and beige walls, unlike our blue kitchen and living room. A mattress expert might have more to say on the bed, but I found it to be incredibly comfortable and easy to drift off at night. The more difficult adjustment was the universal quiet of small-town life. I had lived in cities for the past five or so years. The sound of passing buses, trains and pedestrians was not only common, but relaxing white nose that lulled me to sleep. Pure silence screams MURDER to me. Ciudad Colón after 8 p.m. sounded like the middle of a wooded forest, unless there was a band playing over at the market or a soccer match on television.

The bathroom looked normal enough. That is, until you pulled back the shower curtain and saw the showerhead with electric wires coming out that, when working properly, heat the water. A former Costa Rican transplant later told me these are called "Frankenstein Showers." A monster of reanimated flesh was not exactly what I wanted to think about while washing my nether-regions.

I had actually already read about these being a regular occurrence in other countries. Electricity is expensive and the Tico showerhead heats the water up itself—not in a separate water tank a la the United States. Incoming Americans might find it odd to see electrical wires while showering, but the consensus we came to was that we would have heard by now if there were an epidemic of people being electrocuted from showers around the globe. Of course, that doesn't mean we escaped without a few embarrassing moments.

I remember my first shower being uncomfortably cold after the first blast of lukewarm water.

"Maybe they store the water somewhere and the sun heats it up?" I wondered. "I'll try showering in the middle of the afternoon."

That didn't work, so I tried fiddling with some strange, long hose that came out of the showerhead. I assumed it was for cleaning those hard-to-reach corners of the body without having to maneuver yourself like an Olympic gymnast. However, the duct tape on the hose's nozzle should've been a clue that this experiment wouldn't fare much better. Sure enough, it shot off like a rocket after applying any kind of water pressure, so our struggles with the shower continued for months. Not wanting to seem ungrateful or spoiled by our privileged lives in the States, we kept our mouths shut.

"Costa Rica can be a hot country," we reasoned. "Perhaps the showers are cold on purpose?"

That logic didn't hold up as rainy season afternoons gave way to chilly evenings and Ticos dressing in warmer attire. To our great Gringo surprise, Costa Ricans, too, get cold.

We finally brought up the issue with Andrea, who promptly laughed at us.

"My shower gets hot just fine. Too hot sometimes," she said to our disbelief. She invited us in to check it out ourselves. Indeed, the water was hot. We also noticed the motor in her showerhead was considerably louder than ours, so we went to Carolina, who also laughed at us.

In our broken Spanish, we managed to understand that Carolina wanted to cut the hose to fix the issue of the exploding nozzle. She then melted the open end with a lit candle to seal it shut as it dried.

"Mac-Geever," she said with a smile.

"Mac-Geever?" we asked.

It took a few moments of linguistic limbo, but finally we understood.

"Oh, MacGyver!"

"Sí!" she said, pointing to her MacGyver-esque tinkering that successfully fixed our little rocket-nozzle issue. A mechanic followed shortly thereafter to get our showerhead motor running properly, so it wasn't until January or so that we had a regularly functioning shower with hot water—just in time for Tico summer.

TOILET TRASH

Between the shower and toilet was a waste bin for all your bathroom happenings. Throwing toilet paper in a trash bin was very new to me and I wasn't exactly mentally prepared. Yes, I realize how absurdly privileged that sounds. I'm not trying to be a North American snob, mind you. I can get on board with these kinds of changes; I would just like a heads up when I need to do my business differently. I didn't even have to do this in India, and I think it's fair to say Costa Rica is in general a bit ahead of India in terms of its sanitation system.

The reasoning for throwing TP in the trash is because it doesn't decompose as quickly as waste, so it clogs up the pipes. It felt strange the first, let's say, *time* I used it. But I never gave it a second thought after the first few days.

THE BALCONY

Now back through the kitchen, we head onto the balcony with a second-floor view of the street right outside of our apartment. At this point we were actually above Carolina's house and often chatted with her from above. This was our most cherished amenity of the apartment and was a huge selling point when looking for housing online back in the United States. Many mornings and evenings were spent on that patio, either enjoying a cup of coffee and bowl of cereal or watching the rain pound like clockwork during the rainy season. Speaking of the rainy season...

THE RAINY SEASON

I never tired of that balcony, but the rainy season certainly overstayed its welcome. It left me longing for Cleveland weather. How is that even possible?

"When does the rainy season start?" a student asked during orientation at UPEACE.

"Actually, we're supposed to have rain now," replied the older official toward the end of his presentation. "Climate change has made the rainy seasons unpredictable."

The next day, a Biblical rain came that I swear didn't stop for two months.

Back home it had been sunny and warm with late sunsets that allowed for evening bike rides. In Costa Rica's Central Valley, the torrential downpour started as early as one in the afternoon, and didn't let up until well after the five-thirty sunset. I'd often come home from class jogging, because the rain had somehow chewed right through my umbrella. In those early months, Melanie and I went through umbrellas like rolls of toilet paper.

Who would have thought that the bad weather of Costa Rica would start to ruin my mood, like the bone-chilling winters of back home? I can't even recall how many times we stepped out onto our balcony around twelve thirty in the afternoon, watching the dark clouds roll in over the hillside.

"It's coming…" I'd mutter to Melanie with a cold dead stare as if observing a swarm of flesh-eating locusts.

We tried our best not to let the bad weather bother us, but there was no getting around it. Our days were shorter than we could have ever imagined, and our evenings were spent trapped inside. We tried turning to movies to occupy the time, but more often than not the clatter of rain on our tin roofs would overwhelm the highest volume setting, rendering even English dialogue incomprehensible. Once we even skipped Spanish class, turning back not even halfway into the already short walk because the skies dumped a rainy onslaught on us that sliced through another pair of umbrellas like we were Allied soldiers charging Normandy.

The worst was the foul smell of the rainy season—not to be confused with the admittedly pleasant smell of an incoming or even ongoing storm that reminded me of spring back home. I'm talking about the smell the storms always left behind. What in God's name it was, we'll never know. But something was coming out of the sink. At least that was our best guess. The stinky nuisance became too much when Melanie nearly vomited as she entered the bathroom in the middle of one night.

"I almost puked," she said, running back to bed. "It's the toilet trash. Can you take it out?"

And so I complied, rolling out of bed and into the bathroom, met with a smell that, indeed, was a warm cocktail of rotten eggs, sewage, and Lucifer's own passed gas. Squelching my own vomit, I quickly took the toilet trash out in the middle of the night like a totally normal person.

Frustratingly, the smell remained the next morning and was remarkably stronger since we had closed the bathroom door overnight. Eventually it became ritual that we trapped the smell in the bathroom while we slept. The following morning I would come out of our bedroom, close the door, open all the living room windows and the back door to the balcony, take a deep breath, open the bathroom door, and immediately sprint back to the fresh air of the balcony as that horrific smell seeped out of our apartment. This continued throughout the rainy season and we never did figure out why.

Tourism tries to brush off the rainy season by calling it the more palatable "green season." This propaganda wasn't working on me. Yes, it was green outside for the five or so hours of sunlight we got to enjoy it. But one can only stay inside so long, listening to the hammer of the rain on endless loop, before being driven to insanity.

The rain itself didn't bother me. I can enjoy a good rain, and at times, I was able to enjoy the Costa Rican variety. There were the cracks of lightning that sent a startled Melanie through the roof, and at first, I smiled in astonishment as I recorded one of our very first storms on my iPhone to send home.

"Can you believe it can rain *this hard*?" I'd say.

The novelty didn't last long as I turned into a depressed, lethargic mess. Rain is one thing, but this stuff was turning the two-foot ditches dug alongside the roads around town into heavy streams. And it happened every day! Like clockwork! Oh, and did I mention that the humidity from our daily storms would lead to mold growing on our clothes? Even my baseball hats!

Nobody should have to endure the rainy season. I wish it on no one.

I can feel some American readers scoffing at our living situation. We Americans really are an obnoxiously spoiled bunch, refusing to bear even the slightest inconvenience or discomfort. Feeling the summer heat? Crank up that air conditioning to sixty-five and change the season! Long commute because you choose to live thirty miles from your job? Find a politician who will build you a highway through poor people neighborhoods in the city!

Honestly, I didn't mind the adjustments to living in Costa Rica (the rainy season being the obvious exception). I expected adjustments with an international move. Besides, I liked not having the amount of space Americans have grown accustomed to. When you have space, you fill it with stuff you don't need— Made In China crap that collects more dust than memories.

Without much space, we were more selective. Our Tico

apartment made me realize that I never want to live in a place where I have rooms I don't use every single day. It seems wasteful and inefficient. The average Tico, on the other hand, appears to live rather efficiently starting with the size of their home.

That said, I'd be lying if I said there weren't days when I longed for a return to the apartment we had left in downtown Cleveland. It was one of those boilerplate new apartments popping up in reused urban spaces across the United States. We loved it. But what that Cleveland apartment most noticeably didn't have was a Mama Tica cooking delicious plates of gallo pinto for breakfast.

gallo pinto *(ga·*yo *peen·*to)
noun

1. Costa Rican's signature breakfast, but you're not actually eating a "spotted rooster" as it translates to English. It's a light mixture of rice and black beans occasionally accompanied by fried eggs.
2. Often paired with Salsa Lizano, a type of condiment like Worchestire sauce that is without question *the* nectar of the Gods.

Example: "More Lizano on my gallo pinto, please. I'll tell you when to stop."

Dabbling In Spanish

The sun woke us up, shining brightly through our thin white window curtain as if it were midday. Indeed, it wasn't even six. Being that much closer to the equator meant earlier sunrises and sunsets, and a consistency to the daylight unlike anything I had experienced before, living exclusively in the American Midwest where our time with the sun changes drastically from winter to summer.

As I had surmised the night before, Ciudad Colón was still there when we opened our eyes. We took our time getting out of bed (a bit dehydrated from the prior day's combination of travel and beer). Luckily Costa Rica's water is friendly to Gringo stomachs, the only in Central America, so there was no concern when I started chugging like a marathoner who just crossed the finish line.

A knock on the door finally dragged me out of bed.

"Buenos días!" It was Carolina, greeting me with a coffee pot in her hands. We had briefly chatted the night before, asking about the coffee situation as going even one morning without appeasing our addiction was not an option, lest we commit ourselves to a miserable withdrawal-induced headache.

I caused a bit of confusion in my Spanish, naturally, but was able to understand that she was inviting us down to her place for some coffee that she had already made. I understood this because I think she took pity on me and switched to English, which she spoke quite well even if she would never admit it.

We met Carolina downstairs, who after introducing us to some neighbors, guided us into her house. Like our apartment, it was small by U.S. standards. Then again, what isn't? After all, this is how most of the world lives. Perhaps we Americans with our football field yards that require vehicles to maintain them are the ones living abnormally.

Melanie and I both thought Carolina's home was quite cozy. We sat down at the kitchen table as she poured a couple cups of Café Britt coffee, which I remembered from when my brother studied abroad in Heredia, Costa Rica years ago. My father has imported the beans himself ever since.

Conversation was light at first; both Melanie and myself wondering if we should speak in English or Spanish. Among our reasons for moving to Costa Rica was a desire to improve our horrendous Spanish language skills. My experience was limited to a string of mandatory high school courses that never interested me for a variety reasons. First, it was hard to convince a teenager in exurban Mentor, Ohio the importance of language learning while living in a humdrum American suburb where everyone looked the same. I remember once seeing census information from my school and laughing when it read, "ninety-eight percent Caucasian." Even in my limited worldview at the time, I knew that was ridiculous.

Second, my last high school Spanish professor taught the language with a dry, monotone voice that could suck the enthusiasm for life out of a newborn puppy. His barren classroom was somehow always as hot as a furnace regardless of the season; add no windows and dim lighting and it was the perfect cocktail to turn the Spanish period into the proverbial siesta. (That word, I knew). I left completely convinced I didn't need to learn another language, because "everyone speaks

English anyway." If I could travel back in time and pummel the stupidity out of myself, I would.

Melanie, on the other hand, was the president of her AP Spanish class in high school. But when she moved onto college, she quickly realized just how unprepared she really was for conversational Spanish and bade her adieu to español. The same went for me, having spent just one day in Spanish class at the college level. How I was placed at an advanced level, I'll never know. "Advanced" is not a word that gets thrown around a lot in my presence—unless the topic turns to *Legend of Zelda* secrets, general Teenage Mutant Ninja Turtle knowledge, or walking people through the various plots of the *Rocky* movies.

Put plainly, I was not prepared for a class spoken entirely in Spanish. I dropped out and decided to fulfill my college language requirement by taking an online community college course that would transfer over to my university. I received considerable, let's say, guidance from an older Mexican woman in Southern California when I spent a summer out there interning at a movie studio.

Over time and through travel, I began to see the error of my linguistic ways. Language learning was incredibly important and I threw away some of my best years for improving upon a non-existent yet vital skill set.

As our move to Costa Rica became definite, I decided to tackle Spanish in the most affordable way possible—apps. MindSnacks took a game format to language learning that would have been just as suitable for toddlers as it was for me. Feed a frog by clicking on an image representing the word on the screen. Pop balloons with the matching phrases in English and Spanish. Help a penguin slide along some ice by rearranging words and phrases into the right order. (That game is over when the penguin falls into the water, struggles as the clock runs out, then suddenly remembers, "Hey. I'm a penguin. I can swim," and carries on merrily when the game is over.) For your efforts, you unlock new chapters and watch as your mariachi-dressed monkey-alien avatar hatches out of an egg.

Through forty chapters, I acquired a random arsenal of words and phrases that I was able to later recognize when I switched over to DuoLingo, which taught in a more academic fashion but at least gave me enough sense of accomplishment to continue trudging ahead. (Also, their owl mascot sheds a river of tears if you don't keep up your progress. Motivation.)

Still, my conversational practice was non-existent when landing in Costa Rica beyond writing to and speaking with Melanie, who was not in a position to correct me when I spoke gibberish. If I could play a tape recorder of our initial conversations, I'm sure it would have sounded atrocious.

In Costa Rica, I had no way out. I *had* to speak conversational Spanish and there would be no English prompts or translations to save me when I inevitably hit a wall. At least we had Carolina, patient and sweet Carolina. We really couldn't have asked for a better language partner or teacher.

Still, I was nervous, clinging to my helping of gallo pinto Carolina served us. I desperately wanted to try my Spanish, but I was irrationally thinking I would somehow offend someone. I'm not sure why this notion ever comes across my mind, yet it persists in others languages I dabble in. My French sounds like I'm mimicking Pepé Le Pew and my German like I'm stuck in singsong leading a children's preschool class.

But then I asked myself; am I offended when non-native English speakers try their linguistic skills on me? Of course not.

We started to come out of our Spanish shells when Carolina introduced her daughter and granddaughter. Carolina's granddaughter was just a couple years old and shy around strangers. Not that I blamed her. We very well might have been the first blondes she had ever seen, not to mention my skin is of a particular hue that could damage eyes on a sunny day. I must have looked alien.

Esteban, Carolina's husband who we briefly met the night before, more or less forced us out of our shell by his sheer presence. He came out of the shower with just a towel on around his waist, seemingly unsurprised to see a couple of relative strangers sitting at his table. He also didn't seem to mind being practically naked in front of us. So much for being a conservative Catholic country, I supposed.

After wishing us "Buenos días," he quickly changed and joined us at the table wearing a red polo and shorts. I already began to notice that most Tico adult men wear polos with jeans when out in public during the workweek. On the weekend, shorts are mandatory and shirts are optional for some of the older men on the hottest summer days.

As soon as Esteban sat down, he was off to the races, speaking exclusively in Spanish. Carolina had to occasionally jump in on our behalf.

"Esteban..." she'd start, cutting him off in mid-thought. "Slow down."

"Ah, lo siento... Eh..." I could sense the levers in Esteban's brain trying to pull back like a train engineer coming up on a curve. He'd manage well enough for a while before getting wrapped up in another story, then Carolina would remind him again to back off the gas.

On the whole, I think we managed to hold our own okay. We discovered that both Carolina and Esteban enjoyed spinning, which Melanie mentioned she would be teaching at a gym in town. Esteban also enjoyed mountain biking, but was not shy in admitting that he could only handle so much.

"I think I need to do a little more," he said, patting his round belly and setting up another one of his already familiar Santa laughs.

With that, we thanked our new Tico family for the breakfast and headed back upstairs to our apartment for more unpacking. The fortunate thing about moving into a furnished apartment is how easy it is to get settled. It was something we kept telling ourselves while packing up our lives in Cleveland. At least we could put off moving all the large furniture, we agreed. It would be Future Joe and Future Melanie's problem.

Meantime, we had to finishing christening our move with a proper trip to the grocery store. If it didn't already feel real that we were, in fact, living in Costa Rica, filling the refrigerator with actual food would solidify it.

We found Super Mora to be the easiest transition for fellow North Americans, although there were a number of other stores (or pulperías) in town. Separated aisles with the various toiletries, bocadillos (snacks), and ingredients you need to get by felt no different to us than shopping in the States (save the Spanish interactions at checkout where we quickly learned that the exasperated mumbling sounds made by the teenaged employee behind the counter meant they wanted to see our ID).

Later that day, we started communicating with some other UPEACE students via a Facebook group setup to help make introductions a tad easier and less awkward than inevitable classroom icebreakers. We made plans to meet up with a couple of folks at the cultural center in the heart of Ciudad Colón where families gather for casados al fresco, old friends chat on park benches, and everyone shops at the weekly farmers market. Of those invited, we ended up meeting just Hannah and Lisa.

Hannah won the most interesting background award. She came from Sweden, but had not lived there for more than a decade. She identified as more American than Swedish after getting her undergrad in San Francisco, California, but ultimately she was Brazilian, hailing from Rio de Janeiro.

Although she insisted on needing Spanish lessons, her Portuguese seemed to flow nicely into Spanish without any hiccups, at least as far as I could tell.

Lisa came from France and seemed a bit younger than either Hannah or myself. Likewise, she was looking for a new educational opportunity abroad to further her career, specifically in her case working in Africa. Of course being a manageable trip away from either the Caribbean or Pacific beaches of Costa Rica wasn't exactly a rough selling point.

The four of us walked to a nearby line of shop stalls. These were a set of doors that opened into a small kitchen with a display of options alongside the menu out front. Most were closed for the Mother's Day holiday, but we were at least able to get a juice made from fruits we had never heard of. Hannah did the ordering, hers being the best and most confident Spanish.

I went with cas—a tart juice drink that tasted like a cross between a kiwi and a grapefruit mixed with sugar and water. Delicious. (Bonus points, I learned it's a source of fiber and helps prevent cancer.) We then went for a jaunt around town, locating the gym where Melanie would be working. Along the way we had the obligatory chat about our respective backgrounds before diving into thoughts about the university we had signed up for. Hannah indicated hearing of some issues with the university, but didn't want to turn us off on our decision to come. She promised to share a report written by last year's student union later on—a report I later read and finished with indifferent shoulders shrugged. The gist was a list of complaints students had with the university, including questioning their responsibility for a student's safety off-campus. Evidently there had been a couple of incidents the previous year.

I, however, am not the activist type and was not looking to get heavily involved with student unions or raw-raw fighting for change. Good for those who were, but I didn't see myself having an effective role to offer as a student in an accelerated program who would be gone in less than a year. Plus, there's always the tendency to get involved in as many programs as possible with the excitement of starting something new, only to inevitably have to cut your schedule as you settle in and either find new interests or realize you've taken on too much. Any free time I had would be devoted to traveling and learning as much as I could from Costa Rica, improving my Spanish and writing portfolio along the way. As sublime as the campus was, my sense was always that I would get more out of my time abroad outside of the classroom.

Before heading our separate ways, Hannah suggested taking the bus to San José the next morning after a workout at the gym. We agreed, but Lisa had to pass as she already had plans to tour Guanacaste's Pacific coast. *Poor her*, I thought.

casado (ka·*sa*·do)
noun

1. Literally, "married" in English.
2. The staple dish of Costa Rica, generally comprised of black beans, white rice and meat, (such as chicken, pork or beef), a plantain and small salad.
3. It's the "marrying" together of ingredients.
4. A necessity following any rigorous hike.

Example: "That casado made me hurt so good."

Decapitated Jesus Leads the Way to San José

Most of what I had read about San José suggested avoiding it at all costs. Even the one guidebook that did suggest making a visit did so only because it's the capital. They otherwise made it seem as if stepping foot in San José was an invitation to get robbed.

Tico Thief: Sound the alarm, fellas! There's a Gringo in town!

I'm ashamed to admit that reading these warnings made me a tad paranoid, and I'm usually drawn toward the unknown despite growing up in homogenous, suburbanized America where safety is familiarity. If we had listened to the prevailing *wisdom*, we would have arrived in Costa Rica and locked ourselves away until it was time to bugger off to beaches protected by resort security. It's a mentality I've never understood—the throngs of American tourists who will travel to sealed off resort compounds in Mexico or Central America, surrounded by people who look exactly like them. Why not just go to Florida, the Carolinas, or Southern California if all you want is a beach and sunburn?

The bus was easy to pick up from Ciudad Colón. We met Hannah by the cultural center with two new friends from South Korea. Andrea joined on a last minute invitation. Both Andrea and Hannah had made prior visits to San José, giving us first-timers even less to worry about.

Right on cue, a large Greyhound-style bus colored in orange and white came rolling up through Calle Central. Some Costa Ricans call their bus "la nave," which translates literally to, "the ship." I found this charming not because buses are obviously not ships, but rather it made a certain amount of sense. With no street signs, San José can be impossible to navigate for a novice. The only way to get by is with a captain behind the wheel who has a mental map that manifests three-dimensionally like something out of *A Beautiful Mind*.

Fare was 490 colón, just under $1 to travel twenty kilometers to the capital of the country. Not bad. The driver, a curmudgeonly-looking older man, exchanged our paper bills for change in his wooden box lined with various denominations of colónes coins. Tico bus drivers must have the dexterity of a stage magician the way they handle all those coins, sifting through them and delivering out change to thousands of riders in any given shift.

Without knowing the transit system, one could guess that we boarded near the beginning of the forty-minute route to San José. If you did the math, yes, we were traveling quite slow, our speed dictated by both traffic and somewhat prevalent speed bumps used to slow motorists. The driving reminded me again of Puerto Rico, which was similarly chaotic with a loose observance of stop signs (to put it generously). At least we had those speed bumps to bring some sanity to it all.

We did hop onto what felt like a traditional freeway as we inched closer to San José's inner-ring suburbs, but it didn't seem entirely like the U.S. variety, because the bus was still making stops. In fact, we saw plenty of cyclists and pedestrians mixing it up with high-speed traffic along the ninety-kilometer-per-hour *pista* without a hint of fear. I, on the other hand, was on the verge of empathetically soiling myself.

Along the highway there were the clear remnants of Uncle Sam's handiwork. Auto-oriented plazas with name-brand fast food artery cloggers were aplenty. Entire swaths of land were dedicated to American chain hotels with either an Applebees or a strip mall across from a giant, mostly empty parking lot. I presumed this was to give American businessmen and women traveling to San José the opportunity to continue the perceived safety of the great American suburban bubble while traveling to a foreign country.

Our bus itself was coated in religious imagery. At the front hanging over the driver, there was the image of what I call "Decapitated Jesus," which is Christ's head with the crown of thorns looking sad at all those below him. (To be fair, I'd be sad too if I were decapitated.) Underneath read the words, "El Señor guia mis manos" or "God guides my hands." Based on the more aggressive driving style, I found my generally agnostic-self praying that a deity *was* guiding the driver's hands.

Passengers filled the bus along the route. This was troubling considering it was already quite full by the time it reached Ciudad Colón. Throngs of sweaty passengers shuffled to the back until there was no more aisle to fill. Personal space went out the window. Strangers had to make their peace with the idea of someone's sweaty stomach or groin brushing up against their shoulders, or worse, their face. At least it was all done in as polite and friendly manner as possible under such circumstances.

We arrived at an obsolete Coca-Cola bottling facility after a bumpy, jerky ride through quiet city streets. Though the bottles were long gone, the station and surrounding neighborhood are still referred to as "Coca-Cola." This, of course, proves terribly confusing to foreigners unaccustomed to traveling in a country with no use for addresses. Directions are commonly given using obsolete landmarks and other former points of interest. So if you travel to San José and see a wandering tourist desperately searching for the tree where they're supposed to turn right, you know why.

The station itself was quite lively as it was the end of the line and everyone was departing. Here is where the guidebooks endlessly warned of pickpockets.

Guidebooks: Eyes to the front, hands on your personal possessions, and for God's sake, stay vigilant, man!

Lo and behold, we survived just fine.

Hannah led the way as we wandered through nameless thoroughfares. One aspect the guidebooks did get right is the architecture. It is, on the whole, quite bland. Grey, concrete buildings stood as far as I could see. Traffic was steady with the exhaust of idling cars clouding up the fresh air. Much of San José looked like an image of Soviet-style Brutalism architecture —nothing to write home about.

Before long we happened upon a pedestrian thoroughfare, Avenida Central, which stretched for more blocks than we were even interested in walking. You hardly see this attention to pedestrians in much larger cities in more industrialized nations. It was a relatively recent addition to San José, but certainly a welcomed one.

As we marched forward, a couple of buildings stuck out among the mundane. First, the post office. From a distance I wondered if it was the national theater, a site I had read was the architectural accomplishment of Costa Rica.

Wrong. It was, as signs indicated, the post office. Colonial, large and quite enjoyable to stare at for a few moments as one does when admiring a building. I found it amusing that of all the drab buildings, they really decided to nail the post office. And nail it they did.

We did eventually find Teatro Nacional and it was, as

advertised, a sight to see. It would have felt right at home in some of the most architecturally interesting neighborhoods of Europe. Neo-classical in style with three statues perched on top that look like Michelangelo's handiwork and surrounded by checkered tiles on the front that bleed into the adjacent pedestrian plaza where kids chase pigeons.

Continuing along the pedestrian thoroughfare, I began to notice the businesses whose doors opened right out onto the street. Sports apparel stores and women's clothing were the primary merchants. There were a number of American chain restaurants alongside lesser-known, second-tier chains, and Ticos selling bootlegged copies of DVDs sprawled across the middle of the street. When cops came past, the hagglers were quick to snag their wares and move away faster than a cartoon dash. There seemed to be an unspoken agreement between them and the police. If the authorities truly wanted to crack down on pirated DVDs, methinks those folks wouldn't be camped out along the most popular pedestrian thoroughfare in the capital city in broad daylight. The cops would only swagger through occasionally, perhaps out of boredom.

Then there were the calls of, "Kolbi, Claro, Movistar!" by vendors selling subscriptions to the various mobile and television providers of Central America. Of all my memories of San José, that sticks out the most. There was a calming rhythm to it.

"Kolbi, Claro, Movistar!"

Step, step.

"Kolbi, Claro, Movistar!"

Step, step and repeat.

But the king of Avenida Central? That's the 134-year-old Mercado Central or San José Central Market. The entrance came right up to the street with "Bienvenidos" in distinct red lettering. The exterior wasn't much, but an alluring cacophony of over 200 shops and stalls side-by-side with the sodas awaited inside. Myself, Melanie, and the rest of our small crew shuffled our feet across the concrete floors and through narrow aisles. Experienced Ticos, usually slower and more laid back in the walking department, sliced through our indecision. Eventually we decided to follow the smell of the sodas—namely rice and chicken—and grab lunch.

There was a mixture of stalls where you walk up and grab, say, an empanada and split within ten seconds, but others wanted a more casual sit-down restaurant. Outside the latter, waiters stood with open menus and tried to usher us into their establishment.

"Muy rico!" they'd repeat enthusiastically with a fake grin as if their boss were watching, assuring us of their delicious food we couldn't possibly find anywhere else.

I had never experienced anything like this back in the States. Little did I know that it's how things work in Latin America, especially in tourist corners. In the States, I think most would feel a sudden rush of shyness if someone started bellowing out to them about their *can't miss* restaurant. It took some getting used to on my end, as I found it rather obnoxious, sending me to an irrational fit of rage. My rule became that I wouldn't go to a restaurant if the staff thought I was dumb enough to go in because they yelled at me.

Finally we settled on a soda with stools circling the counter. (They didn't yell.) The servers scribbled our order on a small piece of paper, sent it up a small hand-crank elevator, and it magically returned with food minutes later. Brilliant.

It was here where I had my first casado topped with a healthy helping of Lizano—a staple of Tico tables. I eagerly dove in and fell in love with that first, warm bite. If Lizano were a religion (or cult—what do I care?) I would convert. Casados and I were going to be great friends, I could already tell.

Belly full, we continued back west toward Parque Metropolitano La Sabana having heard it was something to see. Getting there entailed a rather ugly walk along Paseo Colón that would, unfortunately, make any U.S. Americans feel right at home with its obnoxiously wide vehicle lanes lined with a number of fast food chains. We eventually ran into the entrance of the park marked by a monument of León Cortés Castro next to the Costa Rica National Art Museum. I promptly mounted the statues of lions that sat at the monument's base for a photo of the occasion.

Surprisingly, I later learned that Cortés had a connection to Nazi Germany. He served as Costa Rica's president from 1936 to 1940, a standard four-year term for a country that doesn't permit presidents to run in back-to-back elections. The conservative leader did attempt to change the constitution at the end of his term to allow for re-election but eventually backed off. Probably a good thing, ultimately; I know of few countries whose leader changed the constitution to keep them in office and saw it lead to further prosperity. Instead, he left with a reputation of reforming the banks and establishing new ports in Quepos and Golfito. His streak of construction projects gave him the moniker of the "iron bars and cement administration," but his legacy remains tainted due to his interest in European fascism of the era. In fact, he controversially appointed a man named Max Effinger to his government's immigration post. Mr. Effinger was also the head of the Costa Rican Nazi Party and barred Polish Jews who escaped Nazi Germany from entering the country. Hard to believe that Costa Rica had a Nazi Party, much less one active enough to slip its way into actual governance. In any event, for some reason there's a dignified monument to Cortés outside of charming La Sabana. Standing about a hundred feet behind that monument? A Jewish menorah.

La Sabana stretches its roots back to 1783 when the parish

priest of San José, Manuel Antonio Chapuí de Torres, donated the parkland and its surroundings, "in order to favor Costa Rica's interests." For a great while, that meant sports and other recreational activities that sought to preserve the area's green legacy.

Flash forward, the park was home to Costa Rica's second international airport in 1940 under the leadership of the aforementioned Cortés until 1955 when they moved it to its current location in Alajuela. It wasn't until the administration of President Daniel Oduber Quirós, who created the Costa Rica National Art Museum in the mid-seventies, that the ball really started rolling for La Sabana. At the end of his term in 1978, he started construction on the majority of the park's installations with the help of José Antonio Quesada—the architect charged with the task of designing La Sabana. With new trees, shrubs and bushes planted, President Oduber declared La Sabana a Metropolitan Park and the "lungs of Costa Rica." In 2001, the park was declared a National Architectural Heritage by an Executive Decree. (Solid decreeing, I must say.)

We continued through the park entrance onto paved trail alongside rubber trees that appeared to be colored in tie-dye for some reason that wasn't immediately clear. There was a stark juxtaposition between leafy La Sabana and the mess of urbanity that was San José behind us. We quickly began to realize just how enormous the park was, perhaps one of the largest urban green spaces I had ever seen outside of Manhattan's Central Park. (The lungs of Costa Rica, indeed.) Small ponds and trails spread across the park. A pair of Tico couples were out on paddle boats, casual joggers moved swiftly over the running trails, and a small group of old women fed a handful of ducks with their chirping ducklings.

"Que lindo," said one in admiration.

Continuing through the park, it was impossible to miss

Estadio Nacional—San José's most important building if you ask a soccer-obsessed Tico—where La Sele, the national team of Costa Rica, plays their home matches. Since the original stadium's demolition and reconstruction in 2008 (a gift from China), it has also become host to the transfer of power between presidential administrations. Maybe more Americans would care about U.S. politics if we held presidential ceremonies at football stadiums.

Announcer: And here comes the President of the United States, marching toward the fifty-yard line to give the State of the Union! *Are you ready for some speaking!*

As a foreigner whose soccer allegiance to the Ticos can only be so deep, I appreciated more the running paths that crisscrossed throughout La Sabana and surrounding Estadio Nacional. There were basketball courts, a roller-skating rink, and picnic benches that gave Ticos a place to either let out some steam or relax over the weekend. In my travels, I have found that far too few cities value green space. At best, they'll leave a plot of green space the size of a basketball court next to a parking lot twice as large and pat themselves on the back. La Sabana, however, was something special. Something you could come back to time and time again.

We spent our last moments in San José sitting at a park bench, watching some kids practice their roller blading. Runners covered the larger blue track surrounding the rink. Before long, the rainy season clouds rolled in and sent us walking quickly to the adjacent bus stop.

I left appreciating the opportunity to have already experienced something in Costa Rica that the average Gringo tourist skips—San José or Chepe as the Josefinos call it. I can't say I blame them for the misstep. The guidebooks erroneously treat it like an elephant graveyard. With limited time, I get why most would just hop scotch right over to the beach or jungle. Contrary to most travelers, I had the luxury of time, and coupled with a natural curiosity, I was able to get a taste of San José. Besides, it would have been insane for me to avoid it living just twenty-some kilometers away.

Was it a mess? Absolutely. You don't need a degree in urban planning to figure out that much of San José was constructed on the fly. Were there ugly buildings and trash? Yep. But there were throngs of Josefino pedestrians breathing life into the city, pedestrian boulevards, Ticos enjoying a beverage or meal on a restaurant balcony, inviting green space, and a smattering of buildings and monuments that were pleasing to the eye.

Perhaps it's because I come from a city once constantly beleaguered as unworthy of a visit. Indeed, I have found in my travels that I do most identify first and foremost with cities, especially those dismissed as too boring or too dangerous. San José gets a similar rap from Ticos and travelers alike, so maybe it's no wonder I had such a successful first visit. In any event, I already knew a return was in order.

Why not next weekend?

Chepe: Nobody Wants to Get the Gringos

I delayed my first visit to the universally celebrated beaches of Costa Rica for a second trip to Chepe. Like our first visit, the second spawned out of an invitation from fellow classmates, but I also wanted to return for a bit of vindication. You see, I was miffed with myself for traveling so guarded based on the advice of guidebooks when in reality I found San José to be just as safe as any North American city. In fact, they only time I've ever felt mildly threatened in my travels was in Cincinnati. Not Asia, Europe or Latin America—Cincinnati, right in the heartland of America. I was in their Over-The-Rhine neighborhood snapping some pictures for a story when a guy charged toward me from across the street.

"Careful with that camera. There're people here who wouldn't like you taking their picture."

(That aside, both Cincinnati and Over-The-Rhine are fantastic. You should visit.)

Surprise, surprise, we left San José unscathed. There were no invisible targets on our backs, no cries to "get the Gringos!" and steal our cameras. Melanie agreed that the warnings seemed inflated, but I guess that's what you get from a litigious society such as ours where waiters have to remind customers that something fresh out of the oven will be hot.

Yet the idea that strangers are out to get us is the prevailing mindset of far too many back home where we pass off entire cities, countries and regions as too dangerous, all the while we're loading up our tanks to go plummeting down a highway at seventy-miles-per-hour. In other words, I'd sooner spend a day in Chepe than the roads of the U.S.

This time we had accepted an invitation to visit an organic marketplace, because that's what you do in a new environment— you say yes to just about every invitation. Saying no just once or twice puts you at risk of appearing unsocial and makes people think again before inviting you to things in the future. It's a stark contrast to my typical behavior in the States where I'm generally unsocial and reluctant to be around people. I often find people to be terribly selfish, boring and frustratingly stupid. It's people who go on trophy hunts in Africa to kill endangered animals. It's people who deny climate change. It's people who acknowledge climate change and still do nothing. It's people who text and drive, drink and drive, and Pokémon Go and drive. So you see, I'm not wrong about people and that's why I tend to avoid them.

(To be fair, I do find select individuals to be incredibly caring, interesting and frustratingly brilliant. It's the masses that bother me.)

On the other hand, I do enjoy a good marketplace. Any time I can surround myself by the sights and smells of delicious food is a happy day. The market Fería Verde sits in a different corner of San José than what we had seen in our first visit, though the walk did require trekking through familiar territory until we reached Parque Morazán about a kilometer and a half from the Coca-Cola bus station. I was again surprised to see that all the trappings of cities I enjoy elsewhere in the world were alive and well in little ole Chepe, namely Josefinos out and about enjoying the day. In retrospect, I kicked myself for this observation. I mean, why wouldn't Josefinos be out enjoying their city? My skepticism was no doubt left over from the hesitant takes on San José in popular media. In just my second visit, I was thrilled to see that everything I had read was spectacularly wrong (or at the very least greatly uninformed).

Our first pause came at Parque Morazán, which history paints as an important sector of the city. I later discovered a bit of intrigue behind how the park got its name. Morazán takes its name from the nineteenth century Honduran general, Francisco Morazán, who attempted to unite the whole of Central America as a sovereign nation. The decision to honor the general with naming rights over the park toward the end of the nineteenth century was controversial at the time. Here's why.

After the death of President Próspero Fernández Oreamuno (what a name!) in 1885, the political establishment decided to construct a monument in his honor. The bust created by Italian sculptor Francisco A. Durini Vassalli was inaugurated on Augusto 10, 1887 by his successor, Bernardo Soto Alfaro. Their next step was to allocate a variety of lots for public space—the future Parque Morazán. Coincidentally or not, the Honduran general was shot and killed at the nearby Plaza Principal, today Parque Central, on September 15, 1842.

Now here's the controversy of the era. While Morazán was known for wanting to unite Central America, Fernández had been prepared to defend Costa Rica's sovereignty militarily after Guatemalan President Justo Rufino Barrios vowed to reconstruct the previously failed República Federal de Centroamérica by force. Why the decision to honor such stark ideologies simultaneously seems to never have been explained. To Americanize it (because that's what we do), it'd be like Congress coming together to christen public spaces for William F. Buckley and Gore Vidal a stone's throw away from one another. It just wouldn't happen.

In any event, Fernández's viewpoint obviously won in the end, but I have to say Morazán got the better park.

At the center of the park sits the lovely Templo de la Música constructed by architect and painter Francisco Salazar to replace a wooden pavilion previously located in the same spot. The new, elegant pavilion received its inauguration on Christmas Eve in 1920 and is nearly an exact replica of France's Temple of Love. It's been the scene of many political speeches, concerts, and even the passing of power. The morning we arrived, a small band was playing on the pavilion surrounded by twenty or more yoga practitioners for what looked to be a free class.

Nice, I thought. *I'll have to come back and do that.* (I never did.)

In Parque Nacional a few blocks away, a full marching band was out in the morning sun practicing for, I assumed, upcoming Independence Day celebrations. Our small group watched as the band started and stopped, following the conductor's instructions. At this park's center, where the conductor stood in front of his street-clothed students, was yet another monument —a dramatic interpretation of Central American soldiers driving out William Walker, who if you'll remember was the American villain we first encountered in the heroic legend of Juan Santamaría. It's likely not a coincidence that a statue of Santamaría stands just across the street at the Asamblea Legislativa as if he's eyeing Walker down.

Other smaller monuments to influential Latino leaders spread across the park. There's one for José Martí, a revolutionary Cuban poet, the Venezuelan humanist Andrés Bello and Mexican independence leader, Miguel Hidalgo. (I'm now realizing there's a lot of dude-honoring in San José statues, but I'm sure that's par for the course in the world.) In practice, the park is an attractive, shady spot to read the paper and relax away from the beaming sun.

Continuing toward the market alongside the park, we happened upon something exciting for a rail enthusiast such as myself—a train station. Moving to Costa Rica, I didn't expect to find a train network as a key part of the national infrastructure. Instead I assumed I'd find something more in line with the vast majority of the United States—highways, roads, highways and roads. So needless to say I was thrilled when we happened upon Estación de Ferrocarril de Atlántico. Admittedly at first I couldn't tell if it was an active station or defunct. The exterior looked a bit shabby, but so do many of the great train stations of the world that have some years under their respective belts. On closer inspection, I decided it must be some sort of commuter service because the trains looked too well-kept to be garbage, but they clearly weren't actively running that Saturday morning. I then had to hurry away and catch up with my group, who showed comparatively little interest in a piece of transportation infrastructure.

I will ride you, I thought as I walked away from the station. *I. Will. Ride. You.*

As we finally neared the market, nearly another kilometer further north through leafy Barrio Amón, the surroundings were unsurprisingly far quieter than the parks or heart of San José. Soon we began to see other market patrons, who we were only able to identify by their bags full of vegetables. A majority were on the younger side compared to the all-encompassing crowds you'd see at a grocery store. We followed their path in reverse, stepping down a steep line of stairs off an otherwise unassuming and nondescript road. From above we could see crowded shoppers through the tall trees rooted on the hillside and ground below. Moving into the crowd, there was a clear mixture of foreigners and Ticos. Most everyone seemed to be either bilingual or proficient enough to efficiently get the food from producer to customer's mouth.

From here our group dispersed. Melanie and I made a beeline for a bread stand. The owner of Solana bread spoiled us with enough samples to count as an appetizer. (We bought something; the marketing tactic worked.) Then we moved over to the tree-covered section of the market to grab a proper lunch and cool off a bit after a few kilometers of walking in the sun. The steam coming of the grill of a nearby Colombian stand caught our attention. We both went with a plate of gallo ranchero—egg, beans and salsa on a tortilla, the staple ingredients of many a Latino meal. Melanie and I agreed that this was the best meal we had since arriving, and that's not to say we hadn't been eating well.

Just as we finished, the afternoon rain came. It had been stalking us for as long as we had been at the market, quashing our faint and foolish hopes that we'd make it indoors before the rain punished us.

We took cover under a nearby tent as the gentle spray quickly turned to a violent pounding. That's how the rain works in Costa Rica. The clouds warn you, the initial few drops sound the alarm, and then it's no holds barred, every man and woman for themselves. A dry dirt path illustrated the point, for what was dry just moments prior had become a flowing creek right underneath our feet. "El rio!" shouted a laughing Tico who had been sharing a tent with us. Strategic foot placement became necessary to avoid soaked shoes, forcing everyone to freeze as if in the middle of a game of Twister.

As the rain continued, our tent host passed around snacks free of charge. It was a somewhat runny egg wrapped in bread. Our neighbor, a young Latina woman, started chatting us up. Through our brief conversation we discovered that she used to teach in the human rights department at UPEACE before moving on to the international court in San José. She agreed with our assessment that the city isn't exactly postcard material, but has plenty of appealing pockets.

"San José didn't even have an architecture program until the seventies," she said, offering an explanation for the overall lack of artistry in Chepe's buildings. Plus the Spanish largely left the country alone after promises of gold didn't exactly pan out, leaving the country with no modern colonial charm like León and Granada in neighboring Nicaragua or Antigua in Guatemala. (To be fair, the Spanish didn't just show up to those places, hammer out some nice buildings and split.)

Once the rain let up, we continued onward to the nearby Antigua Aduana building—a long and narrow event space created by the Ministry of Culture. The 2014 International Book Festival was ongoing and coincidentally authors from the United States were the year's featured guests. This meant carriers of a U.S. passport received free entry. Sensing an injustice, the group of UPEACE students with us thought it fairer if we split the cost as a group. Don't get me wrong, I can rally behind equality when it comes to larger, more sweeping and pressing issues. But this struck me as a bit nit-picky. Had Korean authors been the guests of honor, it wouldn't occur to me to ask the Koreans to pony up for my piece of an already plenty affordable ticket. Those kind of small gestures, though well-intentioned, smelled a tad self-aggrandizing. To even hint at argument would send us through a rabbit hole I didn't want to enter.

Them: Some people get in free? That's not fair. Let's all split the cost evenly.

Me: Or we can just keep it simple and play by the rules.

Them: Play by the rules? PLAY BY THE RULES!? *Playing by the rules* set by a rotten capitalist, patriarchal society is precisely what has led to the centuries of inequality and injustice that continues to eat at the core of human civilization!

Me: ... We're still talking about a book fair ticket, right?

We picked up a copy of Carlos Arauz's book on Costa Rican

legends appropriately titled *Costa Rica: Leyendas y Tradiciones*. The author himself was present and I explained to him, in bashful Spanish, that we wanted something easy to read for practice. He first offered a book with text in both English and Spanish, the idea being that you could check on how you're doing with a translation after each read. But Melanie and I both worried that the temptation to read the English version straightaway would prove too strong. Instead, we went for the legends book to both tackle our interest in Costa Rican folklore and to challenge ourselves by actually reading in Spanish with no escape.

As soon as we made our purchase, we met up with one Mr. Robert Isenberg from *The Tico Times*. I was first introduced to the American writer following his featured series chronicling his adventure cycling across the country from the Caribbean to the Pacific. Considering this backstory, it came as no surprise to find him a tad sweaty having cycled over to the festival from his Escazú home—some ten kilometers away.

Walking through the festival, we shared backstories that appeared remarkably similar. He hailed from Pittsburgh before his writing career and ambitions to live abroad turned to Costa Rica. When you're thousands of miles away, Pittsburgh and Cleveland are essentially the same thing—old American manufacturing cities. We also shared our interest in writing a travelogue of our time in Costa Rica with Robert lamenting the lack of solid English literature on the topic beyond guidebooks and some take on the whole played out theme of, "I retired in paradise!"

(Not coincidentally, Robert did publish months later the excellent *The Green Season* using a compilation of essays published at *The Tico Times*.)

Robert had also come to the festival for an English-language theater production set to begin in a few minutes. Melanie and I foolishly joined with only an hour to spare before we had agreed to leave with our UPEACE group. When it was obvious that the show would run for more than an hour, we took a brief set change as our opportunity to split.

I grabbed the door handle, pushed, and then pulled to no avail. The door was locked from the other side. This seemed like a fire hazard, but we had no time to ponder flammable fates because the show was set to continue momentarily. Of course it did just that before we could even make a move for another door or return to our seats, both of which required walking onto the stage. So there we were, stuck, watching community theater from the corner as we feverishly texted our friends that we would be missing our two o'clock meet up time. And texting was no easy feat on our Tico phones. This was nobody's fault but our own, since we opted to purchase a couple of brick burners that still used T9 texting. We didn't know anything about jailbreaking our iPhones, nor did we think we'd need anything other than a device to occasionally call each other. After all, our iPhones still worked with Internet. How were we to know we'd find ourselves trapped in the middle of a local theater production?

Despite being momentarily trapped in a theater, Melanie and I agreed our second excursion to San José managed to top our first. We dropped the apprehensions we had before our first visit and allowed ourselves to see more of the color and life in Chepe that escaped our lens last time. More food, more smells, more parks, more everything that draws me to a place. The prevailing wisdom was dead wrong on San José. Not just wrong, but absurdly and incredibly wrong. The kind of wrong that makes you feel a cocktail of stupid and surprise for ever believing the lie.

Truth is, San José is special. The people, the marketplaces, the history, the public spaces—all of it. Anyone who doesn't see that or who would summarily dismiss it because of what they saw on an Internet forum or because it looks different than Cow Town, USA doesn't deserve it. They can go stay at a gated resort on the beach with five hundred other Gringos from basically the same suburb and play pretend that they're in a foreign country. Meanwhile, the cool kids will make some time for Chepe.

Poás: The Disney Volcano

Volcán Poás was and remains the most visited national park in all of Costa Rica. I imagined it would be akin to hanging out with Bruce Springsteen backstage. Catching anyone backstage on that level would be phenomenal, but especially so with *Bruce-freaking-Springsteen*. I built up Poás to be the undisputed rock star of Costa Rican tourism. Plus this would be our first dip into the famed Costa Rican outdoors for which the country is celebrated by millions of tourists. After two successful visits to San José, I had high hopes for Poás to remind me why having an accessible respite from urban life is so important to me.

Unfortunately, I'm afraid to report, Poás was a bit of a letdown. It was a typical Tico day, weather-wise, when we made the trip with a group of UPEACE students from our Spanish class. Needless to say I expected a different experience from anything we had seen up to that point when we pulled up to the park entrance after a ninety-minute shuttle ride through winding rural roads. The lush green landscape, rolling hills that turned into mountains, and fresh country air gave me flashbacks to traveling in India. Temperatures dropped noticeably as we ascended out of the Central Valley; the morning dew settling in and giving a bit of sparkle as the sun peeked through dark clouds. I actually felt a bit—dare I say—chilly to my great surprise.

Signs of tourism hit from the get-go, which coincidentally is also generally a sign that I won't be that impressed. It was early, but a collection of tour buses had already parked, vomiting their packs of camera-clicking tourists onto the pavement. Everything was polished from the walking paths to the welcome center complete with a café and gift shop. This was my first volcano, so I expected something out of a Bear Grylls show, though not quite as extreme. I wanted lightly treaded footpaths in a dense forest and the occasional wooden sign with instructions carved by knife to guide the way. Instead we got the Disney-fication of what decades ago would have been a truly wild experience back when Mario Boza first got the idea to conserve Poás after visiting Tennessee's Great Smoky Mountains in the 1960s.

There was a thirty-minute or so manicured walk to the crater of Volcán Poás from the parking lot. The pathway had been made accessible for most anyone—great if walking's not your thing, not so great if you enjoy a bit of a physical challenge and to be away from swarms of tourists when taking in natural surroundings. At least we arrived early, as numerous tourist guides advised, so that we were actually able to see the crater in all its sunken ground glory. Had we arrived even an hour later, we likely would have been staring at a disappointing blur of clouds.

With the altitude and strong smell of volcanic sulfur fighting its way into our respective nostrils, some began to feel a tad dizzy. I felt perfectly fine in the moment, but I was content moving on rather than risk growing suddenly faint and throwing myself over the guardrail. Besides, I had already decided that Poás was a resounding, "meh." I'm sure I would have felt a hundred percent differently had the view come after at least an hour of moderate to difficult hiking through untouched jungle. It's no different than love. Most men and women enjoy the chase at the beginning of a relationship. The flirting, the *accidental* brushes, the knowing smirks—all of that. There'd be no spark if you met someone and were told from the beginning, "Walk here and do XYZ for thirty minutes and then we'll bang." Poás needed a little foreplay.

We started to head back toward another hike that promised at least sixty minutes round trip. Though still manicured for even the most laid back hiker, this portion at least offered some dense rainforest compared to the lazy jaunt to the crater. One reward was a scenic lake that played second fiddle to the volcano. Pretty for a picture or two, but then I load it onto my computer and realize it looks like any other lake I've seen in my life. There should be signs in Costa Rica that remind tourists: "We know this is Costa Rica and it's incredible, but you don't need to take a picture of every damn thing twenty times."

I hiked the last forty minutes back with my Spanish teacher, María, who put on this day trip with her husband through the tourism company they ran on the side. (Word to the wise: if you own a shuttle in Costa Rica, you too can run a tourism company.) My language skills were actively put to the test. Thankfully she, being a language teacher, spoke with emphasis to clarity and annunciation so even a struggling foreigner with the linguistic skills of a toddler could manage to follow along. I also appreciated her patience and honesty.

During our orientation for Spanish class, María was forward in warning some of the students about how Ticos might talk to them. She was speaking specifically to the women from Africa and Asia, two populations Ticos don't see much of in their country. For instance, every Asian gets called, "Chino," Spanish for a Chinese person.

South Korea? Chino. Cambodia? Chino. China? Chino just the same.

This prompted an African student to ask about something she had been experiencing.

"What is *negra*?" she asked, María's eyes bulging out of her head like she just noticed an oncoming train. "People keep calling me this on the street."

"Negra," of course, means "black." People were yelling, "black" at this young woman from Africa. María explained this as artfully as one could without wanting to make her country seem less than progressive in matters of race. Unfortunately this was all followed by a rundown on Costa Rican catcalling.

"If someone says something to you, just ignore them and keep walking," she explained before qualifying that statement. "But sometimes when someone doesn't say something to me, I go home and wonder what's wrong!"

This left Melanie gritting her teeth.

Walking with María in Poás, she shared that she had spent some time living in New Jersey, but preferred life back in Costa Rica.

"I didn't like feeling like I was living to work," she said in her critique. "That's fine if that's what you want to do, but that's not how I want to live my life. I want to be able to relax."

Some Americans, with their sixty-hour workweeks and corporate policies that barely give women time to recover from popping a human through their vagina, might say María and her ilk are lazy. But I agreed with her sentiment. Over the years with the good fortune of being able to travel to different countries and experience bits and pieces of various cultures, I've always identified with those who generally find themselves at the top of those "happiest nations on Earth" lists. The U.S. rarely fares so well and I find no coincidence that those countries ruling in happiness also take a more nuanced approach to work-life balance with policies in place to support taking extended vacations or paid leave after pushing a human out of your body.

As for me, I've found that I can be a tad hedonistic—for better or worse. Sure, I have what could generally be accepted as noble ideas and intentions for my life. I'd like to leave the world at least marginally less fucked up due to my work and how I live my life. But I'm also very cognizant of the fact that I will only be Joe Baur once for a very finite amount of time (unless all that we know takes an intriguing sci-fi twist, which the nerd in me would celebrate). That aside, I know as my last breath leaves my lips that I will measure success in my life by how I've contributed to the world and how much of the world I've enjoyed—not by the size of the bank account I leave behind. In other words, I know that living in Costa Rica and seeing this volcano (even if it didn't really do it for me) will leave me a more satisfied man at the end of my life than giving my accountant a stiffy as he or she pores over my hypothetical accumulated wealth. (Admittedly, it's much easier to make such a proclamation when you have minimal wealth accumulated.)

Lest I seem like too good of a guy, let me be clear I have no qualm about accepting ridiculously large sums of money for my work. I just like to think I'd do something good with a decent percentage of that sum. The rest is sending Melanie and I to Fiji, because as the wise Truman Burbank once said, "You can't go any further away before you start coming back."

colón (ko·*lon*)

noun

1. The name for Costa Rican currency that stems from
    Christopher Columbus, whose name in Spanish is
    Cristóbal Colón. Tico money can go by a number of
    shorthands that refer to the look of the denomination.
    - Media Teja (*me*·dya *te*·kha) 50 colón coin
    - Teja (*te*·kha) 100 colón coin
    - Rojo (*ro*·kho), literally "red," describes the red
      color of the 1000 colón bill
    - Tucán (too·*kan*), close to the English "toucan," is
      a reference to the 5000 colón bill featuring the
      tropical bird swooping over a pre-Columbian
      stone sphere. (The white-faced monkey, sloth,
      blue morpho butterfly and a number of other
      animals are featured on different bills.)

Example: "I can't believe our currency is still named after that
horrific monster, Cristobál Colón. Let's at least cover the colón
with pictures of cute animals."

Santa Teresa: Just Around The Corner

The first month in Costa Rica flew by like any number of time-themed clichés. We landed in Costa Rica with no definitive plans to see the country, assuming it would just happen along the way. Yet a month had gone by and we had yet to spend a night anywhere other than in Ciudad Colón. We hadn't even seen either coast! What kind of Gringos were we? The only water we experienced were the seemingly lethal pellets shooting at us from the sky during the rainy season.

This felt like a wrong we needed to remedy at the first opportunity. That opportunity came in a UPEACE-sponsored trip to Santa Teresa, a Pacific beach town on the southwestern tip of the Nicoya Peninsula. The trip wasn't so much "UPEACE-sponsored" as it was a staff member at the university offering to shuttle a small group of students to the ferry at Puntarenas that would then take us across the Gulf of Nicoya where we had a connection with a public bus to Santa Teresa. (Seriously, if you have a shuttle in Costa Rica, you can run a tourism company.)

 Admittedly, neither Melanie nor myself were exactly enthralled with the concept of group travel. Absolutely nothing against our fellow travelers, but we had always held our nose up at any form of travel that involved a group of clearly identifiable foreigners pouring out onto the scene together. We were already identifiable enough in Latin America, me with my practically translucent skin tone and blonde hair, without being joined by another eight or ten students. Plus Ciudad Colón to Santa Teresa seemed to be covering quite a bit of land for only one full day. But the benefit of finally seeing rural Costa Rica outweighed any other discomforts and the decision to join came easily despite our initial apprehensions.

Julian, a Tico administrator at UPEACE who wore his short black hair slicked back, met the group at one of the bus stops in Ciudad Colón for an early morning pickup. I thought Julian was a pleasant enough guy when we met, but he had what I found to be an odd habit of commenting on my body. During our first meeting, he gestured toward my arms in a short-sleeve polo and flexed his own.

"Do you workout?" he asked.

I've always hated that question. It should be no big deal to admit to exercising—it's a healthy thing to do!—but at least in American culture, the question "do you workout?" is cached with so many connotations of (and there's really no other way to say this) douchebagery. The question immediately sets a scene in my mind of a bro in a gym, disproportionally huge upper-body to a skinny lower-body, swatting high-fives with his mutant buddies. Their conversations are in general:

"Bro?"

"Bro."

"Bro! Bro?"

"Bro. Bro?"

"BRO!"

So whenever I'm asked if I workout, I feel the need to qualify my response with something that picks away at that stereotypical image. "I cycle" or "Just some body-weight stuff at home," I'll respond. I gave a similar response to Julian, hoping that'd be the end of it, but instead he commented on my broad shoulders. Yes, I do have broad shoulders. Swiss-German ancestry will do that to a guy.

Every time thereafter, Julian, instead of a normal greeting, would push his arms out wide to mimic a bodybuilder instead of a normal greeting. He'd raise his chin slightly, clench his jaw and give me a slight nod like we were the very bros at the gym I've always tried to avoid. I'm absolutely certain the gesture was friendly and well-intentioned, but the joke of "you have broad shoulders" was dead to me before it was ever funny. I always forced a small laugh whenever we passed each other in the hallway. Saying something about how it annoyed me would have been incredibly contrarian to my say nothing, feel nothing Midwestern upbringing where we sweep our emotions under a rug and stomp on them until they go away. You know, totally healthy stuff.

On the morning of Santa Teresa, Julian thankfully skipped over his typical greeting and stuck with mere pleasantries—my wheelhouse—as we boarded the shuttle. (Thank God, because he was otherwise an incredibly kind, thoughtful guy.) The ninety-minute ride to Puntarenas was mostly straight along a relatively young stretch of highway. It was gray out, and I was surprised to see what appeared to be a separated bike lane following alongside the road as we neared the port city.

Julian left us at the ferry where we were instructed to board and pickup another bus at the other side of the Gulf of Nicoya. The rain started to threaten its daily downpour, earlier than usual, as we stepped aboard the ferry. Melanie and I grabbed seats outside the main compartment to enjoy the view and still get cover from the rain. Nearby, a teacher in a small boat led a group of school students with the Costa Rican flag painted on the side. It looked like they had an unlit torch that they were passing around. I wondered if this was the same torch I had read about previously that travels throughout the country in the lead up to their Independence Day celebrations.

(Costa Rica shares an Independence Day with the rest of Central America. Authorities in Guatemala declared the independence of Central America from the Spanish Empire on September 15, 1821 following the final Spanish defeat in the Mexican War of Independence.)

The ferry set off on time and just as the rain started coming down with some force. Our group exchanged snacks and moved bags around to ensure we all stayed out of the rain. The voyage was mostly uneventful, but we were all left surprised at the obvious amount of pollution in the gulf. Entire patches of water were covered by unbelievable amounts of trash—a stark contrast to the image of Costa Rica as a veritable utopia of environmentalism. To be fair, it was impossible for us to know if Ticos created this trash themselves, foreign tourists, a combination of the two or something else. But it set off a conversation amongst the group of our experiences thus far that seemed to contradict the green-friendly image we all had of Costa Rica coming into our year abroad. From Ciudad Colón to San José, we were all surprised by the number of scooters and old cars driven by many Ticos. Melanie and I often wondered how so many of those vehicles could pass an emissions test, if there even was one.

My take was that perhaps Costa Rica's environmentalism is a reflection of political policy and perhaps is not perfectly reflected in day-to-day life. In a simple example, littering is illegal in the States—good, obvious environmental policy. But a walk through any American city shows that not everyone considers themselves an environmentalist with miscellaneous trash, cigarette butts, and plastic bottles rolling down city sidewalks. The stupidity and carelessness of the individual human will always surmount well-intentioned laws.

We left the ferry at Cabo Blanco where a collection of tin roofs kept us out of the steady rain and wooden planks lifted us over the mud as we connected with the bus to Santa Teresa. Costa Rican buses were nearly as diverse as the country's wildlife with more public transportation options than I initially expected, though calling it "public transportation" is technically incorrect since the industry was privatized. That means different fares depending on which company you're riding with and no centralized station in San José. No Union Station or *Hauptbahnhof* equivalent for Ticos. In all it made for an aggravating (and sweaty) experience, running around Chepe to figure out where in the name of all that is *santo* is the connecting bus.

Most notable, however, was how the condition of the buses varied so starkly. Of course the superior buses were reserved for the most popular routes, serving commuters in and out of the capital. The further your bus traveled, the more likely you were to find yourself on the transportation equivalent of a 100-year-old turtle climbing up its last mound of sand to die—the exception being TicaBus for international travel. If your bus was traveling within country, you were most likely in for a treat of sorts.

This was especially the case for the ride from Cabo Blanco to Santa Teresa. The Nicoya Peninsula is already sparsely populated to begin with. A clear majority of Ticos live in the Central Valley in San José or one of the other three urban areas —Alajuela, Heredia and Cartago—that surround it. So you can imagine the quality (or lack thereof) of buses reserved for the least populous corners of the country. To be fair, I was incredibly impressed with just how easily one could traverse the country without a car, reaching some of the tiniest towns in the country with relative ease. (That relativity is compared to the United States. A European or Japanese traveler might balk at my praise for Costa Rican connectivity, but it is without question better connected than most of the United States.) For example, Ciudad Colón is twenty-two kilometers outside of San José and had regular bus service. The same cannot be said for most American cities covering a similar distance, let alone trying to reach something as small as Santa Teresa, originally a quiet fishing village.

That praise aside, the buses could stand an upgrade, and I know many Ticos would agree. Our bus to Santa Teresa was not quite the worst we would experience in Costa Rica, but it was far from an enjoyable experience for Melanie, who suffers from motion sickness on just about anything that isn't a bike or her own two legs.

The bus initially filled up, forcing Melanie to a less than ideal seat in the middle. If bus travel is necessary, she would normally prefer something toward the front in order to see the road and keep her threatened equilibrium at bay. Sitting away from visibility makes the sharp turns and sudden stops all the more surprising, causing her body to unnecessarily sound the alarm. Of course the route between Cabo Blanco and Santa Teresa was full of swinging turns and steep descents as we cut through the Costa Rican countryside over the course of a couple of hours. There's also the ever-present hint of fumes that comes with the rickety Tico buses that have seen better decades. Although the Central Valley had been cool, including our connection in Cabo Blanco, we could feel the temperature sharply rising as we neared the Pacific Coast. Body heat, too, took its toll.

For myself, the growing sweat was a minor annoyance— something I knew would be remedied shortly after our arrival to the beach. Ocean waters have the remarkable ability to rip away all the grime and discomfort of bus travel with a single wave. For Melanie, this couldn't come soon enough. The heat, the bumps in the road and bus ride-equivalent of a roller coaster were slowly chipping away at her well-being. She felt the warning signs of motion sickness on the horizon. This coupled with her growing hunger meant nothing good, and a hungry Melanie leads to a Jekyll and Hyde scenario that would frighten a battle-hardened warrior.

Through it all, she was generally able to maintain good spirits. We had an empty bag ready just in case. Her lips pursed tightly and her eyes winced with each bump. Then the road turned to a mixture of pavement and gravel, tumbling down narrow forested roads that seemed far too steep for a bus the size of a Greyhound. Our only comfort was our assumption that the driver had done this ride more than once. Plus there was the omnipresent decapitated Jesus above his windshield assuring us that *El Señor* would guide us safely.

Ours was the final stop; the bus had emptied by the time of our arrival. We were left on a nondescript road next to a trash container. In Costa Rica, the trash doesn't merely sit out in bins, but often in elevated metal cages. A large iguana was running around the bars of this particular trash container standing outside an empty shopping plaza.

We gave the name of our hostel and the bus driver pointed us further down the road to where he assured us all the lodgings would be. He generously offered to drive us a bit further down, but Melanie had little interest in getting back on the bus. Besides, she had me to drag the bags.

So there we were, our group marching down a quiet road of mixed gravel and concrete. Now seeing the road, we couldn't believe this was what our bus had been sliding down with minimal appliance to the brake. But we were alive and there was a beach that needed to be frolicked upon, so our more morbid thoughts were quickly swept away with the increasing volume of pounding waves.

Two giant dogs greeted us as we approached our lodging, Cuesta Arriba. One especially looked like "The Beast," the gigantic slobbering English mastiff from *The Sandlot*. There was a comfortable mixture of beach town comforts and rustic character. A dirt path led to check-in, passing a small pool along the way. The room was no frills, but why would you need anything more than a bed in a place that demands you to be outside all the time?

After check-in, we made way to the nearest soda around the corner from our hostel, filling up on a healthy helping of rice, beans and chicken. With a full stomach, Melanie seemed to have fully recuperated and was ready for the beach.

We followed a dirt trail off the only road in town, which again was a mixture of pavement and gravel. The path to the beach was modest, no gaudy signs featuring a cartoon caricature of a smiling Gringo with a margarita in hand leading the way. The sound of the waves increased in intensity as we cut through the dense woodland, stepping over lines of leaf-cutter ants and protruding roots. Then, we finally stepped out onto the beach. Our reaction was as clichéd as can be; some of us even gave off an audible, "Wow." The seemingly endless panorama of beach and ocean, our feet sinking into the warm, sun-soaked sand, and the gentle sound of crashing waves onto a sparsely populated coastline filled out the scene.

The water was pleasantly warm, but the floor was covered in sharp shells and rocks that scratched my feet, leaving me overly hesitant and cautious with every step. Meanwhile, the waves pounded into me, one right after the other, tossing me around like a rag doll. Salt water leapt into every orifice of my body. My mouth felt like I ordered super-sized McDonald's french fries and asked them to "hold the fries" while my eyes turned beet red from the burn. This was enough for me to decide that I should go back to admiring the ocean from a respectable distance, prompting a walk with Melanie along the rocky coast.

From certain vantage points, it appeared as if the beach was a secret. Despite it being a holiday weekend, there were but few others outside of our group. There was one individual with what appeared to be a significant other, climbing a large boulder that was sticking out of the ocean like a sedimentary iceberg. I never understood the inclination to climb such things. There didn't appear to be a better view from atop, certainly not one worth slipping and breaking more than a handful of bones on the way down. Was it merely a show to impress his significant other? What ever happened to a good personality?

After losing interest in the climber's motivation, I turned back toward Melanie, who was busy amassing an impressive collection of seashells. No artist could match the designs on these things. Streaks of brown over white, some a light orange like an Easter Egg that ran out of paint, and others that imitated the swirling dark clouds of Jupiter. Sometimes nature just knows what it's doing.

After a warm shower, our first since arriving in Costa Rica given mishaps with our Frankenstein shower back in Colón, we had a couple of beers with the group before heading out to a pizza joint off the main gravel road. Seeking some nightlife, a handful of us split off toward what looked like a pile of bricks with a roof—a bunker masquerading as a bar. Earlier we had seen a sign promising karaoke at night.

Upon our arrival, we could hear the loud drum of thumping music. It wasn't karaoke, but something was clearly going on, prompting us to step in for further investigation. Inside, the music pounded away at our eardrums. A random assortment of colored lights flashed in quick enough succession that it seemed to be on beat with the music. Behind the bar, there was just one bored looking server. The bar or club itself was completely empty save ourselves.

Some took it as an opportunity to bail on the night while a few of us, determined to make something happen, stayed to make the best of it. Melanie, a few others and myself bought an Imperial for a dollar and stood awkwardly on the dance floor as nothing continued to happen. Eventually, Melanie and I started doing our best interpretation of salsa dancing, which for me was repeating the three swing dancing moves I learned years ago, until the sweat we had just cleaned off started pouring through our shirts once more. After about an hour of uneventful nonsense, locals started to trickle in one by one. Before we knew it, the club was steady. So naturally we made way for the karaoke.

Melanie kicked things off with Madonna's "Like A Virgin." A pitter of applause, though only from our little group. Her mic was barely given any volume from the DJ and it became clear that this was not by accident as we passed the mic around. What a shame, too, because I think we did a pretty honest version of "Camisa Negra" and "La Bamba."

Once we handed over the mic to some local patrons, it was obvious *why* our mics had been all but disabled. As it happened, karaoke is no joke in Costa Rica like back in the States. Singers took their songs seriously and proved to be rather impressive. I started to feel a sense of shame looming as I realized that I probably had just displayed the worst of obnoxious American traveler stereotypes for a room full of uninterested Ticos. I opted to slink out of the bar with Melanie as my dignity dribbled onto the sticky floor.

Melanie and I slept that night like a pair of rocks on a morphine drip. We took our time with the morning coffee and toast, the minimalist staples of any hostel. Our day was then spent in search of elusive hiking trails. True to form, no Costa Rican wanted to admit that they didn't know where the trail was.

Instead, they kept telling us, "just around the corner" or "next to the river" or any other number of descriptions that allowed them to pretend they knew what they were talking about. Our last attempt was a stop at a clothing store along the route. I waited outside while friends went inside to ask someone. A young Gringo kid skateboarding around the small plaza over small obstacles and around racks of clothing amused me for the short wait. When they returned, the answer was familiar.

"Just around the corner."

Unable to find the hiking trail in question, we at least found a steep dirt road uphill that led to a small, flat clearing—possibly for an incoming house—that offered a great view of the ocean. That view was enough to convince us to get back to the beach.

After a little more beach time, we paid a visit to the second closest soda to our hostel where I devoured a breakfast burrito and a delicious blackberry fruit drink. The only peculiarity was the endless loop of shark attack footage playing on the television behind the bar. It was "Mes del Tiburón" or "Shark Month," evidently. Regardless of the month, it seemed like a rather odd selection for public display in a beach town that seems to survive off surfers and ATVs ridden by surfers on their way to the beach.

Personally, the beach is not my Valhalla in the way it is for so many other travelers. I enjoy it, but much rather find myself in the mountains. Whenever we do go, poor Melanie must always keep a ball or frisbee by her side to throw it for me to chase, otherwise I risk becoming too restless and annoy her.

Santa Teresa, however, was an exception for me. It was my first time on the Costa Rican coast and I enjoyed it thoroughly. The arduous and long journey from Ciudad Colón to Santa Teresa originally left us questioning whether or not it was worth the effort, especially for just one full day, but we left with little doubt in our mind. Perhaps it was the lack of people. Here, I could actually take in the comforting quiet that only nature can provide. Nothing kills my beach enjoyment more than people—loud, gross, disgusting, stupid people. All of the popular beaches seem to attract the worst of mankind. I'm not saying we should have a purge... But if we did have a purge, we should probably start with the beaches.

Carpe Chepe

I had always treated birthdays with the same indifference as I would a crack in the sidewalk. They exist, sure, but must a shit be given? I say no. There's nothing joyous to me about inching closer to death in what increasingly feels like a living cinematic montage. Nor do I find great achievement in staving off death for another 365 days, especially in my mostly privileged circumstance.

I'm not fighting fires, fleeing war or challenging the likes of Ronda Rousey in the ring. I write, film and travel for a living. My only flirtation with the grim reaper has been certain hikes and long distance bike rides that might disinterest the average person. Those aren't even inherently dangerous activities, which I point out only to emphasize how low I am on the scale of death defying feats. Thus, my surviving another year should absolutely not come as a surprise. No shits must be given on my birthday.

Being in Costa Rica, however, I found an exception to this strict rule of mine. I would mention and exploit my birthday if it led to the promise of alcohol and doing something out of the ordinary that interested me.

In retrospect, I had done this before. Being a September baby, I turned twenty-one before most of my friends in college. Had I stayed in Oxford, Ohio, it would've just been another night in, ordering piss-water beer from the delivery service that was infamous for selling to minors. Needless to say I happily took my parents up on their offer to send me to Minneapolis, my first flight incidentally, to spend my twenty-first with my older brother and soon-to-be sister-in-law. Turning the legal drinking age and living in a new country are the exceptions to my birthday rule.

After turning twenty-one, there's really nothing to look forward to in terms of new legal rights gained through aging. But birthdays can still be trotted out as an excuse to drink somewhat excessively without getting some side eye. They can also be used to score a free drink or two (or five).

Still, it was pretty rare for me to muster up any feigned birthday excitement, even for the privileges that come with it. At best, I'd take family up on a nice dinner then take it easy at home. But as I turned twenty-eight, I made the exception in Costa Rica with a bar crawl offered by a group called Carpe Chepe. They offered a variety of alcohol-oriented tours where, by their description, it wasn't just about pouring booze down your gullet. It was an opportunity to see San José from the perspective of a Josefino and get a little history along the way. The combination of history, booze and being in a city was enough invoke my birthday and get people on board to join for the evening.

The itinerary promised drinks at four different establishments throughout the city, all within walking distance. Andrea and our Filipino friend and classmate Caitlin joined Melanie and myself for an early bus ride over to Chepe with the idea to split up the nearly two-mile walk to the first bar with dinner somewhere along Avenida Central.

Caitlin and I were in the same program and she had quickly become one of my favorite people. A Filipino, she was adorably short and had black hair with bangs that shaped around her wide smile. We shared similar ambitions in terms of what we wanted to get out of UPEACE and what we didn't care for. I was never sure what to make of UPEACE before heading in. Sure, I knew given the overarching purpose of the university that there would be a hippy element. I don't mean to say that in a Reaganite, "Get your paws off me, you damn dirty hippy!" way. Instead, I say it matter-of-factly. I expected to meet students who questioned everything in the spirit of healthy discussion and those who questioned everything to the point of being obnoxious. I expected to meet a fair amount of students with similar thoughts on religion.

Student: I don't identify with an organized religion, but I'm *definitely* spiritual.

You know who I'm talking about.

And I certainly expected to meet some students who already had the whole world figured out (in their mind, of course), appearing every so often only to let us know how brilliant they are before disappearing on some beach trip funded by their parents.

All that aside, I knew there would be a learning curve with UPEACE. Pictures indicated that the campus was one of a kind, perched atop a hill with magnificent surroundings. I found that to be true when a visiting alumnus, Chris, offered to drive Hannah and myself up before our first day at orientation to have a look. Chris had roots in a variety of countries—and two passports—and thus refused to identify with a single nation. I envied him, but it got a little annoying to repeatedly hear his family story whenever he introduced himself.

We get it! You're a citizen of the world. Bully for you!

Chris was, however, helpful in offering a bit of history on the university. We started through the wooded trails of the Peace Park up to an oddly Brutalist UPEACE monument with the busts of various men and select quotes of theirs underneath. The fact that men were the only heroes featured was and remains a sticking point, justifiably so. In fact, the only woman featured was a statue of the Peace Pilgrim, Mildred Lisette Norman. Ms. Norman gained mild celebrity for her walks across the United States in the name of peace. Some say she did the trek more than twenty times over twenty-eight years before she passed away in 1981.

For that, she got a statue under some trees that most people probably miss. Her statue was also missing an arm and it hardly seemed like a deliberate, artistic interpretation. (By the time the year was over, her statue was gone. Perhaps the male busts got together and voted her off their boys' club island.)

While browsing the busts, Chris offered the origins of UPEACE. "The United States had opened a military school in Panama..." he started. I could already sense where this was going. If traveling had taught me one thing, it was that our national history was hardly as clean or gallant as school textbooks and politicians lead me to believe.

"So the president of Costa Rica said, 'If there's going to be a school for war, then we should have a school for peace.'"

Having the university in Costa Rica made sense considering they had abolished their military back in December 1, 1948 following a month-long Civil War. José Figures Ferrer, victorious rebel commander and then president, broke a wall with a mallet to symbolize the end of Costa Rica's military legacy in a ceremony known as the Cuartel Bellavista.

The United States had both supported and played a significant role in Figueres' victory by mobilizing in the Canal Zone of Panama and cutting off supplies to the government's military. This wasn't out of the goodness of our hearts, mind you, but rather concerns that Costa Rica was turning toward communism.

U.S. Government: *Communism!?* We're in! Who do we have to kill?

Following the Civil War, Costa Rica had a front row seat to the U.S.' violent and bizarre overreach in the affairs of Latin America. In the eyes of Costa Rica, this was reason enough to support the creation of UPEACE.

(The president at the time of UPEACE's creation was one Mr. Rodrigo Carazo Odio. "Odio" means "hate.")

The University For Peace can trace its roots back to a UN resolution (34/111, to be exact), which was a treaty endorsed by the United Nations General Assembly on December 14, 1979. In collaboration with the Costa Rican government, the UN General Assembly prepared the organization and structure for what would become UPEACE.

Chris, in walking us through this history, claimed the United States was none too pleased with the idea that the United Nations would support an academic institution.

Oh, for fuck's sake, I grumbled to myself. *Of course we would be against something called "The University For Peace."*

Despite the U.S.'s objection, the UN adopted resolution 35/55 without vote, officially creating UPEACE on December 5, 1980. It was the only dedicated institution of higher education in the field of Peace and Conflict Studies.

A stipulation allegedly made by the United States was that the school would not receive funds from the United Nations itself, which I could at least see an argument for in order to maintain academic integrity. In what little time I had been around, I had already heard rumblings of professors getting the axe for criticizing the United Nations. In fact, the United Nations as a whole seemed incredibly unpopular at its own university, though trouble only seemed to begin if professors recorded said criticisms in research papers and academic articles.

Whatever the truth may be, there was already all sorts of hearsay and rumors spreading around before class even started.

"Did you hear they're getting rid of this program?"

"Did that professor get fired?"

"So, uh, are those two banging?"

There was also sizable portion who wanted to organize some sort of student union or collective modeled after Occupy Wall Street in order to anticipate and respond to some of the concerns the previous graduating class had. Caitlin was at the first voluntary meeting setup by Chris, who was "concerned" about the direction of the university. (How he could afford to routinely hop on a plane from Europe and show up in Costa Rica was never made clear.)

Sitting in a circle, it was a Frenchman in the group who suggested that our format of discussion mirror that of Occupy Wall Street. To show agreement with a speaker, and I'm not making this up, you used "up twinkles" by raising both hands and wiggling your fingers. This was suggested because clapping was too violent—or something. The dreaded "down twinkles," showing the backs of hands and wiggling your fingers toward the floor, meant disagreement. There are at least six more signals, but I'll spare you.

It all reeked like a bag of nonsense to me, but the same Frenchman threatened to drop out of the group if it took a traditional leadership approach instead of the leaderless, all-our-voices-matter-equally structure that made Occupy Wall Street the group nobody talks about today. It took all the strength in my ocular cavities to restrain an eye roll. Caitlin shared similar sentiments and a friendship was formed.

"I just want to get my master's. They can spend their time arguing over nothing," she once told me. More importantly, she revealed herself to be incredibly kind-hearted, focused, but also a fun drinking companion—perfect for Carpe Chepe.

Following dinner, we continued the walk toward a corner of San José none of us had seen, trying to follow the spaghetti streets on Google Maps. It was only a little after 7 p.m. yet we quickly found ourselves alone once we passed the end of Avenida Central's pedestrian-only zone. Our turn south took us to an area that felt more residential with the omnipresent barbed wire that was still taking some getting used to. Seeing as it was dark, well past the year-long five thirty sunset, there was the temptation to hail a cab for the short trek to the bar. In my bravery, I left it to the others to decide if they felt unsafe.

We decided to continue and arrived at Craic Irish Pub unscathed. Despite the quiet that surrounded the neighborhood, Craic was as lively as one would expect in an Irish pub. For a moment, it actually felt like I was back home. The atmosphere felt familiar. The wall was decorated with Irish and Irish-American regale. There was chipped green and white paint, vaguely resembling a battered Irish flag. They even served Guinness. Still, there was that barbed wire outside and the Spanish chirping inside that very much separated this from the Irish pub near my apartment back in Cleveland.

Our Carpe Chepe hosts, steps from the bar and next to a foosball table, had reserved a table for us. Having arrived early, we ordered up some drinks around the table. I was thrilled to take a break from Imperial and went with a glass of Perona IPA from Treintaycinco, a Costa Rican craft brewery. At that point, anything that wasn't mass-produced light beer would have tasted like purified liquid distilled by the Gods specifically for my taste buds. The hops, something I hadn't tasted since arriving, danced on my palate like a Russian ballet.

Meanwhile, I discovered that foosball is a sport some Ticos evidently take quite seriously, as demonstrated by two players who were actually able to pass the ball around whilst seemingly fondling the handlebars to put defenders in the correct position. Both were hunched over the table as if reading a treasure map, intensely focused on the little plastic soccer ball bouncing around on the wooden table. Their cheers and grunts could have been mistaken for actual athleticism.

Eventually, the Carpe Chepe organizers appeared and introduced themselves as they happily collected our money in exchange for wristbands and shots. The shots were apparently included in our payment, and frankly, something I could've done without. That sugary blue alien goo I threw down my face-hole tasted so horribly wrong, I wanted someone to hit me so that I could feel something less painful. I was happy to finish my beer and make for the next bar.

San José was difficult to navigate in the day, let alone at night thanks to the city's indifference to street signs. Thankfully for the navigationally challenged, they have at least mostly embraced a street grid system with exceptions in residential corners. That said, I could not keep track of all the twists and turns we took throughout the night as we trotted from bar to bar. It at least confirmed that we were walking to places we would have otherwise not found, which was half the goal.

The second bar more closely resembled a dive bar I would find in the States. Bar stools were aplenty along with simple square slabs for tables and a consistent red neon glow throughout the establishment. A couple of musicians seemed to be setting up for a gig that never materialized. And from hereon out, we were back to drinking Imperial with the exception of whatever heinous shot that came with the price of admission. In this instance it was, I believe, agua dulce chile, which basically tasted like spicy tomato juice with salt on the rim. I was somehow in the minority in wanting to projectile vomit this awful concoction across the room.

Our third establishment was the swanky polar opposite of the dive. There were sleek tables and stylish chairs throughout, at least as much as a guy who always wears tee shirts and jeans could decipher. Though we seemed to increase in class, those of us still drinking continued with Imperial until our next shot sent us out the door to our final destination of the tour—a club.

At this point in the evening I felt mostly sober with a hint of a buzz. Whiskey neat in a glass is the only thing that can get me drunk anymore, unless I'm purposely trying to inhibit healthy brain activity for some reason. The tour had failed to get me plastered as some might expect for a birthday, but my college days of not recalling what I did the day before are long behind me—and I'm fine with that. I was mostly appreciating the opportunity to see Chepe at night with a pair of young Josefino tour leaders passionate about their city and its history. That said, I felt most at home in the Irish pub where we began. That craft beer was easily my preferred drink of the night.

I didn't have high expectations ending at a club. Loud beats with sweaty male youths trying desperately to sneak their way into a circle of dancing women isn't exactly my thing. In almost any other occasion, I would hear the rattling bass of some repetitive computerized pop song and take that as my cue to head home. I don't want to be at a club and club people don't want me there. It had been a mutually accepted and respected agreement since college. But I had once read someone (Jerry Seinfeld, I think?) saying that the humor behind much of his writing came from saying "yes" to almost any invitation—even if he wasn't really interested.

A Gringo in a Gringo-less San José club. Maybe something story-worthy will happen? I thought.

We didn't stay long as I could only stand so much of the cacophony of beats and grinding genitalia that was required whenever approaching the bar. The space itself was actually fairly interesting. It reminded me of the former industrial lofts back in the States that either become breweries (awesome) or clubs (meh). We had to go up a series of stairs after walking through a dilapidated door that made it feel like we were trespassing. After climbing two or three floors that resembled a fire escape, we found our way into a large space with an extraordinary view of the San José city lights. It at least made for better viewing than the handful of strategically placed, scantily clad women who were thrusting themselves about for, I guess, the enjoyment of people who happen to dance while staring straight up.

We had enough, and Andrea had a pirate taxi ready to take us home. With that, Melanie, myself and two other women whose names I was never able to commit to memory squeezed into the backseat for the forty-five-minute ride home. True to my character, I fell asleep within minutes of the drive, my lifeless head bouncing along with the Chepe potholes and against the poor woman sitting next to me as I snapped in and out of consciousness.

Cañas: Mind If We Take This Land?

While still in my honeymoon period with UPEACE, I eagerly propositioned the environmental department to allow me to join them on a field trip to Cañas where students would be learning about hydroelectric power in Costa Rica. This might not sound inherently enthralling, but I had earlier heard that ICE (Instituto Costarricense de Electricidad), the Costa Rican governmental body responsible for hydroelectric power, was involved in a controversial battle with indigenous Costa Ricans.

For the Americas, it was a familiar tale. The government wanted their land for another project and the indigenous people simply wanted to keep their land. My idea was to tag along and do some research for a possible documentary that would serve as my graduation project.

We left with the sunrise in the now familiar shuttle for a two and a half hour ride up to Cañas, a typically Tico town of about 23,000. Cañas would merely serve as our base for two nights as we moved along the manmade Lake Arenal where ICE operated one of its thirty-some hydroelectric plants. As we neared the plant, the lake peeking into view behind the roadside brush, students wondered if we'd have time to check out the Lake Arenal brewery nearby. (We didn't, regrettably.)

One of the last stories I wrote before leaving the United States was coincidentally a piece about the documentary *DamNation*. The film detailed efforts by environmentalists to dismantle a large number of U.S. dams in order to restore ecosystems to their natural, healthy state. Many had been built during FDR's New Deal period when he was just looking to keep people busy and earning some kind of a wage. By the twenty-first century, many dams long outlived their usefulness—if they ever even were useful. Some were costing more to operate than they even generated in electricity and a number in the Pacific Northwest were damaging the natural habitat. One such example detailed the plight of salmon that could no longer make their usual migrational journey, something that had been embedded into their DNA over millions of years of evolution. Humans came around and promptly screwed it all up, as per usual. This set off a domino effect, chipping away at the wellbeing of the region's ecosystem.

Costa Rica, as we learned, appeared to share some key similarities and distinctions from the United States. Most notably, Costa Rica did not start throwing up dams on every river imaginable for the sake of giving Ticos something to do until economic conditions improved. Every dam appeared to serve some purpose in off-setting the nation's carbon output (these dams later contributed to Costa Rica's globally celebrated lack of carbon emissions to produce electricity that spanned nearly all of 2015).

Costa Rica's dams do face similar criticisms to the U.S. variety. There were environmental concerns and protests from indigenous populations, who of course had to sacrifice their land to power clean energy in San José. Lake Arenal, for example, was a manmade body of water created for hydroelectric purposes. Its creation required the relocation of indigenous Costa Ricans.

The topic came up during a tour of an ICE facility when our host gleefully introduced a worker whose family had been relocated decades earlier in the lead up to the project. The old worker, his hands worn, voice soft and eyes dark, was frank.

"My parents never forgave the country," he said. "But I never would have been able to read, write, or get a good job if we weren't moved."

I struggled for a moment with the response. He works for ICE, I thought. Of course he's going to be mostly positive. Then again, I couldn't imagine he'd work with ICE if he truly had moral objections. Then again, why is it the indigenous populations that historically always get screwed? This gentleman, even if genuine, was hardly the first indigenous person presented by the benefactors as proof that they did the right thing. There may exist a Native American somewhere who for one reason or another looks back fondly on his or her time in U.S. schools, but that doesn't come close to excusing the genocide, both cultural and physical, that native peoples have been forced to swallow.

Now the episode of asking indigenous folks to forgive and forget seemed to be playing out again in southern Costa Rica. The El Disquís Hydroelectric Project between Buenos Aires and Pérez Zeledón has been in the planning stages for years as the government tries to move past indigenous protests. Leaders in the indigenous community claim that the damming of the river basin will flood up to 685 hectares of protected land. This will inevitably send the indigenous peoples of the Bribri, Cabecar, Teribe and Brunka tribes packing.

A 2010 report filed by the University of Texas School of Law's Human Rights Clinic concurs with their claim of human rights abuses, saying "Costa Rica has failed to respect and protect the human rights of its indigenous peoples in the areas of information, property, representation and effective participation in decisions surrounding the [hydroelectric project]... Its national electricity authority, ICE, has not obtained the effective participation of the Teribe peoples as required under international law."

The next year, the Teribe successfully filed a lawsuit against ICE that resulted in a letter from the United Nations reiterating their concerns. If it moves through, El Disquís will be the largest hydroelectric dam in Central America, cutting through over 200 historical sites in the process.

I found it tragically ironic as I learned about this saga playing out. See, Costa Rica supposedly got its name from Christopher Columbus when he stumbled upon (not "discovered," as he so often gets erroneous credit) its Caribbean shores, present day Limón, during his fourth and final voyage to the Western Hemisphere in 1502. During his short visit, he allegedly claimed to have found more gold in his first two days than at any other point in his travels, thus christening it Costa Rica, or Rich Coast. Gold... Rich... Get it? (If only Columbus were a wee bit less genocidal and rape-y, he'd be better remembered for his naming skills.)

In reality there was little gold to be found in Costa Rica, and indigenous populations got off comparatively easy when compared to the human travesty and genocide that took place elsewhere in the Americas.

Of course they didn't get off scot-free. These are, after all, the conquistadors we're talking about. Over about two generations of war, the indigenous population dropped from approximately 400,000 to 80,000. But it still experienced a much slower rate of colonization than its neighbors despite the heinous efforts of the conquistadors.

Gil González Dávila, for example, was a conquistador who in

1522 set indigenous peoples on a bloody march from Panama to the Nicoya Gulf to strip from them what little gold they had retrieved from the rivers of the Osa Peninsula. In the long term, he failed to establish a permanent settlement in the area and instead returned to Spain with embellished stories of triumph, capping his fairy tales with a line that the area should be called "The Rich Coast" for all its gold. Some say it's more likely "Costa Rica" comes from Dávila, accusing contemporaries of favoring the supposedly more romantic tale of Columbus' visit than the rape and pillaging of Dávila. (Both sound like pretty terrible dudes to me.)

On the other hand, it's hard not to get swept away by the engineering marvel of these hydroelectric facilities. Giant tubes the size of the mythical Kraken's arms stretched the length of football fields. Workers hummed along, moving this and that to here and there, punching away at various buttons on electronic consoles. I tried to follow as our knowledgeable host explained the processes involved in churning the waters of Lake Arenal into electricity, but ultimately failed in that pursuit.

I left with a new appreciation for the engineering, yet still entrenched in a moral dilemma. Yes, we need more clean energy in this world, and many individuals whose intellectual prowess far surpasses my own say it's a key ingredient in our future survival off fossil fuels. But good God, why must it be the indigenous populations who we ask once again to suffer for our benefit?

West: We'd like to take a crack at solving a world problem!
Indigenous Peoples: Really? But your record is...
West: Silence! We've already started anyway.
Indigenous Peoples: Okay, well, what should we expect?
West: We need your land.

Indigenous Peoples: Oh for f-

West: We know what you're thinking! It'll be different this time. We triple promise.

I certainly didn't have an answer, but I did know at least one thing. This topic was too large and would need more time than I could manage for a proper documentary project.

Back to the drawing board.

Fighting Mothra

There was always the question of bugs, insects and spiders when considering the move to Costa Rica. For all the promises man has created of a utopia settled in Central America, there was never escaping the reality that paradise is also a draw for creepy crawlers or beasts of the underworld.

Years back I had spent some time on a Tibetan college campus in the northern Indian city of Dharamsala. This place, too, was crawling with spiders as large as a human hand. The American instinct was to immediately introduce these creators to the two-dimensional world as if they had actually threatened me. Of course they hadn't, but such is the nature of the irrational reaction.

We were told early on in our travels that there was a Buddhist monastery on campus and that the monks would not take too kindly to foreigners whacking away at the ground with their shoes to kill, well, anything. Given their belief in reincarnation, it was akin in some ways to smashing a human for the simple crime of being at the wrong place at the wrong time. Imagine that for a moment. You're walking along, enjoying the day in what you believe to be a publicly shared space when suddenly your world is overtaken by a large, Nike-shaped shadow that sends you to oblivion.

Many of us handled the question of spiders by either leaving the front door open in hopes the little monster would see itself out, like an unwelcome party guest, or we used a broom to sweep them out. With the latter, there was the bogus fear that it would somehow grab hold of the broom and crawl up the wooden handle to do God knows what when it reached us noble humans. But after seeing the locals calmly scoop those spiders up with their hands, I decided it was time to take a new approach to insects. By the time of Costa Rica, I had hopefully matured a bit. After all, India was seven years ago.

They're a mere fraction of our size, I repeated to myself over the years. *They're more terrified of us and have more reason to be.*

This worked in theory for Costa Rica. Even better, it all turned out to be a bit of a non-issue as our apartment was on the second floor. Throughout the early months, we had heard stories of scorpions sneaking their way into the warm chambers of a poor, unsuspecting soul's shoe. The worst we had were those army ants, the near-microscopic buggers that would find any crumb left behind on the floor or kitchen counter. They would stretch across entire sections of wall, marching along like soldiers to procure even the smallest droplet of spilt sauce. Annoying, but nothing a little extra scrubbing didn't fix. Other than that, there were the geckos outside our apartment, which we saw as cute, little guardians protecting us from the very insects we feared. We named one Murray, because the idea of a gecko with an old man's name amused us.

We escaped our first couple of months unscathed by the true underbelly of the animal kingdom.

That is, until Mothra.

Just as aircraft in World War I made Great Britain realize they no longer had the advantage of being an island, so too did Mothra change our perspective on the benefits of a second-floor apartment. One otherwise unremarkable night, Melanie and I returned home along with Andrea. As we marched up to our second-floor common space, we noticed something over our doorway.

"Holy shit!" I exclaimed in a calm, definitely not panicked tone. "Is that a moth?"

"Looks like it," Andrea replied, unfazed after having somehow encountered even larger moths during her time working with Doctors Without Borders in the Congo.

Our first mistake was leaving the light on while we were out, which we can only surmise in retrospect drew the beast to our humble abode. Perched above our door, it was difficult to make out much detail other than its color, black as death with two wings spread out side-by-side, the size of a professional basketball player's hands.

Thinking nothing of the situation, Andrea continued into her apartment, unconcerned with the prospect that the moth might follow her in. Her door slammed shut and the moth remained still.

The last thing we wanted to do was panic. Surely this would awaken the moth and begin its fluttering madness. I saw its position above our door as a positive, convincing myself that if it did startle awake by our door, it wouldn't think to immediately pull a mid-air u-turn into our apartment, like an insect version of *Top Gun*.

Clearly I underestimated Mothra.

We calmly opened our door, walked in and slammed the door behind us. Our plan seemed to work. The moth would spend the night outside our door and we would postpone any evening chores, such as taking out the trash, until the next day. This unspoken agreement did not transfer into the language of Mothra.

Later, as these things go, a black blur whizzed across my face as Melanie and I were brushing our teeth. The sheer size of it up close was the stuff of a Japanese horror film.

Mothra perched itself above our backdoor that led to the patio. Neither of us had the courage to swing the door open underneath it and to shoo it away.

What if it decided to attack while we attempted to do the humanitarian thing? we asked ourselves.

Since India, I had practiced a strict policy of trapping and releasing insects whenever they broke previously arranged diplomatic treaties between the bug world and myself. I would take mercy on the troublemakers for the greater good of our coexistence. To this day, I can only recall one instance where I reverted to the horrific child within who smashes firsts and asks questions later. It was in college and one of those centipedes with a thousand legs was racing across my bedroom. After convincing myself it would be impossible to catch (which didn't take much) I smashed it in the corner of my room using a removed closet door, screaming like a warrior on a suicide mission charging into battle. It was one of the more horrific monsters I had ever seen and I do not regret it for a second. That thing had it coming.

Besides, that latter incident was before India. After India, I respected all living things.

But there was something about Mothra. It didn't seem to want to cooperate or go along peacefully. After all, it charged into our apartment when it clearly had no business doing so. It was perfectly welcome to stay outside our door with the bright light that probably attracted it in the first place.

With the rules of the game broken, I decided I had no other choice but to throw a volleyball at it.

Melanie stood by my side as I squared up to the backdoor. I held the volleyball like a basketball player getting ready to deliver a powerful chest pass. After a few deep breaths, I sent the ball soaring towards Mothra.

Miss.

I caught the ball as it ricocheted back to me and fired another.

Miss again.

The beast didn't even flinch! And so, I delivered it again. This time, it appeared to hit Mothra dead on. I was immediately faced with another problem, though, a problem I could only solve in the amount of time it took for the ball to bounce back to me.

In our lives, we experience a handful of moments that play back to us in slow motion. This was one of those moments. Time slowed to the point that the volleyball appeared to be floating. I realized in that stretch of time that I never saw Mothra fall off the wall to its demise nor did I notice it flying away. As the ball approached my hands, I realized it must be flattened on the volleyball. With this disgusted assumption, I quickly stepped away while making what can only be described as an "eww-face" as the ball went crashing to the floor. Melanie and I in our continued bravery dispersed to see what would happen next.

Unfortunately, what seemed like the end was merely the beginning of our evening in Mothra hell.

A few moments later, we tip-toed back toward the volleyball. I poked it using a broom and saw no sign of Mothra. We went back to the corner by the backdoor and saw no remains on the floor. As part of our earlier attempts to humanely remove the beast, we did open the kitchen window over our sink. With no sign of Mothra, we foolishly convinced ourselves that it had flown away to safety after I delivered a strike against its stupid Mothra face.

With a brief moment of calm, Melanie finished brushing her teeth and went into our bedroom. As I went to follow behind, another blur the size of a baseball shot across my face near the couch where the volleyball had landed. Mothra must have been a big Dylan Thomas fan, because it did not want to go gentle into that good night.

All bets were off at that point. We tried to play it civilized, but Mothra did not seem to get the hint. It was the last thing we wanted to do, but we felt left with no other choice.

We brought out the Raid—a deadly spray cocktail of Tetramethrin, Cypermethrin and Imiprothrin primarily used to send cockroaches to their grave. Despite having no indication as to whether or not this worked on moths, let alone moths the size of a dinner plate, I charged forward like a condemned soul into No Man's Land, chasing Mothra into every corner of our 600-square foot apartment. Eventually the spray seemed to be doing its job with the animal fluttering around like damaged aircraft. It even landed a couple of jabs against me in the midst of chaos.

That may seem like personification, but it's not. Mothra punched me in the face. Twice.

However, after what felt like thirty minutes of battle, Mothra remained in our apartment. It was around this point that Melanie realized that wildly spraying Raid in the apartment was probably not a good idea, especially with that label on the bottle warning against breathing those science-fiction-sounding chemicals.

Still, I couldn't control myself. Whenever Mothra approached, I set off into action like a cheetah leaping toward an antelope. In retrospect, I think Mothra was toying with me, flying in close to provoke my attack only to bounce back to safety as I idiotically painted our apartment with deadly chemicals.

This continued for an absurd amount of time. Finally we got it over the sink once again, less than a foot away from the open window that would send this miserable specimen out of our lives for good. Against all logic, I clenched even tighter onto my bottle of Raid. Melanie had the broom. With the appearance of safety that the four-foot handle—plus her arm's reach—provided, she shooed the monster into the blackness of night and quickly slammed the kitchen window shut. Mothra was gone.

In the aftermath of our battle, I flicked on the fan next to our living room window. I cracked open the window just enough to ensure we didn't poison ourselves in the middle of our sleep, but not enough for Mothra to squeeze back through. The next hour or so was spent cleaning all of our plates and kitchen counter where my liberal spreading of Raid may have landed.

Too wired for sleep, we poured ourselves glasses of wine and sequestered ourselves to the bedroom, our door locked in case Mothra came back with friends and decided to wreak more havoc with its supernatural abilities. Eventually, we were able to fall asleep.

The next day, we ran into Andrea in the very hallway space where our battle began. Her eyebrows were furrowed in confusion and the tone of her voice matched.

"Was that you or Melanie screaming last night?"

mae (mai)
noun

1. The equivalent of "dude" among Costa Rican friends, typically of the younger variety.

Example: "Mae, que mierda" or "Shit, dude."

The Ladrón That Never Was

"What was that?" Melanie asked, jabbing me in the middle of the night. "Did you hear that?"

My senses were cloudy on account of the sudden call to wake up. Melanie is prone to nightmares and speaking gibberish in her sleep, so my instinct was to brush it off.

"It's fine," I said, rolling back over. It was around three or four in the morning, and we had a long day ahead of us to get to Bocas Del Toro. Our schedule was comprised of two buses, one confusing walk to the Mepe bus station, a taxi and two boats to get from Ciudad Colón, Costa Rica to our hotel in Bocas Del Toro, Panama. Simply typing it feels exhausting.

"There! That!" she said again. That time, I did hear something. It sounded like metal clanging.

"Maybe it's an animal? Like one of the neighborhood cats?" I surmised.

The sound continued. Neither of us wanted to say it, but it sounded like the gate to our apartment.

"I'll text Carolina," I said, despite the early hour. "Hey Carolina," I wrote in Spanish, "I'm not sure, but I think there's someone trying to get in the gate." I don't remember when, but I specifically used the word *ladrón* (thief). Of course she didn't respond—it was the middle of the night! Plus their bedroom was further away from the gate than ours.

Logic told me that it couldn't be a thief. If someone wanted to break in, they would do it without repeatedly clanging on the metal. Still, I felt overcome with a sense that this was it. I had never been robbed, but I managed to convince myself that it was happening.

I started missing our old apartment in downtown Cleveland. Homes have never felt safe to me. When I hit the age of staying up late for no reason, I would stare out our living room window in Mentor, Ohio, thinking something was out there. If someone pulled their car into the driveway to turn around, my heart would stop. If I saw someone walking underneath the glow of our streetlights, I'd panic. After all, our street didn't have sidewalks, so it seemed weird to see someone walking. I ironically started my life highly suspicious of a lone pedestrian, likely feeding my preference later in life for urban apartments and a constant stream of white noise.

"What should we do?" Melanie asked, visibly startled by the possibility we had concocted that we were being robbed. I didn't want to do anything. Doing something would mean we were those Gringos who made the irrational leap from sound to *they're coming to get us!* We didn't want to be *those* Gringos.

Yet the sound continued. It even seemed to get louder. Finally, I decided I also didn't want to be the Gringos who got robbed.

"I'll push the couch against the door," I said. It wasn't heavy enough to stop someone who wanted to get in, but it would make the initial break in take slightly longer (though admittedly a thief attempting to break our two door locks should have been sufficient notice to get the hell out of there).

With the couch flushed against our front door, I went back to our bedroom and consoled Melanie until we managed to fall back asleep. The next morning, we awoke with the couch just as we left it, our possessions just as they were.

"Joe?" Carolina called from below. I hurried out of bed and out to the patio.

"Morning, Carolina. How are you?"

"I'm fine. Sorry about last night. That was Esteban taking the backseat out of the car." Carolina had the look of an angry wife upset with her momentarily dopey husband. "I told him he can't work that late!"

Melanie and I were relieved. Of course it was Esteban! The man never sleeps. Even if a thief did come, Esteban would know before anyone else. Plus Esteban was our Tico dad at this point, which meant I believed he had superhuman strength like all sons do of their fathers. I'm fairly certain he could handle a couple of measly *ladrones*.

"It's okay," I said, laughing in a bit of a sleepy haze.

At least we could catch up on our missed sleep during Melanie's border run.

A Border Run To Bocas Del Toro

The "border run," better known by foreigners in Costa Rica as "the run," is an obligatory trip across international lines to renew one's ninety-day tourist visa. Relying on the tourist visa is heavily discouraged, but inevitably ends up as the de facto lifestyle for many. Those who have gone through the trouble of gaining some form of residency love to shame those who continue risking it with the tourist visa. They have a point, but for a couple of twenty-somethings who had no permanent relocation plans and wanted to see all that this corner of the globe had to offer anyway, the argument was relatively moot and better suited for Facebook groups where someone always knows better than someone else. You will know when you've found this person, because they will happily tell you so.

Had we planned on a longer commitment to Costa Rica, we would have gladly gone through the proper channels. As it were, UPEACE had already warned that most students don't get their student IDs until May when classes would be wrapping up. It wasn't exactly the most efficient process. Plus, as a native English teacher, it wasn't like Melanie was taking a job away from a Tico.

After about nine hours on the road, we arrived at Sixaola to the border crossing between Costa Rica and Panama. The Mepe bus dropped us off along a nondescript road adjacent to the highway. There were no signs, but our smiling bus driver was happy to point us in the right direction with a cheerful "Allá!"

As we neared the actual border, a local holding a stack of immigration forms chased us down, trying to hand us one for a price and usher us into a nearby building. His baseball cap, shorts, tee shirt and sandals didn't exactly scream "immigration officer," so I opted to verify with a nearby uniformed officer. After all, no one really talks to you when walking over the Canadian border at Niagara Falls—my only prior experience with international land crossings—except maybe a tourist asking for help taking their picture.

With our exit stamp secured from a grumpy-looking border agent, we continued ahead to the infamous Sixaola Bridge. Had there not been hundreds of people already crossing this dilapidated structure, humorously referred to as a piece of international infrastructure, I would have assumed we were on a hidden camera show, waiting to be gagged. The fact is, Costa Ricans and Panamanians cross with ease as if they had the holes of the bridge down to muscle memory. Only we Gringos, foolishly dragging wheeled luggage, had to take our time, watching every step with the same meticulous care a doctor takes during open heart surgery. This was a shame, not only because of the brief glimpses of certain death below, but because the landscape is actually quite delightful with the sun setting just over the Sixaola River. Not to mention the historic bridge itself was clearly a looker in its day and possibly could be again with a little financial love.

Turned out that this crumbling structure of wooden planks and metal was actually once an elevated railroad. A closer examination of the bridge revealed dusty tracks that had long been ignored. Suffice it to say, the bridge looked its age. This *puente ferroviario* or railroad bridge was first constructed in 1908, and any passerby can see it has largely been left to rot despite maintenance being the shared responsibility of the Costa Rican and Panamanian governments.

The respective national governments did come together in recent years to build a new $3.2 million bridge at 260 meters long over the river with an estimated lifespan of twenty-five years, hoping to eventually find a more permanent solution. This unremarkable (yet much more stable-looking) bridge stood alongside its older sibling, but was blocked off from pedestrian use. Rumor was that the new bridge was already having issues, giving merit to existing concerns over its brief estimated lifespan.

But as we had been learning in our initial travels throughout the region, pedestrians were trained by birth to be accustomed to inconvenience. Sidewalks were limited to city centers and optional everywhere else, forcing people to walk alongside high-speed vehicular traffic on highways and to dodge cars that see stop signs as suggestions. Puente Sixaola may look as if it will go the way of the Millennium Bridge at any moment (sans Death Eaters, of course), but at least it can't sideswipe you off the street. Thankfully, we managed to get across without taking a dip into the river below.

What followed was more confusion and more men not dressed in uniform insisting they wanted to help us. One such gentleman, noticeably taller than anyone else in the vicinity, pointed us into another decrepit building. This at least had "Bienvenidos a Panamá" painted on the side with a rustic beauty to it that clashed with the surrounding area, and offered some assurance that the following proceeding would be legitimate.

Inside sat two immigration officials looking as equally disgruntled as the Costa Rican we had just left. With minimal conversation, we received our stickers—yes, stickers—for Bocas Del Toro and were off.

This is when disaster could have struck. A casual traveler

might think that was all that needed to be done, but we were warned by previous Bocas travelers not to have such crazy thoughts. In fact, this is merely step one of two. After retrieving the Bocas sticker, we were meant to head down a makeshift staircase constructed alongside a tiny hill, continue past a gravel parking lot and finally to the lower level of what looked like one of those heinous, architecturally insulting shopping plazas my home country has had the misfortune of bestowing upon the world. This is where we were to actually enter the sovereign nation of Panama by explaining our travel plans and receiving our entry stamp (not to be confused with the sticker, you silly and foolish person). Basically, it boiled down to charging travelers to Bocas a little extra in taxes, but you absolutely cannot confuse the two (and nowhere is this plainly explained).

From there, the aforementioned large gentleman who guided us to the immigration building had already reserved a taxi for us —$15 per person to the coastal town of Almirante where speed boats finish the trip to Bocas Del Toro. Travel guides said we could get a taxi for less, but it felt weird to haggle over $10. Plus we knew the drive was supposed to be an hour and we were informed that the last boats would be leaving Almirante in forty-five minutes. We were in no place to barter when there was already someone in front of us more than willing to drive recklessly through the northern Panamanian countryside to ensure a couple of Gringos successfully completed their poorly-planned trip. And drive poorly, he did, turning what should have been at least a sixty-minute drive into thirty minutes of terrifying speeding down the Panamanian coast. Tight turns were handled by taking up both lanes, assuming nobody would be coming from around the corner. This gentleman operated as if he were in a real life Mario Kart race, though I was more concerned with an actual crash than being hit by a flung reptilian shell.

Thankfully for our sakes (and that of potential oncoming drivers) we arrived to Almirante unscathed and in time for the final connection of the day by boat to Bocas Del Toro.

Isolation. The only hint of life in coastal Panama came from the *acuaticos* or water taxis shuffling tourists from the mainland to the archipelago chain of islands known as Bocas Del Toro. The sun had set during our thirty-minute ride from mainland Almirante to Bocas Town. Then it was just us and the captain, or guy with his hand on the engine, on our little rusty *lancha* as we drifted a few minutes further from the main island of Colón to Carenero. No roads, no cars.

We pulled up to a dock. It was pitch black. I could see hints of a pavilion with a hammock. Clearly we were supposed to get out of the boat. But go where? We started by marching along the hundred-foot or so wooden walkway over the quiet sea toward what little light we could spot. Finally, we made out something in the darkness that appeared to be our lodging for the evening, Hotel Tierra Verde.

Moving from stone step to stone step, our hosts greeted us out on the patio.

"You made it!"

I hope that wasn't in doubt, I thought to myself. But considering we just barely caught the last acuatico of the day, I suppose there was a point in which our arrival could have gone either way.

Having survived the day on Nature Valley bars, we were quick to drop our bags, clean up and get back out the door to the nearest restaurant. Luckily there was Bibi's on the Beach, just a five-minute walk away from our hotel. Even in this brief walk, we got a sense of how rugged life could be on Isla Carenero. There were no lights or signs guiding the walk, only some sand, old wooden homes that appeared to be full of traveling (or squatting) surfers, and crabs large enough to rustle the surrounding bushes.

Bibi's appeared just as our hotel did—out of nowhere amidst the darkness. Sitting down, we were alone.

We'll take all the food and beer, please, we were both thinking. Luckily, we toned down our stereotypical American appetites for a simple plate of Chicken Criollo to go with our respective bottles of Balboa—one of Panama's national beers and our server's drink of choice. Balboa, like most things in Panama, is named after conquistador Vasco Núñez Balboa. His namesake beverage proved a hint stronger and darker than its Tico counterpart of Imperial or even the American water-beer heavyweights. But after a long, sweaty day of travel that took us over a questionable bridge before dropping us off with a Panamanian NASCAR driver, most any beer would have sufficed.

Sitting on the patio out on the sea, we finally had a moment to take in our surroundings. On Carenero, it was complete and utter silence. Below, a sting ray was cruising around in the clear waters along the shore, illuminated by the restaurant lights. The transport was exhausting, but Bocas was already proving itself.

The next morning we headed into Bocas Town for our first real walk around the small Caribbean city with no plan in mind other than a noon yoga class.

It doesn't take long to feel like you're in a beach town. Bocas is, thankfully, not some gaudy tourist resort where travelers are left isolated in a fort with their silly island drinks, but I could easily see the dichotomy between the haves and have nots. Gringo tourists were aplenty; marching down Main Street (or Calle 3) with backpacks half their size. They passed by the local bocatoreños selling their wares at Parque Simon Bolívar— another common namesake in these parts for his own place in

Latin American history. Bolívar was the George Washington of Latin America, if you will, a military and political leader in the revolution against colonial Spanish rule to liberate Gran Colombia—modern-day Venezuela, Colombia, Bolivia, Ecuador, Peru and Panama. Bolívar gets bonus points for freeing slaves, but he didn't see eye-to-eye with Washington on the role of the president, preferring lifetime terms where the outgoing president could select the next one.

Although a traveler from so-called developed countries (a distinction often made by the so-called developed countries) might sense overwhelming poverty, Panama did rank first in the world in Gallup-Healthways' Well-Being Index, so who's to say who's doing better? Hostels, hotels, restaurants and tourists shops line the streets of Bocas Town center, open and ready to serve. Drivers and trip leaders tracked us down from the main port.

"Hola! ¿Cómo está? ¿Inglés? What's the plan today, man?"

The aggressiveness was off-putting, like at the market in San José, but I reminded myself that it's a different culture, and more importantly, their livelihood. I was at least thankful that the money appeared to be going to the local Panamanians and not some foreign corporate chain sequestered from the community.

With nothing but time, we walked a bit off the main strip to find a different kind of Bocas. Here we saw an even greater contrast between the freshly painted Caribbean-style wooden buildings of Main Street and the homes of bocatoreños in the backdrop of ongoing development projects. But Angie, our contact with local tourism who helped plan this little Panamanian jaunt, told me that most locals welcome the tourism after the banana economy crashed at the turn of the twentieth century thanks to the "Panama disease," which issued a devastating blow to Bocas. The fungus wiped out an entire type of banana from the world, outside Asia.

With that behind them, Angie struck an optimistic tone.

"Looks like tourism is going to put Bocas on the map again and they [locals] want the old good times to come back," she said. "It all started when Tito Thomas, owner of Gran Hotel Bahia, the oldest building in Bocas Town and ex-headquarters of the old United Fruit Company started bringing groups from the old Canal Zone [U.S. military personal] on planes to Bocas for the Feria Del Mar."

Backpackers followed suit in the following decade, and even tourism darling Costa Rica started marketing the island chain as a destination that could be reached through their country. Angie herself came in the '90s when there was just one disco, a supermarket and a handful of hostels.

"After the U.S. military left in 1999, Panama started investing a lot more in tourism and Bocas started growing as more expats started moving to Bocas, opening businesses."

There's always the question of finding the right mix of development while maintaining the soul of the existing community when you talk about tourism. While you can only learn so much with two full days, Bocas at least seemed to be doing it infinitely better than other tourist towns I had visited over the years. For that, it seems to me they deserve some credit.

The grey skies of the morning had turned to rain toward the end of our aimless walk around town. Luckily it was just about time for our yoga class.

The studio was housed in a two-story wooden home colored purple with a painting of a deity underneath a simple wooden plank reading, "Bocas Yoga." The trim of the sign celebrated the colors of the Panamanian flag—red, white and blue. Our host and teacher, Jennifer, greeted us on the front patio with a wide smile, deep brown eyes and curly brown hair. Her father served in the U.S. military, which was why she was born in the Panamanian Canal Zone and permitted to hold dual citizenship. Eight years before, she took advantage of her Panamanian passport and opened a yoga studio in Bocas.

Our session was unlike any I had ever done before, from India to back home in the States. That's because we did partner yoga with myself sitting across from and facing Melanie, or as Jennifer referred to her for the duration of our session, my "beloved." It was difficult for both of us to keep a straight face. We're not exactly the type to refer to one another as "beloved." But when in Bocas Yoga, I suppose.

The practical purpose of partner yoga was to mirror the person across from you, which we were able to handle reasonably well without too much laughter. Discomfort only arose when Jennifer used me to give a demonstration of one of our poses. The position involved me on my back, knees bent to the side and the soles of my feet touching together—something of a two-dimensional seated lotus. The partner, Jennifer for the sake of the demonstration, places their hands on their partner's groin and holds a push-up position, putting some weight behind the stretch for the partner lying on the ground.

This sounds innocent enough, but while holding the position, Jennifer shuffled her hands closer to my nether regions, saying "Don't be afraid to get closer to your partner's energy for a better stretch."

I could only imagine Melanie's reaction, sitting across from me while an older woman inched herself closer to my "energy." And let's not forget that yoga shorts aren't exactly the most conservative attire to begin with. Usually there's an agreed upon "don't look" policy. For males, you'd have to try and spot something given the location. But when your legs are spread open in a position that naturally starts to thrusts your hips in the air, there's not much room for the imagination.

Then it was my turn to try it on Melanie. I started with what I thought was respectable hand placement for the confines of a classroom. Jennifer, though, nudged my hands closer to Melanie's groin, insisting that I not be afraid to get to "her energy."

To be fair, it really was a fantastic stretch.

Encroaching on the late afternoon, we purchased a six-pack of Balboa and headed back to the hotel for a little relaxation out on the dock, watching the acuaticos zip back and forth across the sea. Here was when I discovered my love for hammocks. How have I not embraced this before? The gentle swing, the light suspension, the comforting cocoon when the sides begin to slightly wrap around you. Who could hate a good hammock?

Adding to the enjoyment was watching a group of neighboring bocatoreño kids out on the adjacent dock, spending their time diving into the water and fishing with nothing more than a string and a plastic bottle for a reel. Nice to know we had a recycle-friendly community there.

This reminded me about the Well-Being Index. Who's doing better? The American kid playing video games all afternoon, cursing at inanimate objects because they got sniped in a virtual recreation of war (because war is fun! ...?), or a bocatoreño turning their surroundings into a better playground than Toys 'R Us could ever imagine? I know who I would want to hang out with. Though who knows—maybe those kids would rather play video games than fish.

The night was spent back in town where we caught a fire dance performance in between power outages at a large outdoor restaurant that at least gave off the appearance of being for an upscale crowd with its modern decor and waiting staff dressed to the nines as if they might be joining their customers later on. I don't know what it is, but the fearlessness of hurling flaming balls like they were made by NERF or swinging an engulfed hoop around the hips is pretty freakin' impressive to me.

Then, just before calling it a night, we stumbled upon a local band equipped with a variety of drums and bugles entertaining passersby in the middle of Parque Simon Bolivar. This chance encounter proved to be our most memorable of the trip. You could sense that everyone, the musicians especially, were enjoying every beat, bouncing from side to side to the encouragement of the crowd.

Unfortunately the fun sputtered to a sudden silence once the cops showed up. I suppose I don't know for sure that it was the cops, but the bugles came to an awkward crescendo and the drums fell silent as soon as a couple of gentlemen sporting uniforms came wandering in. You do the math.

Our final day on the horizon, we awoke to crystal clear blue skies and a powerful sun just in time for our planned tour around Playa Zapatillas. Evidently, the beach had a connection to the hit CBS show, *Naked And Afraid*. For those unfamiliar, the premise sends one naked man to meet one naked woman in a dangerous location armed with only their survival skills. Apparently, one contestant had to call it quits after suffering from one too many mosquito bites at Zapatillas. Naturally this is where we decided to spend our day of relaxation. Of course we were guided to a much safer slice of the jungle and were allowed to keep our clothes on. After all, nobody wants to leave tourists with tales of itchy privates (nor do we want the image).

First, en route to the beach, we spent thirty minutes or so looking for good 'ole flipper in Dolphin Bay. This consisted of about six or eight speed boats, full of photo-starved tourists— Gringos and Latinos alike—motoring around in circles every time someone spotted a fin breaking the surface.

"Over there!" a tourist would shout, standing up and rocking the boat as the guide angrily reminded everyone to stay seated and keep the weight balanced. One boat would rush over to the sighting, prompting all of the other drivers to follow suit. I couldn't blame the drivers, though. They probably didn't want to deal with some entitled tourist, yell-asking in English, why they weren't doing everything they could to get them a selfie with a dolphin.

Minutes went by without another sighting as we bobbed around the waves created by other boats, breathing nothing but exhaust. No surprise, the dolphins would always be gone by the time we got to where they were spotted. But what could we expect a dolphin to do with a bunch of boats speeding after it as soon as it comes up for air? Strike a pose? Dolphins are smart. They're not going to make like a Kardashian, throw a fin to the hip, and toss their, I guess, blowhole back for someone's Instagram account.

Moral of the story, we would have happily found another way to Zapatillas if we could have skipped that inane side-tour, because the beach itself was definitely worth the excursion. Just as I had been previously introduced to the wonderful world of hammocks, I was now learning about the wonderful world of snorkeling. This whole having the ability to breathe whilst underwater thing was a foreign concept to me and one which I now love. Truth be told, I could've spent hours just staring at the Bocas seafloor full of vivid coral and fish that reminded me of my childhood fantasies spurred on by *The Little Mermaid*. Alas, we eventually did have to get back to civilization.

We had missed out on a proper celebration of Costa Rica's independence day, so I was thrilled when we caught some of Panama's Separation Day festivities. Our cab left early from Almirante to ensure we got to the border with plenty of time to cross back into Costa Rica and board our bus to San José. Traffic bottlenecked in a few towns along the way with marching bands and school children dressed in matching uniforms taking over the streets to commemorate the November 3rd holiday that marks Panama's separation from Colombia.

"Today is Separation Day," our driver told us with a hint of pride, his Panamanian flag dangling around the rearview mirror.

Indeed, it was on this day in 1903 when Panama formally separated from Colombia to become its own Republic of Panama. The formal separation was preceded by the Thousand Days' War between conservative and liberal factions in the newly created Republic of Colombia. The conservative government won in the end thanks in part to threats from U.S. President Theodore Roosevelt's navy in the region. Teddy, you see, was protecting his interests in the future construction of the Panama Canal. In fact, the final peace treaty was signed on an American battleship, the Wisconsin, marking the end of the war on November 21, 1902.

Less than a year later, a separatist movement in Panama had gained strong support. Colombia deployed troops from Barranquilla to depose Governor of Panama José Domingo de Obaldía and General Esteban Huertas, but faced delays along the way thanks to Panama Railway authorities who sympathized with separatists. Teddy's USS Nashville, still with an eye on the future canal, did its part to interfere with Colombian troop movement in the region. With Colombian troops suppressed, the Revolutionary Junta declared the separation of the isthmus and the independence of the Republic of Panama. (News of the separation didn't even reach Colombia until three days later thanks to issues with submarine cables.) No surprise, the United States quickly recognized the new Republic of Panama on November 6th (unofficially) and 13th (officially).

This marked the beginning to a complicated—and more often than not—one-sided relationship between the United States and

Panama. Melanie and I knew that we would find our way to Panama City to explore the canal and more of this history before our time in Central America came to an end.

Meantime, we turned our attention back to the happier moment at hand. Panamanians had lined the streets with parked cars, finding space wherever they could throughout all the small towns we passed on our way to the highway. Many, we imagined, were parents cheering on their sons and daughters marching in the parades. Most everyone was wearing a smile and old women clapped their hands to the beat of the music. Small children climbed onto their fathers' shoulders to see over the crowds, and the trumpets continued to provide a delightfully cheerful soundtrack to put a cap on our first visit to Panama.

Coffee, Waterfalls and Football

In early November, Melanie's parents came for an impromptu visit. Melanie and her mother, Helen, have always maintained a close relationship often more reminiscent of blood sisters than that of a typical mother and daughter. Whereas most mothers would be satisfied to hear from their offspring a few times a month, Melanie and Helen chat almost every day—so long as they can find a mobile or internet signal. They don't do it out of obligation. No. They do it because they actually enjoy talking to one another *every single day.*

Needless to say it came as a bit of a surprise to Melanie's close, ancestrally Greek family when we decided to move abroad. This is a family and culture that still embraces and expects regular attendance at the Sunday family dinners. Hugs and shared feelings are the norm—a huge contrast to my more typical Midwestern upbringing where emotions are a wild beast to be domesticated and caged. Once when I thought my father was mad at me, I sent him a text.

"Did the Cavs win last night?"

He responded quickly in the affirmative, offering a brief analysis of the win and how they'd been looking as a team. This meant we were cool.

The reaction on my side of the family when we shared the news about Costa Rica was more matter of fact.

Baur Family: Okay. You're an adult. Do whatever you want. That's love, people. That's love.

Melanie's side of the family were just as supportive, but there were far more expressions of feelings and emotions than would ever happen on my side.

Helen planned to visit alone at first, but Melanie's father, Patrick, was able to join at the last minute thanks to a healthy dosage of airline miles. The pair had made it to Central America before—Guatemala—following a family recommendation. Even before our own plans to move to Costa Rica, we had often heard the story of how the guys on the trip were thrilled beyond belief to stumble upon an Ohio State football game in progress at a bar in town. On a more somber note, Patrick admitted noticing a stark contrast in wealth among the population.

"They have some of the best golfing I've ever seen, but what Guatemalan could actually afford it?" he wondered. He was also notably surprised by how welcoming they were of U.S. Americans, considering our not-so-stellar history with them.

"We gave them syphilis!" he'd say in surprise. "I wouldn't blame them if they hated us."

Record scratch. That's right, the U.S. government deliberately gave innocent Guatemalans a sexually transmitted disease. During the Truman administration, doctors led these human-led experiments by infecting everyone from soldiers to prostitutes and mental patients with syphilis—without informed consent. The goal was to study the disease and its treatment. By the end, it resulted in eighty-three deaths. The U.S. finally formally apologized to Guatemala in 2010 via a joint statement from Secretary of State Hillary Clinton and Secretary of Health and Human Services Kathleen Sibelius. President Obama also apologized to Guatemalan President Álvaro Colom. I can only imagine how that conversation went.

Obama: So, about that report saying we purposefully gave

your countrymen syphilis. That's messed up.

Colom: Yes. Yes it is.

Obama: I mean, human-led experiments with a sexual transmitted disease? And at the same time Nazis were being tried for their fucked up experiments? Seriously, messed up stuff.

Colom: Yep. Messed up. Think we've got that covered.

Obama: So we're, uh, going to go ahead and formally apologize for that.

Colom: And compensation for the families?

Obama: How about some M&Ms with the official seal of the President of the United States?

Patrick and Helen are more inclined toward European and North American travel, but their positive experience in Guatemala had them looking forward to visiting another Central American country. Not to mention I'm fairly certain Helen would charter a rocket to visit Melanie on Mars once interplanetary tourism becomes a thing.

Given the impromptu nature of this trip, nothing too significant was planned. We spent Friday afternoon and evening touring Colón before grabbing a couple of beers in town. Saturday was just as relaxing with a visit to the town farmer's market in the morning, a short hike around a park in El Rodeo and an agreeable dinner at fancy-schmancy Vino Mundo in nearby Brasil de Mora. Sunday, however, was a day to explore a bit of the Central Valley, starting with a tour of the Doka Estate coffee plantation and La Paz Waterfall Garden in Alajuela.

Coffee and Costa Rica are synonymous nouns for Gringos. The two are always six degrees of separation from one another, like any Hollywood film actor and Kevin Bacon. We could be talking about a volcano eruption and somehow find ourselves talking about Tico coffee by the end of the conversation. Or to turn it around, we might be sipping morning coffee in Cleveland and thinking about the beans back in Costa Rica.

We were saddened to hear rumblings that Costa Ricans don't even get the best batches of their own coffee production. While serving us a morning cup during one breakfast, Carolina confirmed that the tastiest stuff gets exported to North America, Europe and Japan. I haven't the faintest idea how one determines which beans are better, but the fact that someone goes through the trouble of making sure Ticos don't get the best brews is disheartening to me. Could you imagine how the French would react if some overweight American in a button-up Hawaii shirt had first dibs on their best cheeses and wines? There would be riots.

All of this was confirmed at the Doka Estate coffee tour where our Costa Rican guide walked us through their process and shared that they do, indeed, send their best work out of the country and give Ticos the leftovers. Also curious was her description of the bean picking process. It truly is arduous, backbreaking work. And it's work the Costa Ricans leave to immigrant Nicaraguans.

Costa Rica and Nicaragua have a similar relationship as the United States and Mexico. Stereotypes are generally less fair to the latter. Depending on who you talk to, Nicaraguans are painted as lazy criminals.

"Things were good around here... Then the Nicaraguans started moving in and now there's crime." I had heard some iteration of this from various Tico tour guides and taxi drivers. I never understood the lazy stereotype. Remind me again who are the ones taking some of the most difficult, thankless jobs in the coffee industry, working long hours underneath a punishing sun? That's right. Nicaraguans.

Most laughable in our guide's description of the Nicaraguan role was that, "Costa Ricans don't like picking coffee. But Nicaraguans don't mind."

Sure they don't, I thought.

The La Paz Waterfall Gardens were paired with the Doka Estate tour thanks to a manageable distance between the two. Neither particularly excited us, but it was at least an excuse to get around the valley a little bit with visiting family. One can only do so much in Ciudad Colón.

By the time we arrived at the gardens, the weather had taken a turn to its rainy season schedule. I myself planned poorly and was shivering from exhibit to exhibit. Luckily for my sake, most seemed a little underwhelmed or at least uncomfortable with a majority of the exhibits and were happy to move along to the waterfalls. It's hard to tell from the name, but the gardens turned out to be something of a code for zoo. Seeing some of the creepy critters was interesting, I suppose, but they couldn't overshadow the depressing sight of a jaguar circling back and forth, smacking its head against the window frame in a clear show of insanity. I wanted to play the role of Chief from *One Flew Over The Cuckoo's Nest* and send the big cat free. But I can't exactly throw a sink like a rag doll, nor do I think the law would look too kindly upon me freeing a large, wild, carnivorous animal in public.

Zoos weren't really my thing back in the States either, so it's no surprise I didn't take to this mini-version in Costa Rica. Melanie and my in-laws concurred that the experience could have probably done without the jaguar slowly losing its sanity. The waterfalls, on the other hand, gave us more of what we were looking for even if it was a tad overdeveloped for our liking. Essentially we had a string of waterfalls, each one more dramatic than the last, as we hiked down a manicured path. I couldn't help but constantly wonder what it all looked like before money came in and someone decided to profit heavily off the area.

Like Poás before, the experience would have been

tremendously more enjoyable if I could have earned the sights through a rigorous hike. Seeing throngs of tourists and gaudy fake-jungle infrastructure surrounding the falls takes away from the journey, not to mention that those completely against any form of remote exercise had the option of taking a bus to the final and most dramatic waterfall. This Disney-fication of nature is why the earlier trip to Poás struck me as underwhelming. To see La Paz before the tourism development would have been a real treat.

Our evening plans took us back to Esteban and Carolina's for what promised to be a thorough test of my improving linguistic capabilities as I translated back and forth between our Tico hosts and visiting family. Esteban greeted us as boisterously as always. For the men, it was a handshake that quickly turned into a big bear hug with a couple strong pats on the back that tended to scare the air out of your lungs.

"Hola! Como estás?" he'd say in his baritone voice. "Pasa, pasa!"

As Esteban grew more familiar with me, it'd often be one powerful slap on the back, a definitive, "Joe" and slight nod.

Carolina greeted with a gentle hug and the typical Latina kiss on the left check. It was always sweet and actually felt welcoming. Prior to Costa Rica, I had always felt exceptional discomfort with hugs for greetings, much less a kiss. I don't have a drop of Mediterranean blood in me.

It was interesting to watch the interactions between two sets of people meeting for the first time, mostly unable to verbally communicate. I was more accustomed to either being involved or causing the linguistic confusion, certainly not being the translator.

Carolina's English was always better than she let on. It felt hesitant when she spoke and she usually reserved her English as a last resort when we'd hit a linguistic speed bump and one of us couldn't understand the other. My in-laws, however, had to dig out high school Spanish that had been long at rest. Patrick was especially interested in learning some basic pleasantries, like how you greet a passerby on the street. (It was also a cultural lesson as Helen prompted the "delicate question" of whether or not you flush the toilet paper.)

Translating between the two groups was surprisingly less of an exercise than I had expected. That's not a testament to my improving Spanish but rather the beauty of non-verbal communication. After offering us seats on their couch around the television, Esteban retreated to the kitchen to pull out some cold cans of Imperial. With his hand, he made a symbol for drinking, which for him was a mixture of slugging a bottle back and the Hawaiian gesture of "hang loose."

Conversation was simple, too. While translating, you see how simple initial conversation tends to be. Nobody talks in book-speak with vivid descriptions. The bulk of conversation surrounds "I like..." and "Do you like...?" Naturally, Patrick became inquisitive as to whether or not Esteban had ever embraced American football—though the question was admittedly more of an in to asking if he could put on the Ohio State game.

Shrugging his shoulders, Esteban said, "I've seen it, but we mostly watch soccer."

"Well, there's a big game going on tonight with a team from our state," Patrick explained through me, which was more than enough to launch Esteban out of his chair to grab the remote and find the game for us Gringos desperate for some high stakes, uncompensated, college-aged, man-on-man smashing.

It took Esteban mere seconds of clicking before he got the game up on the television.

"Alright!" Patrick exclaimed. "Now we're talking."

See? You don't really need to translate that. It's joy, pure and simple.

I initially felt a bit embarrassed about asking to get the game on television. *Did this hit some kind of American stereotype of television worship*, I wondered? As much as I had traveled, being invited into someone's home was rare. I always assumed that watching television was less of an event in other countries. Then again, I recall a number of quiet evenings suddenly interrupted by the screams of Esteban and his fellow soccer fans celebrating or bemoaning a goal. Perhaps the emotions of men across the spectrum of national and cultural boundaries are ultimately controlled by the ability of their team to score points.

As the game went on, Helen and Carolina discussing their children, Patrick noticed Esteban leaning toward the television with an intensely focused stare. I could see a cartoon in his head of someone shoveling coal on a steam engine train as he tried to make out what was happening on the screen. Finally, the furnace burst.

"No entiendo," Esteban admitted in defeat. "I don't get it."

Who would? American football, unexplained, is a bizarre athletic endeavor. Men, eleven on each side for some reason, are covered in bulky equipment for the purpose of bashing into one another as one side tries to cross various lines measured in yards —a unit of measurement nobody uses in daily life.

Then there are the penalties. Something seemingly good happens, only to be met by groans when a wadded up yellow napkin is on the field. Points are measured in increments of six, three and then you get an extra point after scoring six unless you decide to go for two by running a play you would similarly run to get six.

I don't blame Esteban for a second.

tuanis (too·a·nees)
adjective

1. Basically, it means "cool."
2. Something the young kids are saying these days when they aren't busy twittering and Snapchatting.
3. Its origins are not Costa Rican. Nineteenth century Salvadoran General Francisco Malespín created a linguistic code that rearranged and switched various vowels. "a" for "e," "i" for "o," "b" for "t," "f" for "g" and "p" for "m," and vice versa. When you apply his system to the word, "bueno," you're left with, "tuani," which added on a final "s" at some point during its trek south to Costa Rica. (Hat tip to *The Tico Times'* Katherine Stanley for researching and publishing that interesting tidbit.)

Example: "You're writing a book about spending a year abroad in Costa Rica? Tuanis!"

Running with the Ticos

Ticos are not a lazy bunch. In fact, in my highly anecdotal experience, they put the average American to shame.

Back home, exercise always brought to mind a few stereotypes. First, the runner who drives to the treadmill. (Anyone driving to the gym, for that matter.) Second, there's the Frat Bro with his knack for sacrificing safe posture for more weight and taking long breaks between sets that nearly nullify the workout. Then there's the unnecessary gorilla-grunting after each rep that sounds like a roid rage orgasm. Frat Bro's time would be better spent in front of a full-length mirror in a private room with a neon sign flashing above that reads, "YOU'RE AWESOME!" complete with a mixed playlist featuring Creed and Nickelback.

Last, we have the talker, someone who treats their workout like a wine social. They'll hunt you down with the eyes of a hawk in the middle of a workout and demand conversation even if you've given no sign that you're interested in talking.

Now I can't say without exception that none of these stereotypes exist in Costa Rica, but I had yet to see it. To the contrary, Ticos appeared to take their workouts rather seriously. Sunrises were always around five-thirty and Ticos were up with it, charging up the hills in their running shorts and tank tops. Cyclists would set out on their rides even earlier, in the interest in covering more kilometers before heading to work. There was also Zumba, which is essentially an excuse to dance and call it a workout. I didn't meet a soul who didn't enjoy Zumba at some level. Then of course, most anyone from the age of a toddler to teenagers had some soccer background. Volleyball and even roller skating proved to be exceptionally popular, as well.

If that weren't enough, many even extended their workout to include their morning commute. Carlos, a volunteer firefighter and UPEACE employee, rode his mountain bike up the steep, winding road separating Colón and UPEACE in El Rodeo over about seven kilometers. None of this is to say that Costa Rica was absolutely absolved of baffling laziness. Those with a car, seemingly older generations, would insist on using it everywhere, even for the shortest of walks. One of Melanie's English students, an otherwise kind woman in her forties, overheard that we were going to the farmer's market after class one morning.

"I'm going, too! Do you want a ride?" she asked.

"Oh no, thank you. We're okay," Melanie replied.

"Are you sure?"

"Yeah, we like the walk."

The walk was no more than a couple of blocks. There's no doubt in our mind that driving and looking for parking would have taken considerably longer. The offer was obviously coming from a good place. But apparently it's not uniquely American to have car ownership make you forget about the wonders your legs can accomplish in moving the body.

On the whole, Ticos struck me as an admirably active group of people. Often their level of activeness made me feel like I needed to get off my ass and do something. That was largely the impetus for our signing up to run in Santa Ana's annual Lindora Run, a ten-kilometer trek through the popular San José suburb. Both Melanie and I had missed the thrill of an organized run and joining a small race seemed like a nice way to see something most never do when traveling abroad. It was an opportunity to see the Tico take on something we loved doing back home.

The race called for an early morning rise. We had been through the area before in between airport runs and our bus trips to San José, but we couldn't figure out if the bus actually dropped off where we needed to go seeing as many of the bus companies have yet to discover the beauties of the World Wide Web. For safety's sake, we opted to use the same pirate taxi as Andrea had called for our ride home following Carpe Chepe. Andrea warned us to give this particular driver an extra fifteen minutes, which ended up being a good call seeing as I'm almost certain I woke him up when I called to remind him he was late.

Turned out we could have easily taken the bus, but doing so would have required a decent walk alongside Lindora, Santa Ana's very American-style, high-speed thoroughfare through the center of a recently developed area where the race started. Inhaling some muffler farts didn't exactly sound like a great way to warm up for a 10K, so we were plenty happy with our decision. (In retrospect, I realized we were contributing to the problem of runners breathing muffler farts by taking a taxi.)

We had no fantasy that this race would be the most scenic available in Costa Rica. What little we had seen and heard of the area indicated that it would be a rip-off of the worst in American development. That was, a multi-lane, high-speed road with fast food chains and the occasional bland plaza with parking in the front. Our suspicions were very much confirmed. Sidewalks appeared to be an endangered species here. The area was designed hostile to pedestrians.

What better place to hold a road race?

The story behind Lindora is rather intriguing. Kevin, a Canadian professor in his thirties at UPEACE, shared that the Lindora land was originally supposed to be home to the university's new Earth Charter Center. An odd choice for a location considering it's an easy thirty-minute drive from campus, I grant you, but hang with me.

As the story goes, UPEACE received the land as a donation explicitly for the Earth Charter, but then President of the Council, Maurice Strong, later decided to build on campus and instead sell the Lindora area to developers. When Strong left Costa Rica, there were still authorities who wanted to ask him some questions. Rumors speculate that he was persona non grata.

It might be hard to jump directly to accusations of wrong doing by Mr. Strong when looking at his résumé. The Manitoba native grew up impoverished through the Great Depression and worked his way up to become the first executive director of the United Nations Environment Programme and national president and chairman of the Extension Committee of the World Alliance of YMCAs. The International Union for Conservation of Nature even recognized him as a leader in the fledgling environmental movement.

Mr. Strong's work was not completely altruistic. He was also an oil entrepreneur working in the Alberta oil patch and eventually achieved the presidency of the Power Corporation of Canada until 1966. Skipping ahead, UPEACE hired him in 1998 to clean up a bad reputation plagued by mismanagement, misappropriation of funds and incompetent governance.

Around the same time, the Oil-for-Food fiasco was developing in which it was alleged that Mr. Strong accepted a $1 million check from the UN-sanctioned regime of Saddam Hussein. That same year, in the polar opposite end of the nefarious spectrum, he became known as the "godfather" of the UN's 1997 Kyoto treaty.

Following his mysterious death on November 25, 2015, Claudia Rosett of the Foundation for Defense of Democracies had this to say: "He had a piece in scandals ranging from North Korea to Iraq to the climate business to this bizarre university that he sort of revived with UN funds from UN organizations he helped to found." She continued alleging that he abused the United Nations and served the interests of UN insiders. "This was one of the great scam artists of the modern world."

Who are we to believe? It's said the political left of Canada will overlook the bizarre Hussein allegations in favor of his environmentalism. The political right, such as Ms. Rosett's foundation, are generally no fans of environmentalism and skeptical of international bodies like the UN to begin with. Perhaps Strong got the last laugh.

Despite the Lindora development, the race itself was quite enjoyable. The energy from our fellow racers was exactly what we had been missing from our running back home. It didn't take long for the course to whisk us away from the nonsense and onto the leafy, windy roads of Costa Rica that I loved so much. It's here where I could always find fresh valley air, a cool morning breeze, clear blue skies and the meditative quiet of the Costa Rican countryside.

There were just two notable oddities. One, volunteers handed us water in plastic wraps to be popped open for a quick blast of hydration. I had never seen anything like it and was never able to figure out the most effective method of delivering the water to my mouth without first spilling it all over myself.

The second came at the post-race celebration. Lindora Run ended in a parking lot for one of the shopping plazas. Parking spaces had been taken over by a stage featuring an enthusiastic host cooling down his adorning crowd of racers with some post-race Zumba.

That's right, Zumba. To relax after running ten kilometers, throngs of runners were gyrating their hips to some high tempo Enrique Iglesias and the encouraging chants of their instructor on stage. The writer in me should have jumped right in for the sake of the story and getting the full experience, but after ten kilometers of hilly running, the writer begins to fade and make way for hunger.

So instead, Melanie and I finished the morning by continuing with our own tradition, a post-race brunch mixed with a little taste of our new home—gallo pinto. By the time we finished, paid our bill and headed back out to catch the bus home, post-race Zumba was still underway.

Seriously. Ticos are not a lazy bunch.

El Triángulo De La Solidaridad

UPEACE operated classes differently than most master's programs. Rather than a typical schedule of multiple classes over a semester, students took just one class over two or three weeks for about three hours a day with the expectation that the rest of the day would be spent catching up on reading and studying. By November, I had already completed a small handful of my courses. I had a strong start, captivated by the coursework and excited to be learning again full-time.

Naturally, my initial enthusiasm hit a lull within the first couple of months, which was to be expected. School is still school, after all. But the obvious culprit for my growing disinterest in schoolwork was without question a course on how to conduct academic research. Simply typing that sentence made me yawn. Thankfully, that course was followed by something in my wheelhouse—media production. The final exam was essentially presenting a short documentary project.

Score! I thought. *I'm going to nail this.*

My mind immediately raced toward various project ideas. I was determined to tackle something profound that would move my audience to think, perhaps even to tears. It was the kind of stream of consciousness many artists are guilty of before finally realizing how naive and self-inflated such illusions of grandeur are. The course did lead to one proverbial blessing in disguise, however. It sent me to a slum of San José.

That's probably not the combination of thoughts one would expect. "Blessing" plus "opportunity" does not usually equal "visiting a slum," but in this case it all added up. I always had an interest in stories not yet told. One of my most important assignments before moving to Costa Rica was a story I had written looking at a U.S. drone strike in Yemen that allegedly (and very likely) hit an innocent wedding party. I spent days researching and interviewing subjects via Skype who had spoken with families on the ground in rural Yemen. The final product was something I was quite proud of and suggested I might be interested in a career that fed my travel itch by going to those places less traveled and telling their stories. What better example of this than visiting a slum in a country best known for tourism, beaches and jungle?

The project idea came from my partner, Valerie, who knew a Costa Rican student, Davíd, who also worked at the non-profit El Niño y la Bola (The Boy and the Ball) in San José. Our project, she thought, could be a simple documentation of their efforts in the slum of El Triángulo de la Solidaridad just north of central San José off Route 32. The unplanned community was home to approximately 2,000 people and some 520 families, largely Nicaraguan.

We planned to visit on a weekday afternoon, first with a stop at El Niño y la Bola headquarters to meet staff and conduct a video interview with a resident. Our subject was in his early twenties and from the Nicaraguan capital of Managua. He was shy and spoke rather quietly, but was frank as he shared his story of being taken to Costa Rica by his family in search of work. They landed in El Triángulo with no options and it had been his home ever since he was a small child.

His prospects for a stable future seemed bright, however. He was the first from the community to be accepted into a university—the highly competitive University of Costa Rica, no less.

Once the camera (my iPhone) stopped rolling, he opened up a bit more over some standard small talk.

"Do you cheer for Costa Rica or Nicaragua?" I asked since it was just five months ago that Costa Rica made a historic run in the 2014 FIFA World Cup.

"Nicaragua is terrible," he laughed. "I prefer baseball."

"You know Dennis Martinez Stadium, right?"

"Yes, of course."

"He played for the baseball team in my city back in the States."

"Wow! He's like a hero back home."

Our chat came to an abrupt end, as it was time to continue with two additional interviews before moving over to El Triángulo itself with Davíd. He drove us through steady San José traffic en route to the slum, complaining about the congestion as we bounced over a set of railroad tracks.

"I wish we had more trains," he lamented.

We knew going into this that getting to El Triángulo would be a bit of an experience in and of itself. It's not like there's parking there, after all. So we parked across the street from El Triángulo at a gas station. A tech company headquarters next door provided the juxtaposition. Davíd pointed it out as an obvious metaphor of inequality. Behind him there was also a sign about an upcoming roads project that would displace the people of El Triángulo with four kilometers of new highway to connect northern and western sectors of San José. My strong bias against highways, with their history of steamrolling cities back in the States, already had me fuming.

At the time, Davíd and El Niño y la Bola were fighting the government in the courts, arguing residents had not been given enough notice to find new housing. It seemed as if the powers that be didn't feel it entirely necessary to worry about the residents given that the sum was technically illegal. They did end up offering housing, which some from El Triángulo had accepted, but others were left concerned that it was too far from San José and any prospect of employment.

Davíd and Valerie took their time minding the traffic of Route 32 as they ran across the highway. I stayed back and filmed what appeared to be a game of Frogger brought to life. Coincidentally, a group of uniform-dressed elementary school students were walking back to the slum simultaneously. Even though I didn't have the opportunity to meet those specific children, I always think of them whenever I now see a child back home complaining about being forced to eat dinner or wanting something shiny because... it's shiny.

I caught up with my colleagues, running across the highway and meeting them alongside a dirt path where the first buildings of El Triángulo crawled up a small hill of green grass. For as much as some might pretend a place like El Triángulo doesn't exist, it very much does. You can't miss its makeshift homes and stores created with strategically placed wood, tin and whatever other scrap materials residents can find.

Davíd didn't expect problems; crime had been known to happen in these corners, though primarily at night. He expected we would be fine, but advised to be courteous and not film without permission, something I was happy to obey anyhow.

El Triángulo's infrastructure is made up of dirt paths carving the way in between homes and the occasional store selling basic necessities. Particularly muddy areas had planks of wood placed overtop to make walking a bit easier. Though we were lucky that it had been rather dry for some time, one could easily imagine how difficult it is to get around El Triángulo with any amount of rain hitting the ground.

The community is incredibly dense. At some points, I could touch both sides of the "street" with my arms stretched out (though had I actually done that, I would have accidentally tripped up some kids running by).

It was obvious early on that Davíd was a regular as he was immediately recognized and greeted by one of the residents. The man's stoic children looked on with curiosity, presumably confused as to why their father was speaking to us. After all, we were probably a confusing group to look at from their young perspective. Davíd, a Tico, was mostly bald with skin as fair as mine, and Valerie had a darker complexion and hair to match thanks to her Venezuelan-Honduran parents. Then there was me, who couldn't possibly look more foreign.

Walking along, I couldn't help but be impressed by the construction of the community. Of course the exteriors aren't aesthetically pleasing; it's a community made up for survival, after all, not visual inspiration. These folks weren't getting help from some government or private entity with money to build their community, yet everything appeared sturdy and plenty insulated, and I doubt the folks who created El Triángulo had access to the best material or a building contractor. Usually I'm one to walk with tunnel vision when in delicate circumstances, wanting to mind my own business and not peer into someone's property like I'm at a zoo, but I couldn't help but steal the occasional glance. If I would have taken a still photograph of some of the interiors, one might mistake it for a modest abode. Inside one room, I noticed an older woman, perhaps a mother, watching television on a flat screen with a handful of smiling toddlers.

One woman, heavier set with a piercing voice, joined our meandering tour to offer her own insights as we shook hands with various residents. Stories were often similar. Life is hard, but you make the best of it. Nobody complained and nobody asked for anything, though I did give a coin to a little girl with a sparkling crown and a flowing white dress. She had just celebrated communion and it's tradition to make a small offering of money, I was told.

We left El Triángulo having enjoyed our walk and the omnipresent peaceful calm despite the community's uncertainty. Though the Housing Ministry continues to move residents, others have successfully held up the project due to environmental concerns and opposition to being moved to publicly funded homes far from the capital and its employment opportunities. Others have blocked busses carrying residents of El Triángulo from visiting their neighborhoods in San José where they might have the opportunity to move. The infamous "not in my backyard" mentality knows no political boundary.

Meanwhile, Davíd and his colleagues have since made our little tour into an official enterprise, offering tourists looking to see more than beaches and jungle the opportunity to visit El Triángulo. For just $12, El Triángulo residents will guide visitors around the community to showcase a different yet equally important side to Costa Rica. I for one can say that my jaunt around El Triángulo has been more impactful in my life and in shaping my worldview than seeing yet another beach.

That said, it was time to head to the beach.

Patacones and Bad Weed in Puerto Viejo

Puerto Viejo is, for the most part, thought of and advertised as a party town.   Surfers lazily flip-flop around the old port toward the infamous waves of Salsa Brava, take a siesta and come out once more to rage through the evening and into the morning. Bob Marley's greatest hits are heard throughout the day and into the night, whether you're at a Gringo-run bar or a family-owned restaurant just off the main strip. Beach bikes roll across the narrow roads as travelers and locals alike navigate from the black sands of Playa Negra to the more popular Playa Cocles. Short jaunts north and south along the coast leads to the impressive Cahuita National Park and the more remote Playa Manzanillo. That's Puerto Viejo in a nutshell.

This admittedly did not sound like my scene nor Melanie's. Each birthday seems to knock another ten minutes or so off our tolerance for staying up late. Nonetheless, we're just about always game for taking the reviews into account and checking things out for ourselves.

After seeing how gloriously wrong people were about San José, perhaps Puerto Viejo, too, would yield something special beyond the reviews. Besides, if worst came to worst, there was always the beach. And after experiencing an MTV-esque spring break in Panama City, Florida during my collegiate years, Neanderthal men hosing off intoxicated women on a concert stage and all, I'm confident I will never find anything as obnoxious.

Mepe, the same bus that took us to the dying bridge at the Panamanian border en route to Bocas Del Toro, left us at the edge of the main strip. With the crashing waves to our backs, we began our short march south to our lodging at Cashew Hill Jungle Lodge. Sidewalks quickly disappeared as we passed a few restaurants, shops and a grocery store. Soon we were in the residential part of town, walking past the school and soccer field where a pickup game amongst a few local kids was underway. The hike up the gravel road to Cashew Hill, our suitcase in my arms for an extended bicep curl of sorts, served as my workout for the day.

The effort was worth it. We decided early on without hesitation that it was one of the loveliest lodgings we had ever stayed. This place was designed in a way that felt like nature could easily reclaim it if not for the care of its groundskeeper, Edwin. Unsurprisingly, we were told it was a lot of work to maintain the perfectly manicured gravel paths that crisscrossed between shrubs, flowers and fruits as if in a mini-greenhouse. Caring for the cabins themselves seemed to be an ordeal in and of itself. Luckily Mark, the general manager, had Edwin on hand to assist, a Tico with a perpetual broad smile whose family was still in San José, but longed to move to Puerto Viejo.

After admiring our ocean view from our perched location, hunger called us to town. We quickly stumbled upon Soda Guetto Girl One Love, a basic-looking wooden shack with Caribbean character. Clearly this was a family business; a baby was sleeping in a crib next to an empty dining table in the middle of the establishment. No menu, only Bob Marley jammin' and casados.

Costa Rica, for some reason, doesn't seem to have the greatest food reputation. Tico cuisine often elicits an "eh" from foodies busy adjusting the tint on their next Instagram post. I find this unfair. That said, we had been raving about each casado as our best casado in Costa Rica, one right after the other since moving there four months ago. The casado con pollo at Soda Guetto Girl was no different, with the chicken not just falling off the bone, but damn near diving into my mouth. The salsa caribeña did things to my palate I had not experienced since my first helping of salsa Lizano.

Original impressions conjured up a rather sleepy town with little to do outside of grabbing a tasty casado and hitting the waves. To the contrary, even a slow Tuesday night proved rather lively. Vacationers and locals alike were trotting around, enjoying the warm sea air hours after the sun had set. An intense ping pong match was underway at Lazy Mon between two men who seemed to be treating their little competition no differently than an olympian would with a medal on the line. There were plenty of makeshift stands and shops with various inexpensive beach-y merchandise. There was a distinctly Jamaican vibe.

The Jamaican culture clash comes from the Costa Rican Caribbean's history with cheap labor. With the constant drum of reggae and prevalence of English, one might wonder if this is more Jamaica than Costa Rica. After all, this area was historically English with Puerto Viejo known as "The Old Harbor," nearby Cahuita as "Bluff" and Bribri "Fields." This changed when Spanish was institutionalized by the central government. The Caribbean province of Limón has battled politically with San José ever since, claiming neglect and charging racism.

Not that they don't have a point. While Black Costa Ricans technically had the ability to gain the right to vote through citizenship, naturalization was made legally difficult through discriminatory laws. This explains why only twenty-five people of West Indian nationality had become naturalized Costa Rican citizens by 1927, a rather large discrepancy considering the vital role they played in the development of the country.

Things started to change following the month-long civil war in 1948 when the victorious President Figueres abolished the army and created a new constitution (which finally gave women the right to vote). Like a true politician (think JFK and African-Americans), Figueres recognized the electoral possibilities of embracing West Indian immigrants. One source even claims that he endeared himself to the West Indies voting bloc by dancing with the voters, speaking English, and even kissing their babies. It just doesn't get more *politician* than that, folks.

Sitting on the beachside patio of Lazy Mon, enjoying a cool Imperial, it was easy to imagine the other side of Puerto Viejo, the "party town" we had read about. You could see a hint of it in the few bars blaring club beats for an audience of solely employees. Thankfully for our preferences, crowds were modest and the vibe followed as such. We went to sleep pleased with our destination.

It bears repeating that Cashew Hill alone is a sight to see. We took our time the next morning to further explore the property, following the pebble trails into the surrounding flora and variety of stone statues fashioned by indigenous Bribri. Pineapple, star fruit, mango, lime and banana trees could also be found along with the occasional sloth sighting.

"Being here is just about relaxing," Mark told us during our morning walk.

On cue, a light rain started that necessitated us putting this relaxation business to the test.

Eventually, we meandered back into town for yet another

casado con pollo to fuel our mile-long hike to Playa Cocles. Walking out of town, Puerto Viejo turned into the more secluded beach town we had previously found in Santa Teresa, with just one unmarked road tracing the coast and the occasional hostel or restaurant along the way. It was all very subtle with nature as the focal point.

We later learned from Mark that Costa Rica has a maritime law explicitly to protect their coastline from development. Few exceptions are made, which is why you'll rarely find a restaurant or hotel right on the beach in Costa Rica. In April 2012, some local residents and business were informed that the government would be evicting and demolishing their properties due to violations of said law. The feeling was that you're never sure what the government is going to do or why. Rumors abounded that the government was giving into so-called foreign-financed "Mega Marinas." Almost two years later, ground had not been broken and the Costa Rican legislature approved a law to allow the residents to stay put.

There is certainly little development surrounding Playa Cocles —a modest slice of sand full of sunbathers and surfers. The waves were perfect for surfers, but the undertow proved too strong for my toddler-esque swimming skills.

Our beach needs fulfilled, we headed back to Cashew Hill for a sunset yoga session with Sean, a college lacrosse buddy of Mark's who followed the road to Central America after feeling burned out by corporate America. Sean helps out around Cashew Hill and serves as the on-call yoga instructor. The class was plenty enjoyable, but later offered fodder for snickers as we recalled his calls to different deities in between positions.

Sean: Taurus, I open my groin to you in the spirit of joy and devotion.

Something like that.

He also had the distinction of training with Costa Rica's

national lacrosse team.

Oh yeah, Costa Rica has a national lacrosse team.

Sean, with a bit of a professional background back home, was even invited to join and play for the Ticos in Denver for that year's World Cup of lacrosse.

"I almost said yes for the story," he told us over drinks at Cashew Hill. "Gringo who doesn't speak Spanish on the Costa Rican national lacrosse team. Would've been funny."

Thursday morning was somehow even lazier than the morning prior. We lingered on our first-floor patio, drinking coffee, eating breakfast, doing a bit of work and enjoyed the light breeze off the Caribbean Sea. Hours later, we headed out for a bit of sloth sighting around the hotel grounds before heading down into town for lunch at Soda Shekiná.

Noticing my camera, the staff invited me into the kitchen to meet the chef and see how patacones are made—a delicious Latino snack where one essentially fries and salts smashed plantains. Add some refried black beans and queso and you have yourself a new Super Bowl snack.

From there we moved onto Gecko Trail Adventures to meet with Leah, a Swiss expatriate who was in the process of becoming an official Tica by way of her husband when we started exchanging emails. Leah found us a guide for some hiking around nearby Cahuita National Park.

Just outside the heart of Cahuita, a quiet Caribbean town about a half-hour north of Puerto Viejo, sits the humble entrance to the national park alongside the coast. We paid our suggested donation of one or two bucks, then followed the sandy beach trail through the quiet jungle with our eagle-eyed guide. Thanks to his assistance, we saw troupes of white-faced monkeys prancing about from tree to tree, like ballet dancers on the jungle vines. It seemed choreographed and not just a mindless way for them to spend the afternoon.

We also saw many lizards, spiders, crabs, snakes and sloths. Though I have to be honest about the sloths, the animal mascot of Costa Rica plastered all over tourist merchandise and information. Our patient guide would continuously point to the sky, spotting them like a beagle in the middle of a hunt. My vision not being what NASA would require for astronaut training, it all looked like a tree bark-colored blur. At least Melanie was able to see from afar, but we never did get close enough to make out the details of the sloths' relaxed goofy grin. Instead, my enjoyment came from planning my future trail runs around this superb path. Flat with the feeling of being completely alone, this is where you want to run and never look back. Though for us, we did have to look back when a guard informed us the park was closing.

One of the warnings you get before heading to just about any Gringo-covered beach town in Costa Rica, namely Puerto Viejo, is that locals will try to sell you pot. I've dabbled over the years, but the whole inhaling thing really isn't for me. Once in a blue moon, edibles make for a more enjoyable evening—except for that one time I ate too much and told Melanie, "I think I'm sinking into the couch" and then saw a giant baseball coming out of the wall.

With those warnings also comes the disclaimer that the pot being sold wasn't exactly top-notch. This made it that much easier to decline when a couple of young locals paused their one-on-one soccer match to offer us some of their stash.

"Hey! Hey, man!" one called, running over with bare feet, shorts and tank top. "You want weed?" Want weed?"

"No gracias," I offered in a terse reply as they leaned against the chainlink fence surrounding the field.

"You smoke? You smoke?" they continued until we were out of

sight. Back at the hotel, Mark confirmed the rumors.

"Yeah, the stuff they're selling is no good," he said. "If you want pot, I'll get you pot."

"I'm not crazy about inhaling," I started. "But for the story..."

Turns out, I still don't like smoking pot.

Perfect weather is never a guarantee along the Costa Rican coastline, despite what the postcards may suggest. Luckily, the fantasy was a reality on our final day in Puerto Viejo. Doubly lucky was that we were with a couple of locals who knew where to go to best take advantage of the perfectly blue sky. Otherwise, we may have ended up wandering around Playa Cocles again or frolicking in the black sands of Playa Negra. Both perfectly suitable options, but they quite simply do not compare to Manzanillo.

Sean drove. Eventually, the road turned into beach trail similar to Cahuita's. Every time I thought we had arrived to Manzanillo, Sean continued navigating the narrow path until we found a small, makeshift parking lot along the coast. An older gentleman working as both *guachimán* (parking attendant) and vendor served us a couple of pipas—coconut water—sliced open with his machete. Sipping our coconuts, we continued marching south along the beach trail into the coastal jungle.

The trek was terrific. We found ourselves on the kind of secluded beaches where not more than a dozen people were. Melanie and I hung back to admire the view from a piece of land that offered a phenomenal 180-degree view of the southern Caribbean coastline. Ocean water with hues of light green and blue; tall jungle trees; dramatic, jagged rocks off the coast—this really could be a postcard.

A brunch of eggs, potatoes, chicken sausage and a French press coffee at Bread and Chocolate capped our visit to Puerto Viejo. This rustic little beach town gave us precisely what coastal travelers are looking for when they come to Costa Rica—a piece of natural serenity not too far from jungles teeming with wildlife. Most tourism brochures jump off the deep end when it comes to describing their destination.

Tourism Brochure: Nature, city, adventure, wildlife, shopping, food, buzz word-buzz word-buzz word—WE HAVE IT ALL!

This brochure usually comes with a young couple on the cover —probably white—caught in mid-laugh as they eat up paradise. Puerto Viejo, on the other hand, was the rare example in which the promise and expectation matched our experience.

brete (bre·*te*)
noun

1. The Tico take on *trabajo* (work).
2. Another invention of General Malespín's linguistic code, like *tuanis*. Apply the code to *trabajo* and you get *breteji*, which got shortened to *brete* for the purposes of satisfying slang.
3. Often used to show gratefulness for having a job that'll feed the family, e.g. "Mucho brete, gracias a Dios" or "I have a lot of work, thank God."

Example: "There are things I'd rather be doing than wait for this marshmallow of a Gringo tourist to waddle up the trail. Oh, well... At least I've got brete.

The Tico Times

Melanie and I had been eyeing a possible move to Costa Rica for two years before the actual move. Before landing on graduate school, I thought perhaps working for English-language media could be our ticket to Central America. To my initial surprise, I found a wealth of English media down in Costa Rica. Admittedly, many came off as passion projects created by North Americans enjoying early retirement—not something that would be willing to give me some form of monetary compensation in exchange for work. They say not to judge a book by its cover, but anyone who's worked in freelance writing can look at a website's homepage and get at least an educated hunch as to whether or not they pay. Considering many welcomed their visitors with what I could only generously characterize as one step above GeoCities, I felt safe in my assumption that nothing sustainable lay ahead with those outlets.

One, however, did stick out. Everything on the site indicated that it was an actual news outlet. Words were spelled correctly and real stories were breaking. I'm referring to *The Tico Times*.

The name initially threw me off. After all, there's no *Yankee Daily* or *Canuck Chronicle* covering all your "moose on a highway" traffic news. But it only took a few minutes of jumping into *The Tico Times* to see that this was a verifiable operation with reporters and editors who appeared to be taking home enough colón to buy a casado and beer at the end of the day. Even before knowing about UPEACE, I had my eyes set on *The Tico Times*.

As luck would have it, I happened to be connected via Twitter to a former managing editor, who despite knowing nothing about me beyond my 143-charactered profile description, was willing to connect me to the current managing editor. This connection paid off when Costa Rica became a reality and I was introduced to Caitlyn. After exchanging a few emails upon my arrival, she agreed to meet with me about possibilities.

We met at the café attached to the national theater just as it opened for the morning. The meeting was brief with Caitlyn walking me through some recent changes at the paper. Most notably, they stopped printing and were focusing solely on the Internet. Additionally, she was returning from Miami after having previously worked for *The Tico Times* and appeared happy to be back in Costa Rica with her Tico husband. She was also spearheading JumpStart, a free intensive English language camp for Ticos with hands-on development for teachers coming out of low-income rural and urban areas. This, it became clear in conversation, was the strongest passion in her admirable career.

Caitlyn offered me the opportunity to pitch her on what I saw as my skill set and how I could fit in. I quickly suggested a topic that had become a passion of mine over the past couple of years —urbanism. Now I by no means counted myself as an expert. My shtick had always been to start by admitting that I'm not an expert, but rather a mouthpiece for a variety of experts who in general have something to say about how we've been (poorly) designing cities in the United States around cars. While the state of American infrastructure remained in a sorry state by the time I left for Costa Rica, there was no shortage of people to complain about it with who were more interested in moving around by train, bike or those two wobbly things under your waist.

Urbanism became a niche of mine over at one website I had been writing a weekly column for, so it was my hope to continue that in some form down in Costa Rica.

I shared some of my initial impressions of San José from an urbanism lens with Caitlyn, namely how I felt that despite not exactly being a postcard city, Chepe actually had a lot going for it in terms of being a comfortable place to walk compared to so many more widely known U.S. cities where highways blaze through city centers and you need a car to cross the street. At the very least, San José had that lovely pedestrian street right through downtown. Few cities in the world can claim such a feat.

The idea appeared to strike a chord with Caitlyn.

"Everything we hear about San José is negative," she said with her hands wrapped around her coffee. "It'd be nice to put something positive together for once."

"Absolutely! I can do that," I responded enthusiastically.

That meeting led to my first piece with *The Tico Times*, which published within a couple of months of our first meeting. I was able to follow that up with another urbanist look at San José. Both stories did quite well in terms of reader engagement. Turns out Josefinos themselves were thrilled to see "San José" surrounded by words other than "dirty," "dangerous" and "ugly."

In late November, I received an email from Kevin, the managing editor of *The Tico Times*.

"Hey Joe, I never heard back, so wanted to make sure you saw this gig for covering real estate. I know you've been looking for something steady, so wanted to give you a first stab," the email read.

I immediately went into something of a mild panic.

Never heard back? I repeated in my head. *I don't remember getting anything and this certainly would've gotten my attention.*

I quickly solved the little mystery by noting that my last name was spelled wrong in his initial email. My mind went paranoid for a moment, wondering if I had missed out on other career opportunities because of my Swiss-spelled last name that's just one "E" away from the terrorist-thrashing star of *24*, Jack Bauer. It would be impossible to figure out, so I was at least thankful in that moment for Kevin's electronic persistence. We setup a meeting at the office for the following week.

Melanie joined me because we're gross and can't stand being apart. Plus it's never a bad thing to have a second pair of ears in the room. I do admittedly lack a business brain and often falter when discussions turn to dollars and cents. My gears are generally too busy churning away on what I think would be a great story, not what will put more food in my stupid face hole.

Kevin and I had exchanged emails, but never met face-to-face. He met me down at the lobby and immediately reminded me of Johnny Depp's turn in *The Rum Diaries*. Not because Kevin looked like Johnny Depp, but he seemed like he belonged in the newsroom depicted in that book and movie. He was wearing an untucked, short-sleeved button up, had a full black beard, and had something to his voice that implied he had heard some bizarre stories, even lived through some of them.

We pretty much got straight to the point. The gig was managing a new real estate section of *The Tico Times*—nothing sexy and Kevin described it just the same. He slid a piece of paper across the table with a list of topics that the editorial team thought would be a good start.

"We're looking for four to seven stories a week," he said. "Interested?"

"Yes, absolutely," I replied with my usual excitement for something new. He then casually threw a number at me for my monthly rate, which seemed fair (though as we've already established, I have the business acumen of a starfish). I was, however, able to add to the deal that we could call this an "internship."

Internship, you might be wondering. *Why in God's name would you want it to be an internship?*

Up to this point, I had been struggling to identify what my final master's project at UPEACE would be. I liked the idea of taking on a short-documentary project, but I also don't like taking on projects that I can't give a hundred percent. If our bank accounts were bottomless, perhaps I could have dedicated the right amount of time to put together a compelling documentary I could be proud of. In reality, I needed to earn money. The time I needed to spend working would make my documentary project suffer.

There was, however, another option. An internship of at least three months rather than a project would also fulfill my final obligations with UPEACE. It wouldn't change my work in the slightest with *The Tico Times*, yet changing the semantics behind my new position would save me a significant amount of stress in finishing my master's.

I was euphoric. And from our conversation, it was clear that this could be a lead into other opportunities at *The Tico Times*. A new editor would be joining in the next few months to start a travel-specific section of the website where I would also be able to contribute. Traveling Central America and writing about it for money—that's the definition of a dream job.

The pay was also enough to be the final hurdle in convincing Melanie to quit her job teaching English in Ciudad Colón, something she had come to loathe to the point that it was negatively impacting her enjoyment of living in Costa Rica. There had been too many no-show students and higher-ups who couldn't give a damn to let her know that her class had been canceled before she planned and arrived for the day's lesson.

As much as I despise linking happiness to anything monetary, human civilization has unfortunately yet to craft a utopic society in which goods and services can be exchanged for hugs and smiles. With this job at *The Tico Times*, things were taking a financial turn for the better. I was set to start the following week with the flexibility to work remotely from Ciudad Colón, and Melanie and I would no longer have to worry about paying the bills.

Fruit Ninja in the Valle De Orosi

I wanted to make a special effort to take the train at some point despite its limited service and the fact that, logistically speaking, it didn't make much sense coming from Ciudad Colón. We were twenty-two kilometers west of San José with the nearest train station over another kilometer away from our final bus stop. Taking the train would require a very specific purpose.

Nearing our holiday return to the States, we decided to look for someplace in the central valley we could visit for a quick weekend getaway—something the typical traveling tourist doesn't know about quite yet. Somehow that loose criteria led us to a hostel in the Orosi Valley, just outside Cartago. I knew the train went as far as Caratago, so this would be our excuse to hit the rails.

A word on Costa Rican trains: The modern system is merely a shadow of what it once was, which could be said throughout the Americas outside of the major North American rail hubs of New York City, New England and Toronto. Tico trains started back in 1873 when the government put in a line connecting Alajuela to Puerto Limón through San José. General Tomás Guardia Gutierrez got the job done with some British civil engineering, courtesy of one Edmund Wragge, though more credit should go to the Jamaican workers who were brought in to clear forests and build the tracks, repeating the all too familiar story of richer nations abusing poorer black laborer. This immigration, followed by future migrations to work on banana plantations, helped settle the Afro-Caribbean culture so prominent in the Caribbean coast today.

Remaining sections of the first lines were not completed until 1890 to connect as far as Cartago. The Pacific Railroad joined the roster of trains in 1910 with Maria Cecilia, the first steam engine, departing Puntarenas for San José moving a mixture of passengers and cargo. This transcontinental railway was especially important in linking to neighboring Nicaraguan and Panamanian lines.

Things moved along with various ups and downs, as trains do, throughout the twentieth century until they hit a financial point of no return sometime in the 1980s around the same time José María Figueres was appointed by Costa Rican sweetheart President Óscar Arias to overhaul the national system, Instituto Costarricense de Ferrocarriles or INCOFER. The suspicion goes that Figueres had a buddy in the national trucking industry and so he ceased all commercial railway activity when he became president in 1994. Slowly but surely, trains disappeared as the country turned toward more vehicular-oriented development as other wealthier role model nations had done in the Americas, namely the United States, which by the '90s was a solid four decades in to promoting a dream life where car ownership was a staple.

The system then largely fell into disrepair with a completely gutted INCOFER all but handcuffed to do anything about it. Only a select number of freight and passenger trains passed the still functioning tracks. The Costa Rican rail system was basically abandoned.

Then in 2005, trains began to make a comeback, starting with passenger urban lines between San José and its suburbs of Pavas to the west and San Pedro to the east. They're still working to rehabilitate the lines with commuter service returned to the main urban centers of the central valley, including Heredia, Alajuela and Cartago. Those rehabbed lines to Cartago served as my excuse to ride the train, connecting us to the Orosi Valley.

We hopped on the train at the Atlantico station that we previously noticed during one of our first trips to San José. The train was full with standing room only, but at least there wasn't the unintentional rubbing of genitals all too common on packed Tico buses.

The train passed through a number of neighborhoods and the Universidad de Costa Rica where students filled the train even more. From there, we started to climb into more rural, scenic corners of the valley. Some of the lush, green valley views reminded me of riding trains in Switzerland—until we arrived in Cartago.

Interestingly, Cartago was the original capital of Costa Rica until 1823—just a year after suffering the first in a series of devastating earthquakes. The city's bad luck continued when republican leader Gregorio Jose Ramirez moved capital honors to San José, punishing a Cartago that wanted to unite with Agustín de Iturbide's Mexican empire. San José and Alajuela supported a Republican system, and that's precisely what they got.

The final train stop left us near the famous Basilica de Nuestra Señora de los Ángeles or Our Lady of the Angels Basilica, a byzantine-style cathedral mixed with colonial elements. Legend has it that in 1635 a young peasant woman by the name of Juana Pereira found a statue on a small rock of the Virgin Mary carrying the infant Jesus. Each time she brought the statue home, it mysteriously reappeared back at the rock the following day. The object's seemingly inexplicable divine boomeranging turned it into the subject of worship.

Over time, worshippers of the statue attributed a number of miracles to the image. So as many-a-Christian story goes, a hermitage was constructed in its honor followed by sturdier temples in 1675. Monseñor Anselmo Llorente y Lafuente (one person), the first bishop of Costa Rica, erected a basilica.

Unfortunately for Mary and her adoring public, an earthquake on May 4, 1910 destroyed the temple. Construction on a replacement began in 1912 by the architect Lluis Llach Llagostcra, whose preference for the byzantine style remains as resplendent and impressive as the man's wonderfully alliterative name. Further legend says that earthquakes continued to destroy the basilica during construction until they moved it all to its present location. Many, such as religious affairs expert Andrea Meszaros, believe the earthquakes were not-so-subtle instructions from the Lady of Los Angeles herself on where she wanted the basilica to be built. I'm sure a less violent message delivery system would have been appreciated, but at least it wasn't a great flood or plague wiping out first borns, I suppose.

The basilica is worth the trip to Cartago alone. Somewhere around 2 to 3 million Costa Ricans make the pilgrimage during Romería in August to give thanks to the Virgin Mary's black statue, nicknamed La Negrita, housed inside the cathedral. Particularly devout practitioners finish the final twenty-two kilometers by crawling on their hands and knees as a sign of piety. Luckily blonde-haired heathens are still welcome to approach by foot.

When it's not the season for pilgriming, the basilica remains open to believers who will bring a silver medal representing a body part they're concerned about and leave it with La Negrita in hopes of scoring a cure. After a certain time—perhaps enough to give said curing a shot—the medals are collected and some are stored for visitors in the museum. Architecture and design aficionados will at the very least appreciate the striking white and grey colors that envelope the massive complex.

Earlier on the train, we met an American who had called the Cartago area home for some time. He pointed us in the direction of buses that would finish the trip to our hostel, El Salto. I, unfortunately, came unprepared for the drastic change of climate in Cartago compared to Ciudad Colón and San José. Clouds blanketed the sky. The misty air left the concrete and surrounding buildings looking a bit soggy. It all had the feel of an Irish city yet the familiar architecture and city planning of a Tico town. The main difference here compared to any other city in Costa Rica was that Cartago was the first to install protected bike lanes with help from the Dutch Embassy. (Coincidentally, an employee of the Dutch embassy who assisted with the project lived in Ciudad Colón and joined us on a couple of occasions for some volleyball.)

As a result of my poor packing, I was left shivering in a tee shirt and jeans as we strolled about Costa Rica's County Cork. We opted for a cab to finish the journey, especially since the prospect of lugging a rolling suitcase over uneven slabs of sidewalk was unequally unappealing.

Reaching El Salto was no easy feat. The manager left explicit bus and driving instructions on the website that came in handy when it came time to blurt out, "Ir a la derecha!" (Go right!) off the highway, just passed the Mirador of Ujurrás overlooking the colonial valley. Posted signs directed the next two turns and recent landslides covering the road ensured we didn't miss our stop at the white gate.

The manager met us at the gate and joined us for a short and very steep jaunt down a switchback driveway. Instructions asked guests to wait five minutes after ringing the doorbell and it was easy to see why. Rocky in his prime would need some time (and raw eggs) to get up this thing quickly.

El Salto appeared after a few turns down the driveway, a modest looking three-story development made of wood, stone and the typical Tico-style tin roofs. A couple of bust sculptures that looked like they belonged in ancient ruins stood outside the entrance. Small wooden directional signs donated to El Salto gave a glimpse of some previous visitors. Tehran, St. Gallen and Hochdorf were among the collection.

After showing us to our room, essentially a concrete box made with simplicity in mind, we took a moment to admire the view outside our door of the Orosi Valley. The star of the view was a thundering waterfall that could be heard quietly drumming all through the night. It was relaxing to someone who needs a little noise to fall asleep, but easy to ignore for others. Given my hatred (and illogical fear) of pure silence, the waterfall-infused soundtrack was a welcomed surprise.

After admiring our view, we turned back past a couple of hammocks, up a set of concrete steps and through a faded wooden door held open by a small boulder to the common area and kitchen space. The manager sat us down with a shot of "illegal moonshine," as he put it, for our sipping enjoyment as we chatted.

The manager, hailing from central Mexico, was a slender gentleman with a commanding voice and wavy black hair not unlike Javier Bardem. He had a plan to travel through all of Central and South America, ending in Buenos Aires, when he ran out of money in Costa Rica.

"I thought I better start making some money," he laughed.

This turned into managing a San José hostel where he had been staying. Eventually, this led to Brewha, which was rebranded earlier that year to El Salto to cater more toward families, couples and the occasional backpacker rather than exclusively backpackers. As such, rooms previously made for throngs of hostel travelers—with all the interesting smells that brings—had since been converted.

A home cooked meal for dinner ran at a reasonable $12 per plate, served around eight o'clock. Our host made an exception to serve an hour earlier for a visiting Swiss family with three brightly blonde-haired kids that looked like they came out of a Heidi story.

The kids were busy swinging around the hammock with *Madagascar 3* playing in the background as our host prepared dishes of chicken and fettuccine alfredo. He recited lines and laughed as much as the kids.

"I love those movies," he said.

Dinner also came with the option of purchasing a bottle of his homemade beer.

Don't mind if I do.

I opted for the chocolate stout. A bit smoky at first, but it mellowed out to offer an enjoyable taste I hadn't found much of in Costa Rica's sea of Imperial, Bavaria and Pilsen. Plus, knowing where your beer comes from, as is the case with food, makes it all the better.

Breakfast the following morning came with vanilla and chocolate pancakes, strawberry jelly, honey and butter, and a bowl of fruit. The property owner, a chain smoking Frenchman with a stubbled beard, joined us. He wore sunglasses despite the thick gray clouds covering the sky and the fact that we were indoors. In my experience, only two types of people wear sunglasses indoors—celebrities and douchebags.

While discussing his career in real estate, I noted that I had just started covering real estate at *The Tico Times*.

"If you have any stories you'd be interested in sharing..." I started.

"Oh, I have tons of stories."

The next thirty minutes were filled with insults of just about everyone, most notably Ticos themselves. His earlier comments lamenting the influx of arabic peoples into his home country of France were starting to make sense. This guy was *terrible*.

After several poor experiences, he explained, he will never hire another Tico. One of the said "poor experiences" involved an employee who evidently took him to court after he didn't offer health care or vacation. Granted I have no idea whether or not it was explained to the employee upfront that he cannot provide health care, nor do I have any idea what the law says, but the Frenchman's demeanor in retelling his stories did not leave much room for ambiguity or doubt as to who the reprehensible human being was in this equation.

He went on to complain of other Ticos who have had the gall to demand health care in exchange for, y'know, working for him. It was a profoundly bizarre experience where Melanie and myself nodded politely for what felt like eternity as we tried to ask the manager, the guy we liked very much, if he thought the ground was too wet for the planned hike.

(Weeks later when the article I had written on our weekend in the Orosi Valley published with *The Tico Times*, I was told he complained that he wasn't mentioned... Poor thing.)

While the morning meal was certainly agreeable, the weather was not. The manager had warned us when we first exchanged messages that the rain could make the path too slippery. I brushed off the written warning before seeing just how incredibly different weather in Cartago can be.

But this was why we came to the Orosi Valley. We wanted a serious hike, something slightly masochistic. The kind of athletic endeavor where you have earned your beer at the end, or in this case, a belly-splitting casado.

I could tell he didn't have the heart to tell us "no."

"Let's wait until nine."

Nine came.

"Let's give it until nine-thirty."

Nine-thirty came.

"I don't know guys," he said, shaking his head. But he still couldn't flat-out deny us the trail.

As Melanie and I worked on a Plan B, I noticed a bit of blue sky off in the distance. This was enough to send Melanie over to the manager's office with the hope of a small child on Christmas morning. Her face said it all when she returned.

"We're good to go!"

Knowing how quickly the weather could turn, the manager wasted no time changing into a pair of heavy duty hiking boots, and we were off within twenty or so minutes.

The trail, created and maintained by the manager and his gardener, starts right outside the front door, meaning it truly was an El Salto specialty. This trail, it should be pointed out, is not of the manicured variety we found at Vólcan Poás and the La Paz Waterfall Gardens. This is a trail that would be reclaimed by nature in no time if not taken care of meticulously.

Branches, tall grasses, leaves, trees, small rocks, boulders—everything one can imagine in a rainforest trail was there. And let's not forget the anthills, which covered the trail like organic landmines that could unleash thousands of microscopic insects ready to burn your skin. You know someone's been attacked if they suddenly slump over their legs, smacking at them wildly, and yelling any number of expletives.

Thanks to the consistent mist and rain of the Orosi Valley, the path was as muddy as forewarned. Mixed with sharp declines and loose stones, taking a spill was a constant concern. At times, under the manager's instruction, we purposely allowed ourselves to slide with some steering and control offered by adjacent, sturdy branches we would hold onto for nature's helping hand. After Melanie did in fact take a hard fall down a switchback trail covered in slick mud, we always made sure a hand was offered.

This especially came in handy (no pun intended) as we scaled boulders along the banks of a river and again when we finally crossed the river. The knee-high rush of water was ready to sweep our feet from under us, but the manager's experience of covering this trail as much as three times per week wouldn't allow for anything remotely catastrophic.

Our first highlight came after about an hour's worth of downhill hiking—the waterfall that could be seen from our hotel balcony. This is the kind of natural wonder you hear about in Costa Rica. The kind that renders you speechless until your brain flickers on again like a laptop covered in spilt water. Though we had seen impressive waterfalls before in Costa Rica— namely at La Paz Waterfall Gardens—there was no park staff, paved path or bus ready to come hold our hand. Finally, here was a waterfall, a view, a moment that we earned.

The rigorous portions of the hike over, we were guided to a squash farm. Now away from the river and hillside, it was smooth sailing over flat, gravel terrain as we admired the surrounding farms and fruit ripe for picking. The manager, saying he had permission to grab what he wants, picked us some oranges and cas. He was also kind enough to lend us his machete for, as he put it, "real-life Fruit Ninja." Both Melanie and the manager allowed for plenty of space, giving me a baseball-like soft toss as I did my best to mimic the expert swordsmanship of a samurai warrior. As fantastic as I felt, video replay later showed a less flattering image, but then what could I expect as a Gringo who thinks he's a samurai when he holds a machete.

This all led to the small town of Ujarrás, whose crown jewel is the Ruins of Ujarrás—Costa Rica's oldest colonial ruins. Estimates say the ruins, a church by the name of Iglesia de Nuestra Señora de la Limpia Concepción, was built at some point in the late sixteenth century, housing the miraculous statue of the Virgin of the Holy Conception of Ujarrás. The statue allegedly protected the area from pirate attacks, but natural disasters and disease were evidently not covered in the statue's insurance policy. The site was abandoned throughout the late eighteenth century, forcing the local population (along with their holy statue) to relocate and create nearby Paraíso.

The church stands out as one of the few architectural reminders of Spain's conquest in Costa Rica. Today the preserved ruins (made ruins by periodic earthquakes) are surrounded by a scenic park enjoyed by far more locals than backpacking tourists. The culture clash of the day came just around the corner from the ruins where a group of Ticos were playing football—American football. One even had a pretty tight spiral.

By this point, we had truly earned our casados. Thus we parted ways with the hotel manager, who had an appointment with a "chicken lady" to get back to, and we helped ourselves to a heaping pile of casado con pollo at La Pipiola just down the street from the park. Our waiter confirmed our suspicions that the squash served came from the farms we had just hiked through.

The Orosi Valley, thanks to our Mexican guide, had given us what we long desired—a hike that put us on our respective asses in tired awe. Not only had the valley challenged our bodies, but now it was nourishing us back to health through its natural bounty. There must be a metaphor in there somewhere, but the Orosi Valley left me too exhausted to wax poetic.

Don't Feed the Animals in Manuel Antonio

Imagine tropical sandy beaches lined with rocky shores and steep cliffs, teeming with wildlife, including three different species of monkeys (mantled howler, squirrel, capuchin), iguanas, snakes, bats and even the occasional migrating whale.

And then there are the tourists, featuring just as much diversity as the pristine rainforest they can be found traversing. Some wear oversized straw beach hats; some bright, multi-colored swimsuits. Others wear something resembling a swimsuit that *just doesn't quite* cover enough. They bark English to a Spanish-speaking audience, confusing volume with comprehension. They buy a baseball cap featuring the national beer logo as a frankly odd reminder of their time in Costa Rica. There are bratty children who don't realize how goddamn lucky they are to be traveling in a foreign country and honeymooning couples trying to avoid their spoiled screams. Above all, no matter what category the tourist falls under, they all take hundreds upon hundreds of photos they'll (maybe) look at once after coming home. That's Manuel Antonio.

Costa Rica is rightfully celebrated for its national parks. Manuel Antonio warrants this acclaim and then some. Dedicated in 1972, the park has since enlarged itself to sixteen square kilometers. Though this makes it the smallest national park in the country, it clocks in as the second most visited, behind Poás.

Melanie and I had plans to spend our honeymoon just outside the park over New Year's Eve. Although most would consider moving to Costa Rica a honeymoon in and of itself, they're wrong. A honeymoon is a vacation after the wedding that sets a ridiculously misleading tone for the marriage. The formula is, in general, an expensive party full of friends, family and booze to celebrate one's nuptials. This is followed by a romantic vacation that creates an unrealistic bar for what the rest of your life is going to be like together. It's not all beaches and silly island drinks, folks. There are bills, bank accounts, and if you're an American, student debt.

Moving to Costa Rica itself was not a romantic vacation. The actual act of relocating our lives to a foreign country was stressful. Granted things were generally great once we settled down in Ciudad Colón (and we've always been exceedingly fortunate in the grand scheme of things), but it's not like we hopped off the plane and into our beach gear when we moved back in August. Our visit to Manuel Antonio for New Year's Eve, however, most certainly was a honeymoon, especially so thanks to a gift card from aunts and uncles that would cover our stay at La Mariposa Hotel, perched alongside the Pacific Ocean.

One of Melanie's aunts had noted that the hotel's location put it on some list of places you need to see before you die thanks to its perfect vantage point for watching sunsets. Indeed, the vivid sunsets that sent a mixture of warm red and orange hues bouncing off the horizon elicited a round of applause in every instance from admiring visitors. Originally I found it odd to be applauding a sunset, something we all know will happen every evening. Were they surprised? Did they think there was someone pulling the strings who would appreciate the applause? Had we all indulged in one too many fruity beach drinks? Whatever the case, I appreciated that we were collectively applauding something at least worthy of marvel and contemplation rather than, say, a 6' 10" 300-pound monster of football making silly putty of a wide receiver's brain when he was caught off guard looking the other direction. (Guilty.)

La Mariposa is one of countless hotels off the winding and narrow Route 618, just a hair over three kilometers from Quepos—the main town and transportation hub of the region. Free shuttle service meant easy access to the region's storybook beaches, but hiking the road was an equally popular option for those traveling without children. One such childfree traveler that comes to mind is a forty-something-year-old woman who shared the hotel swim up bar with Melanie and myself and confided (without provocation, mind you) that she was there celebrating her recent divorce.

"And what brings you here?" she asked.

"Well, we're on our honeymoon," I responded uncomfortably.

"Oh, gosh! The last thing you kids probably want to hear about is some lady's divorce while you're on your honeymoon."

Righto.

Thankfully a group of young men—whose unbuttoned shirts screamed "Here to party!"—took her attention away from us as drinks were exchanged.

Before visiting the park, we hit the public beach of Playa Espadilla. Vacationing foreigners and Ticos could be seen dotting the shore. Adventurers parasailing, adults, and families all had a place at Espadilla. There were some folks trotting around the beach in hopes of hocking their small goods off on tourists, but nothing overly aggressive. A polite, "No gracias" always did the trick. It appeared we had come before the tourist season really kicked off, which we counted as a blessing. Going into Manuel Antonio, I was prepared for some sort of Gringotopia complete with all the kitsch and obnoxiousness that that it entails. So long as I can mentally prepare for such surroundings, I can usually leave without falling into an anger-hole and perhaps even have some fun.

Only a few blocks away from Playa Espadilla, we found the entrance to Manuel Antonio National Park. Admission was $16 per adult entrance, which seemed steep but ultimately worth it considering that's what we were there to do. Nationals, however, paid a substantially lower fee. This bothered some, but I frankly could not muster the energy to care. I understand and largely agree with why visiting nationalities pay a higher entrance free. Even if I didn't, I can't imagine a Tico official at admission would be swayed to suddenly change policy because some sweaty Gringo started mouthing off as if some grave injustice were really at hand.

Bird watchers were already out in full force with their guides and comically large telescopes by the time we entered around eight in the morning, clearly eager to see as many of the estimated 350 species as possible. A few guides made a modest effort at offering their services, but we declined. Having experienced Cahuita National Park with a guide, I had no doubt in their eagle eye-ability to spot plenty of creatures we would otherwise miss, but we preferred to work up a sweat and move at our own pace rather than spot wildlife.

With approximately sixteen kilometers worth of trails, hiking came as a highly recommended option for spending a day in the park. It was also a way to weed ourselves out from the crowds. The avian enthusiasts dominated the initial trails, wide and flat enough for vehicular travel. Sendero Perezoso (Sloth Trail), indeed.

An out-and-back option sprouted off the main route to an underwhelming waterfall overlook, and another was a boardwalk trail that inevitably bottlenecked with beach-bum traffic. A group of Ticos heading to the beach with a packed cooler had some fun with bird watchers marching on a parallel trail separated by bush, shouting out their own bird calls to the confused tourists.

Both trails eventually came to an unavoidable junction where we were able to ditch the crowds by turning left and taking on some actual hiking trails that left us each with a pounding heart underneath our sweaty shirts. There were two very lightly populated beaches welcoming those willing to put up with a bit more effort. The way they appeared suddenly through the dense rainforest reminded me of the idyllic setting in director Danny Boyle's *The Beach* (minus the Thai drug lords and general chaos).

Capuchin, known for their white faces, and squirrel monkeys were in large numbers, swinging from tree to tree like in a children's book. Howler monkeys could be heard emitting their terrifying cry far from afar. Had we not been in a well-established national park, I might have been just a tad more terrified by their ferocious call. I assumed we wouldn't be allowed to freely roam had they actually been dangerous animals. Besides, considering that their howl can travel for three miles (loudest animal in the Western Hemisphere!), it's hard to say if you're even near one when you hear one.

Unfortunately when it came to the monkeys, some tourists left us disappointed. Only those with vision impairments had an excuse for missing the ubiquitous signs reading, "No alimente a los animales," or "Don't feed the animals." Considering how well some of those tourists were able to spot the monkeys and call them over with food in hand, I suspect their vision was just fine and that simple human idiocy was the problem. I found myself quietly rooting for one of the monkeys to bite or at least smack one of the tourists upside their stupid, stupid head.

By the end of the day we had hiked almost every stretch of trail within the dense rainforest of Manuel Antonio, and our legs most certainly felt it by dinnertime at El Avión.

You know you've reached El Avión because there's a Fairchild C-123 aircraft sitting alongside the road as casually as a parked car. This is the twin sister of the infamous C-123 shot down over Nicaragua by the Sandinista army in 1986.

In 2000, the proprietors of El Avión purchased the Central Intelligence Agency's second aircraft, which had been abandoned at the international airport. They converted it to the bar and restaurant we know today. Cheeky signs, like the "Contra Bar," make light of the establishment's backstory.

Within the hull of the aircraft, we enjoyed an icy cold Imperial and watched college football. (At least we applauded the sunset first.) Ohio State was busy carving a path to the national championship. Children, meanwhile, were busy climbing into the cockpit for a few moments of make believe as they pressed every button they could find before their parents beckoned them to turn around for a picture. Melanie and I waited eagerly for our turn.

"We should probably not stand in line behind kids," Melanie suggested.

I agreed. And so we sat with something resembling patience until the last kid left without another in line. With our own childlike wonderment, we hustled up the narrow ladder into the cockpit and pressed every button we could find before Melanie asked me to turn around for a picture.

The next morning, with our bus departure approaching, we took our time at breakfast, and packed our bags. Our lazy morning quickly stretched into the early afternoon when we decided to have a little lunch to hold us over the bus ride back to San José. We landed at a nearby Israeli establishment for some hummus and pita, a decidedly non-Tico ending to Manuel

Antonio. All was perfectly enjoyable, save some foreign tourists dressed in banana hammocks taking what felt like the better part of a decade to decide on their order.

Perfectly satiated, we took our bags aboard the hotel shuttle, made our way down to the beach drop-off point, and waited for our first bus into Quepos to get the connection to San José. While we were waiting alongside the road, a rocket-sized tourist bus pulled up, unleashing a crowd of confused-looking travelers wearing matching tee shirts.

We were leaving Manuel Antonio in the nick of time.

llevarla suave (ye·*var*·la swa·*ve*)
verb

1. In English, "carry it soft."
2. Ticos might use this during vacation or when they're feeling overworked to mean, "take it easy."

Example:
Tico 1: I've gotta walk the kids to school, find time for breakfast, get to work before rush   hour, file a report, make reservations for the hotel, buy an anniversary gift, and somehow in   the middle of all that I'm supposed to squeeze in time for a workout, because the doctor says   my heart's going to explode if I don't lay off the *carnitas* and run around the block every   once in a while.
Tico 2: Whoa, calm down, man! Carry it soft. Llévela suave.

So We're Going To El Salvador

I knew nothing about El Salvador, and as far as I'm concerned, that's reason enough to visit. Okay, I knew some relatives back home might not be happy thanks to disparaging media representations, but I sensed there was more to the country than drug-fueled gang wars, just as there's more to Cleveland (or pick your city) than any number of less-than-flattering stories that any competent Internet user could find in a quick Google search. Even better, I saw that we could combine El Salvador with Guatemala for just about the same price.

Two countries, one week each, we decided.

Unsurprisingly, we were met with some raised eyebrows. One day after returning from class at UPEACE, Melanie said her mom went speechless when she shared our travel plans over Skype. A fellow student, a Latin-Canadian married to a Salvadoran, cautioned me against going several times—this despite never having been herself.

"You're going to stick out, man," she once told me. "Like, you're really white. You won't blend in."

She wasn't wrong. I am very white and I didn't expect to blend in. I just didn't think of that as an imminent threat.

Her well-intentioned reminder that I would be traveling in Latin America and not Switzerland only fueled my interest in El Salvador. With that, I started researching and reading everything I could on the topic. Joe Frazier's (not the boxer) *El Salvador Could Be Like That* proved particularly useful in educating myself on the country's brutal Civil War that only ended relatively recently. Oliver Stone's *Salvador* left Melanie in tears.

"They're going to hate us," she said after watching the film, which depicted American support of an extreme rightwing government in El Salvador that used death squads to murder their own people.

While I was confident we would return to Costa Rica in one piece, I didn't want to come off completely naive. I decided to work with a travel company in planning an itinerary that would show us the diversity of the country over our seven days. This all entailed countless emails back and forth between the company and myself, researching their suggestions and responding.

With less than forty-eight hours before our flight, I received an email notifying me that the provider was canceling the trip. No reason was provided. The gentleman playing the role of messenger seemed somewhat sympathetic in his email, but it did little to ease my burst of rage. Said rage quickly turned to fear. Not for our safety, but that something could go wrong to make the trip regrettable. Instead of convincing others to travel to El Salvador themselves, we would suddenly become the second hand reason for friends and families to steer clear and stick with familiar waters.

This certainly did not fly with Melanie's code of "Prior Planning Prevents Poor Performance." We were suddenly left without a plan. But to her credit, and maybe this was months of Costa Rica mellowing her out a bit, she remained relatively calm and confident that I'd figure something out.

The night I received our cancellation, I fired off emails to as many hotels around El Salvador as possible. On the bright side, the company had steered us around some of the destinations we were originally looking forward to visiting. Again, not for safety reasons. They just assured us that their itinerary would be a better experience.

"Well, screw that," I thought.

So I went back to my original plan of Santa Tecla (which I heard was an exciting slice of urbanity just outside of capital San Salvador); Suchitoto to see a colonial city; somewhere in the middle of Cerro Verde, a national park; and finish in the beach town of El Tunco where we could get a shuttle up to Antigua, Guatemala.

(For Guatemala, we decided early on to just stick with the tourism favorites assuming we'd be exhausted after El Salvador.)

Luck (or something) must have been on our side. We found an affordable private room at a new hostel in Santa Tecla. They were even able to arrange an airport pickup, an agreeable addition considering the forty-minute drive between Santa Tecla and El Salvador's international airport, which is oddly placed near the Pacific coast an hour outside the capital, San Salvador. Before we even left for our flight, we also had a place lined up in Suchitoto that experienced travelers had described as the finest hotel in the country. From there, a new AirBnB option up along the side of Cerro Verde offered to host us in exchange for some professional photos.

Can do! I thought.

Nothing for El Tunco yet, but I knew that it was arguably the most touristy town in the whole of El Salvador. We could find something last minute if need be.

As we boarded our flight, I felt a sense of relief and confidence. What could have been a disastrous start to exploring unfamiliar territory in Central America had been salvaged. At the very least, we had someplace to sleep for five of the seven nights.

Santa Tecla: A Mi Me Gustan Las Pupusas

I was struck by just how green and alluring the Salvadoran countryside appeared from the plane. This was hardly the active war zone I was encouraged to expect by media representations and various concerned parties. Then again, aerials often paint a different picture than the ground. You don't get the streets, the traffic noise, the city chatter, the crimes, the hugs, the kisses, the love, the hate—none of that. Up close, you're more likely to find the faults. Earth looks mesmerizing from space, but zoom in too much and you'll catch some pretty gnarly stuff. There's a safe neutrality to distance. El Salvador wasn't any different. Of course it looked fantastic from the sky, most anything does! I've never flown someplace, looked out the window and thought, *Well, that's just hideous.*

I often have to remind myself, in my disdain for humanity at large, that the world is mostly good and that those cheerful people and their stories and experiences are out there embedded into every country and culture. But in order to see them, you have to get up close. That's why I'd rather be on Earth than witnessing it from the moon. That's why I'd rather land than stay hovering above ground. That's why I was going to El Salvador— to meet people and find those real stories and experiences, share them, and do my part in changing unfair perceptions, because it's those exchanges that have killed and that will continue to kill those baseless fears we harbor of one another across manmade boundaries. It's those exchanges and those exchanges alone that will save humanity from itself and make people like me a little less pessimistic about our future.

(I'd also kill to go to the moon sometime.)

Passing customs and security was as unremarkable as any other international airport. El Salvador's was noticeably small, but it's not an incredibly large country. Most Americans compare it to the geographic size of West Virginia. From there our driver, a young man probably in his early twenties, was easy to spot. Either he was shy, quiet or uninterested in chatting, because the forty-minute or so drive up to Santa Tecla was like sitting in a library. Typically I take an apprehensive if not downright hostile approach to small talk, but I do enjoy chatting with local drivers (if I must start my trip by getting into a car).

Instead, Melanie and I peered out the window as we worked our way through the countryside and into the city. Before long, we found a familiar face painted along highway walls, city streets and printed onto tee shirts—Óscar Romero, the fourth archbishop of San Salvador who spoke out against social injustice in the lead up to civil war despite threats to his life. An assassin fatally shot him at mass just a day after giving a sermon that called on soldiers to stop carrying out the government's violation of human rights. Today, his calm expression adorns everything from murals to tee shirts just like Che Guevara does in Cuba and counterculture shops in the States.

Our driver left us at our hostel and we arranged plans to be picked up again the next morning for our trek up to Suchitoto. With that, we checked in, left our bags in our modest room, and headed out to the nearest pupuseria per the hostel hostess' recommendation. It was a familiar joint after having lived about four months in Costa Rica. Open space, benches for tables, cheap national beer and quick service. I was glad we arrived with empty stomachs to be filled immediately with the quintessential food of El Salvador. Pupusas are essentially a thick corn tortilla filled with cheese, beans and protein. I was over-eager and burned my mouth on the first bite. Once the steam let out, I was able to enjoy and bask in the glow of pupusa glory. We then headed back the two blocks to our hostel to meet with Roberto for our city walk.

With slick black hair pulled back into a small ponytail and a wide smile, Roberto proved to be an encyclopedia of knowledge when it came to Santa Tecla and his home country.

Just southwest of San Salvador, Santa Tecla was formerly known as "Nuevo San Salvador" due to its role as the capital in the mid-nineteenth century. The name Santa Tecla comes from Saint Thecla, a saint from early iterations of the Christian church and follower of Paul the Apostle. She's doesn't make an appearance in The New Testament (perhaps an editorial decision?), but is featured in the apocryphal Acts of Paul and Thecla, believed to have been composed early on in the second century.

Roberto was happy to brag about a nascent art scene, and his passion for Santa Tecla was palpable as we worked our way around the city.

"People are moving to Santa Tecla, because they want to be here," he said. "They want to be in El Salvador and be part of the future of this city and country."

Roberto's sentiments were a stark contrast to the typical Salvadoran narrative we're fed back in the States in which certain politicians play off xenophobic populism to scare white people into thinking they're being overrun by foreigners. (First, who cares if that were true. Foreigners are awesome and sometimes I am one. Second, it's just statistically not correct.)

I must admit I was taken aback by what I was seeing in Santa Tecla. From the moment our taxi pulled in, I was thoroughly impressed by the city's architecture. Santa Tecla felt like an actual city with its narrow streets covered in road bumps to slow aggressive traffic, giving pedestrians a sense of ease when traversing the city—something that much of the auto-oriented world unfortunately lacks. Buildings had a sense of design and purpose. They were covered in turquoise, gold, maroon, beige, orange and light brown colors one right after the other—easily one of the most colorful cities I had ever seen. The streets were lined with impressive-looking restaurants I could hardly wait to peek into. That familiar Central American smell was in the air, a mixture of something cooking, a nearby public market and an overall fresh quality that, for me, is unmistakably linked to the region. One might be tempted to call this the "Brooklyn of El Salvador," if the New Yorker trend of comparing any revitalizing cultural neighborhood in the world to Brooklyn weren't so damned annoying.

As we explored, Roberto shared a bit of his own story.

"I was born in San Salvador, but spent some time in Minneapolis to improve my English." Indeed, his English was impeccable—certainly superior to my Spanish, even if he did humor my linguistic ego by giving a good chunk of the tour in Spanish. Now he's happy to be back in El Salvador, this time in Santa Tecla where he runs the Mango Inn, our hostel, and a nearby restaurant.

Daniel Hernández Town Square and José María San Martin Town Square are two fantastic public spaces in Santa Tecla with no shortage of locals either relaxing on park benches or chatting amongst themselves into the early evening hours. The latter was named in honor of José María San Martín, who while president of El Salvador in 1854 issued the decree to temporarily move power to Santa Tecla while San Salvador recovered from the earthquake. (Again with those pesky earthquakes in Central America.) Hernández was also a teacher who contributed significantly to then-Villa Tecla's urban design while the city served as the capital, which I presume is why he was rewarded with such an attractive park off a little thoroughfare known as the Pan-American Highway.

A reasonably tall (perhaps fifty feet?), white monument that almost looks Roman stands in the center of the park surrounded by large pockets of fenced-off green space where trees tower to shade hundreds of passersby. At nearby Daniel Hernández Town Square, a white and tan pavilion anchors the park, large enough to welcome the strings section of an orchestra. Steps surround the structure with locals, mostly on the younger side, talking to friends or scrolling through their phones. It also unfortunately appeared to be a target of pigeons with more than twenty perched atop and many more roaming around on the ground. Apparently rat-birds are the scourge of attractive urban spaces the world over, not just New York City and London. Thankfully the smells of the adjacent Mercado Municipal de Santa Tecla made the scene pleasant again.

Following our tour, we returned to our hostel to meet Patricia, a language exchange friend I had made online who lives in Santa Tecla. She took us for traditional Salvadoran ice cream on the outskirts of downtown. It's still not clear to me what was Salvadoran about it, but you can never go wrong with ice cream served with fruit and a crunchy cone.

Patricia is the friend everyone wants. She always has a smile on her face, even when she's talking about the often discouraging local news and ongoing struggles of life in El Salvador. You want her to follow you around for a confidence boost, because she's always willing to laugh at your bad jokes.

Following our ice cream, we continued to a bar for a quick drink. Here the bartender caught wind of our plans to explore the country over a week, offering his own suggestions on where to go. This would be a theme throughout the trip. Salvadorans everywhere were eager to know more about why we were visiting. Then they'd give their own itinerary, and sometimes even thanked us for visiting despite the unflattering international reputation.

We finished at Pizza Italia, a rather bizarre iteration of a pizzeria. It looked as if a cultural bomb had gone off. At least two Elvis posters adorned the walls, surrounded by countless more of random celebrities and Italian memorabilia. Outside, kids were playing on one of those plastic playground sets you typically see in the backyard of North American suburbs. Back inside the large town hall style eatery, a Johnny Cash tune was playing.

Before parting ways with Patricia, she managed to top off her generosity with a small book on Iglesia El Rosario.

"I would like to give you this book on a church in San Salvador," she said. "I'm not religious, but it's always been special to me."

I regretted not having anything to give in return for her generosity.

Suchitoto: In the Heart of Guerrilla Country

We were off early for the approximately two-hour drive up to Suchitoto. Less than twenty-four hours into our week, we were already finding a stark contrast between El Salvador's international reputation and our experience. The warnings we had received from friends, family, and acquaintances had thus far proven to be off base. We had not been caught in the crossfire between rival gangs and national police, nor did those mythical Gringo-hunters snatch us right off the street. To the contrary, I already knew El Salvador was going to be a special experience that would shape my worldview for years to come.

One of El Salvador's selling points is its density. Not its population density, mind you, which is the highest in Central America at 301 per square kilometer. (The United States is about thirty-two and a half). Population density has historically caused issues with neighboring Honduras. Attracted to the less populated, larger land mass, poor Salvadorans immigrated to Honduras and became squatters. This culminated in the 1969 Football War or 100 Hour War that kicked off (no pun intended) with riots during a qualifier match for the 1970 FIFA World Cup. The Salvadoran military briefly invaded until the Organization of American States negotiated a ceasefire. Approximately 130,000

Salvadorans fled or were forcibly expelled as a result.

El Salvador's geographic density, however, is very much a selling point. Mountains, rivers, coastline, and an ocean are all within an easy day's reach. In just an hour's drive north from San Salvador (with the same silent driver as before), we were already in the colonial village of Suchitoto.

Bouncing on cobblestones, we hopped out of the car and into the decadent entrance of Los Almendros de San Lorenzo. Inside we caught our first glimpse of how the rest of the world sees El Salvador. After passing through a decorated gate and magnificent hallway covered in impressive paintings that just as easily could have been in an art museum, we caught the front page of *La Página*. Two cops had been killed; one served as a witness against a gang. They weren't even the first cops to be killed in the year, and it was only the middle of January. Still, we felt perfectly safe as we had no plans to get involved in the local drug trade overnight.

With its cobblestone streets, it was immediately clear that Suchitoto is a city full of history. The world "Suchitoto" itself translates to "Bird-Flower" in the indigenous Náhuatl language. Pipiles, indigenous Salvadorans, get credit for first settling in the Cuscatlán region in the eleventh century where modern Suchitoto sits. History shows that they were one of the most formidable foes of the Spanish conquistadors. Unfortunately for the Pipiles, history also shows that there's a simple reason why these men were known as conquistadors: they conquist-ed.

Following Spanish control, the region became known for its indigo trade. The industry eventually collapsed once synthetic colors were discovered in Europe, thus forcing Suchitoto to reinvent itself—a historic theme for the city, though no event forced change among the people of Suchitoto quite like the infamous Civil War that ravaged El Salvador between 1980 and 1992. Approximately 80,000 died as a result of the conflict, creating an additional million displaced peoples both internally and internationally.

Oddly enough, there are very few signs of leftover conflict to the untrained eye (i.e. my eye), especially if you're not looking for it. Of course we know that many Salvadorans still feel the sting of conflict. Many of those involved with the infamous *maras* (gangs) that the world associates with El Salvador are former soldiers who seemingly have no other way of making a living. Not to mention the nation's youth unemployment rate of about ten percent lends itself to creating more chaos.

Despite it all, Suchitoto seems to have successfully come out of the ashes of war to become one of, if not the, top places to live and travel to in El Salvador. The colonial town remains a stronghold of the Frente Farabundo Martí para la Liberación Nacional (FMLN), the leftist political party that started as a guerrilla movement during the war, but this is only apparent through political signs and flags around town—not bands of marching militia.

Today, it would be difficult not to enjoy yourself in Suchitoto. Melanie and I spent countless hours walking the quiet cobblestone streets, enjoying the homes painted in brilliant shades of orange, red, blue and white that made Suchitoto pop to the eye. One of our hosts at Los Almendros, Fernando, explained to us that the town had traditionally been painted entirely white. The decision to add color to create a visual sense of vibrancy was recent and by most accounts, welcomed.

Like Roberto, Fernando is a native to San Salvador who spent a considerable amount of time overseas. Impressively, Fernando served his country as ambassador to Europe. It was in Paris where he learned his French and met Nathan, his co-partner at Los Almendros.

Over dinner at the restaurant within Los Almendros, Nathan shared his love for his adopted country. The people and density of the country, he said, were natural selling points. Though now in the tourism game, he questioned the seriousness of those in charge of promoting the country. Perhaps it's inexperience; the ministry of tourism only launched within the past decade. The lack of tourist infrastructure didn't bother us. Unlike the touristy corners of Costa Rica, you will be expected to speak Spanish. Any passersby will jump into conversation with you assuming you speak the language much like any American in the U.S. would English.

Just like in our last stop, every Salvadoran we met asked us what brought us to their country. This wasn't as standoffish as the question might suggest, but seemed to be out of genuine curiosity. They wanted to know where we were from, where we were going, where we planned to go, and tell us where we should go next. Perhaps most importantly, they wanted us to share the experience with friends and family back home, so they too would plan a visit to El Salvador. My only hope is that El Salvador maintains its sense of self that, at least for me, has separated it from other experiences in Central America and worldwide. Most travelers can think of a city or town that has completely changed itself over time for the sake of tourists. Worse, it's not entirely uncommon to read about a stretch of pristine beach once enjoyed by the public being quarantined off for a resort catering primarily to foreigners. As of this writing, Suchitoto very much remains a Salvadoran town.

At dinner, we discussed what we had planned for the rest of our trip. Our hosts at the AirBnB in Cerro Verde would be sending a driver to pick us up. From there, we would be off to El Tunco where we had yet to secure any kind of lodging. Without even asking for help, Nathan and Fernando said they had a friend in El Tunco working for a new hotel that just opened up. He promised to send an email introduction, and by the next morning, we had our last two nights taken care of.

Formally retired, Fernando spends his time giving back to El Salvador. One of his pet projects has been to restore Teatro Alejandro Cotto, a theater he hopes will be used to give local children an outlet in the arts. Speaking of the arts, there's also Centro Arte Para La Paz launched with the help of an American nun named Meghan. The Center works to, among other things, prevent violence against children and women. This helped explain the ubiquitous stencil drawings outside of local homes, taking a pledge to end violence against women.

Erick, a Suchitoto native working at the center, was kind enough to give us a tour, sharing El Salvador's progress and history through a variety of displays and short documentaries. Here it seemed as appropriate as it ever to ask about Salvadoran opinion of U.S. Americans. Most of us (myself included before reading Frazier's book) are unfamiliar with the objectively heinous role our government played in El Salvador's civil war. For the United States, this was the last actual battleground of the Cold War. Of course it wasn't Americans or Soviets who were suffering. It was the approximately five million people of El Salvador.

(Cue Uncle Sam awkwardly murmuring chants of, "USA!" underscored by a sad trombone.)

In short, the Reagan administration was funneling a million U.S. dollars a day to the far-right ARENA government—the same government known for sending death squads throughout the country. President Jimmy Carter had halted funding to the Salvadoran government when he learned of these atrocities (and after a plea from Óscar Romero), but that all changed with the inauguration of President Reagan. If only Salvadorans weren't so busy being bombed by an American-funded military, they could have looked up to see Reagan's shining city on a hill.

Salvadoran 1: What's that bright light beyond the smoke and rubble? Is it... freedom?

Salvadoran 2: That's a glare off the tank. GET DOWN!

Thankfully for us and other American travelers, Salvadorans like Erick are able to distinguish the American people from the government. We had noticed this to be true throughout Central America. Considering our abysmal history in the region—from purposefully infecting Guatemalans with syphilis to regime change—we would have been back stateside long ago if we were held personally accountable.

People like Meghan are also brilliant reminders of the good work U.S. Americans and other foreigners can do in the region. She ended up in El Salvador after working in South America. Meghan and her fellow nuns wanted to be closer to home, and Central America is closer, relatively speaking. Like Nathan, Meghan fell in love with the people of El Salvador, and so she stayed—before, during, and after the war.

In passing, Meghan lamented the ongoing crises of the world: war, poverty, climate change. She apologized for the dysfunctional planet her generation has left us with, but remained confident in the next generation who would be inheriting the problem. As the topic turned to El Salvador, she thanked us for not listening to the many who strongly cautioned us against visiting.

Pointing to my camera, she said in her thick New England accent, "I hate to use the word 'weapon,' but that thing is a weapon. Use it."

Leaving Suchitoto was tough. I knew immediately that I was going to miss this town. I would miss the hilly side street our hotel apartment was on, crammed in between a row of homes that some local kids turned into their playground. I was overcome with a moment of guilt. How could people back home and throughout the world think this place isn't worth visiting or living in? Could they tell those kids that? To their face? Think about the countless big-box suburbs and exurbs that exist from California to Maine that look exactly the same. There's more character and life here in Suchitoto, I promise. I, for one, left envious.

We spent our final night taking one last walk around Suchitoto, admiring every uniquely built door we saw and hanging around the town square after a delicious dinner at La Lupita del Portal. Families were out in larger numbers than previous nights, presumably because of the coming weekend. Parents watched their children play on the cobblestone plaza, which was anchored by a magnificent white church constructed with perfect symmetry. I'd almost consider going to church if this is what it always looked like.

Before setting off the next morning, we took a quick trip a couple kilometers outside of town to a waterfall that, we were told, would make for excellent filming. Unfortunately this was the dry season and there wasn't a drop to be found.

There was, however, Cesar, who popped up from a ledge of rocks. If I had to guess, I'd say he was around five-years-old. He assured us that this dry patch of cliff was, indeed, the waterfall we had been sent to see. Perhaps sensing our disappointment, Cesar was quick to guide us to another nearby sight. He sprinted barefoot across the rocky trail as if he was running on pillows. First he took us to a tree he likes to climb to pretend that he's a monkey.

"Soy mono!" he shouted in between his chimpanzee mimicry.

Next he took us over to another cliff with a more open view of the vista ahead. A couple of picnic benches sat just ahead of the ledge. This, Cesar shared, is a good place for a nap.

Duly noted for future reference.

The Drug Lords Of Cerro Verde

Our next stop promised to be a stark contrast to the cozy colonial town we had just left in Suchitoto. Next we were being dropped off in the middle of a Salvadoran national park, Cerro Verde or Parque Nacional Los Volcanes. Even the Spanish novice can sense plurality in the latter name. "Los Volcanes" refers to the three surrounding volcanoes of Cerro Verde, Izalco and Santa Ana. Reaching our AirBnB required a steep climb up a winding road that continued well after the asphalt and concrete rubble turned to dirt. Afterward it was hard to imagine any vehicle, even the Volkswagen pickup truck we were riding, on the narrow patch of jagged dust we had just climbed. This looked more like a hiking trail, not a thoroughfare.

If the ride itself didn't clue us into just how high we were, we knew it as we stood practically eye-level with Izalco—a rather young volcano, geologically speaking. Izalco formed in just 1770 and erupted constantly until 1958. Its tendency to remain aglow gave it the nickname "Lighthouse of the Pacific," which is more charming than the fact that it killed fifty-six people while burying the town of Matazano in 1928.

There were no Internet or phone signals during our time at the B&B. But why would you need them? The land itself was a playground for adults and kids alike, though admittedly aimed more towards children with the mini-canopy tour and playground equipment adjacent to the main house. Still, this was a time to stare at nature and let your mind wander to the world's most perplexing questions, like "How the fuck did this all get here?"

We awoke early the next morning to prepare for a hike up Santa Ana. Guillermo, a caretaker at the B&B, joined us as a guide with his machete equipped on his side (obligatory fashion in rural Central America). There was some confusion regarding when and where to start the hike. See, you're actually supposed to be escorted by a police officer, but nobody was where Guillermo had thought to be the meeting point.

Instead we ended up spending a considerable amount of time wandering through a few abandoned farm buildings and a church that were left after the last eruption in October 2005. Fun for us, but hardly so for the two people who lost their lives and seven who were injured by rocks the size of cars that were shot as far as a mile away. Volcanoes can be quite terrifying. Just ask the fine folks of Pompeii.

With time to kill, I decided to ask Guillermo about his experience during the civil war. Because what better way to spend a sunny afternoon than to recount one of the most horrific times in your life with a curious Gringo?

Guillermo shared that he, indeed, fought in the war.

"I was a soldier," he said in Spanish.

"Do you mind if I ask which side?"

"For the government," he replied, pausing a moment before gesturing northeast, back toward Suchitoto. "FMLN's on that side of the country."

What struck me as remarkable was the nonchalant tone in his voice. He spoke of his position in the war in the same unremarkable tone I use to specify *café negro* over *café con leche*. I didn't hear the animosity in his voice I somewhat expected, considering the position on FMLN was once that they're a bunch of commie bastards thirsty for innocent capitalist blood (though there is the possibility that he just didn't feel like getting into it with someone he knew for a whopping twenty-four hours). It spoke to me just how far El Salvador had come since that horrific chapter.

Eventually we ran into the right people who were able to point us toward the trail entrance, which had a park ranger of sorts holding down the fort. He told us a group just left with a guiding officer and that we could probably catch up. This supported my theory that the constant recommendation to hike with an officer or guide throughout Central America is less about the actual threat of crime and more to protect their image on the rare chance someone does get mugged and posts a one-star review on TripAdvisor as if there's an epidemic.

Sure enough, we caught up and were able to ascend Santa Ana in about two hours. What I loved about this hike was the diversity. We started our hike in dense forest with dirt-covered paths. About a third of the way up, dry and loose rocks covered the paths and the forest cleared up, allowing us a glimpse of the view that awaited us at the summit. Suddenly we felt like we were in Phoenix, climbing lifeless Camelback Mountain.

Nearing the crater, life, as John Cleese would say, ceased to be. Nothing but wide expanses of rock could be seen like a panorama from Mars without the red hue. Hikers started to follow the path of least resistance rather than any formally marked trail.

Finally at the summit, the wind picked up. Guides expecting over-eager photographers ushered us to where the wind was blocked, allowing us to peer over the edge to see the crystal clear view of Santa Ana's crater instead of being blown into it for a more intimate look, albeit brief. With the 360-degree view of the surrounding area—the bubbling turquoise waters in the crater; the rocky trail we just hiked; the bright green, rolling countryside; Izalco and even the Pacific Ocean an hour's drive away—Melanie and I quickly agreed this was up there with Orosi, perhaps even better. Vale la pena or "worth it," as I told ascending hikers on my way back down.

On our first night, we discovered we were not alone. Melanie threw together dinner while I setup a movie on my laptop in the living room. Guillermo helped start a fire before he went off with his family for the evening. While eating, we heard a repeated clanging sound coming from the kitchen. We paused the film each time, listened closely, and it went away. Then the clanging returned with the sound of something being dragged.

Finally, we went back to the kitchen to investigate. Nothing appeared out of the ordinary, so I started to head back to our meal when Melanie shrieked as if she just locked eyes with the devil himself.

"What's wrong!?" I yelled back as I grabbed her in the middle of her sprint out of the kitchen.

"There's a rat!"

While I wouldn't say I have a friendly relationship with vermin and creepy crawlers, I hardly harbor anywhere near the same level of fear as Melanie. Yet that fear has the ability to transcend any rational behavior going on in my brain. She has the ability to make *me* afraid of things. I can feel her heart racing as if it's my own when I'm sent to investigate something, such as an alleged rat.

I peeked around, keeping my distance of course, and didn't see anything. As Melanie approached, it sprinted out from behind a bowl she had used in her cooking and scampered behind the counter.

That was enough to send us straight into a state of irrationality, but thankfully we behaved better than with Mothra.

We immediately shuttered the kitchen and placed heavy objects in strategic places to ensure, against all reason, that it wouldn't pry itself out. Whatever hell it would wreak, it would do so in the confines of the kitchen.

The next morning, Melanie tiptoed into the kitchen. The rat had left a trail of droppings around the countertop and chewed through our bag of coffee. Guillermo did his best to find it to no avail. It appeared we would have another night with the rat. Except this time we were prepared, removing everything we would need for the evening well before night to ensure the rat would not cross paths with us.

But it was also that night we received a call from Henry, the husband of our AirBnB contact Laurie. I thought it was odd that he was calling, considering I had only previously corresponded with Laurie. Plus I had already spoken with her earlier that day. She asked if we could stick around for breakfast on that final morning, which we were happy to do as long as we could get to El Tunco by the time our next hosts were expecting us.

Guillermo handed me his phone.

"Hello?"

"Hey, Joe. It's Henry. Laurie's husband."

Skipping the pleasantries.

"So look, we're going to be a little later tomorrow. How about lunch?"

This caught me off-guard, but I tried to remain polite.

"We'd love to, but we already told our hosts in El Tunco we'd be there by noon."

"Well, considering everything we're doing for you, I'd think the least you could do is wait for us."

Now I was truly caught off guard. Henry had skipped beating around the bush and bluntly demanded that we wait for him, regardless of our schedule. From his perspective, we owed him something. Never mind we were already doing some work for him. Perhaps he was unfamiliar with the digital age and expected physical copies of the photos before we left?

Considering we were without phones or Internet, I didn't exactly have any bargaining chips. So I agreed to meet whenever they could. Then it occurred to me. We didn't have any Internet or phones. What if something happened? Who were these people anyway?

It took every fiber in Melanie's being to convince herself that they were *not* drug kingpins. In her mind, we didn't know what they did and they were clearly very wealthy. Every bad script would say that they were, indeed, drug kingpins.

Since we thought we would be leaving early the next morning, we made no plans. Now that we had to wait, we made a late breakfast, took our time packing, walked around a bit more outside, and watched movies until they finally showed up—later than promised.

Laurie looked sweet, like a young mother who could double as a soccer mom back in the States. Henry was shorter and stocky. He moved confidently and deliberately.

We sat inside and chatted a bit while their staff setup our fried chicken lunch. This felt strange. Very strange. I'm not at all accustomed to having a waiter or caretaker, and I feel incredibly uncomfortable being served anywhere outside of a restaurant. Even then I like it when it's as informal as possible. I'm also the guy who fights with hotel staff when they try to carry my bag for me. (I have arms and am capable of lugging twenty pounds myself, thank you very much.)

Henry was interrogating me a bit, asking about what I do and the arrangement we made with his wife.

"Now what am I getting out of this? I mean, we let you stay at this place. What're we getting out of it?" he asked on more than one occasion.

"Well, we're taking photos of the place. Laurie wanted to use that to help promote the property."

"I see. And like what, you'll put this on your website or

something? And then what, people come and stay here?"

"Well, I'll be sharing the photos with Laurie and she can do whatever she wants with them."

He absorbed it for a moment. "I don't really get it, but that's why I leave it to her. I'm more of a business guy. I like to know how this is going to make me money."

Suddenly Melanie's drug kingpin suspicions didn't seem too far off. Laurie, meanwhile, was as sweet as she appeared, gushing about the view as if it was her first time seeing it.

"We only get out here maybe once a year," she shared, which explained why she wasn't sick of the view. "That's why I listed it on AirBnB. It's so beautiful out here, I didn't want it to just sit here. I want others to come and enjoy it."

Okay, maybe not drug kingpins.

El Tunco: How To Make The World Suck Less

El Salvador, for us, would end on the beach. Perhaps appropriately so since what tourism has existed here has been a result of surfers who historically pay little attention to the local situation or international reputation if it means finding a good wave. More practically, this is where we could pick up a shuttle to Antigua, Guatemala where we would be spending our second week of travel.

The ride to El Tunco from Cerro Verde speaks to the, let's call it, dense diversity I have been mentioning. Within a couple of hours from urban Santa Tecla, we were in colonial Suchitoto. Another couple of hours, Cerro Verde where the temperature dropped to the low fifties at night. Then not even two hours away we were in sweltering hot and humid El Tunco on the Pacific Ocean.

Our final stay was at Boca Olas, referred to us by our hosts back in Suchitoto. We walked into a gorgeous complex geared toward longer stay travelers that had just launched within the new year. We were more than willing to help break it in.

After a quick jaunt across the rocky Pacific coast that was our backyard, we joined Lisa (who worked in marketing and PR for the hotel) and her husband for a drink at the hotel bar. Cadejo

Brewing Company from San Salvador was generous enough to leave a six-pack with a few different flavors upon hearing of our visit. Damn fine stuff that could stand up to most American craft breweries. Lisa shared that Cadejo once ran a satirical campaign for president. Who wouldn't want to support a brewery like that?

Joining Lisa were her in-laws who had worked in the government during the Civil War. They have since moved up to Houston to be closer to grandchildren, but were in town to visit Lisa and her son who live in San Salvador. Lisa herself comes from the States, but you can tell she considers herself just as much a Salvadoreña in the way she talks about her adopted country. When the conversation inevitably turned to the Civil War, Lisa admitted some frustration with how foreigners continue to perceive El Salvador.

"This country could really use some good PR," she said with a bit of a sigh.

She wished El Salvador would get some credit for absorbing the guerrillas of the FMLN as a viable political party rather than continuing the battle. In fact, the FMLN has now held the presidency multiple times, and their far-right rivals in ARENA are still around as well. No war would have clearly been preferable, but you get the point.

As one of the older tourism stopping points, we saw more foreigners in El Tunco than anywhere else in El Salvador. Ultimately Lisa sees El Salvador as a melting pot, and it surely is in El Tunco. Boca Olas alone is full of foreign staff mixed in with Salvadorans. At the front desk we met Laura, whose New Zealand accent threw us off when she told us she's from Switzerland. Like other foreigners who have landed in El Salvador, she fell in love with the place during a backpacking trip through the Americas. She's since gotten married and was happy to call El Salvador home for the foreseeable future.

El Tunco struck us as a beach-town unlike any other we had

seen, especially within Central America. The town is essentially one narrow street lined with a mixture of homes, hostels, shops, and restaurants that lead to the *calle peatonal* or pedestrian street. This "street" is simply a strip of sand surrounded on both sides by an even larger mixture of businesses to poke in and out of that eventually lead back to the beach.

Unlike the rocky corner of the beach near our hotel, we now found ourselves on a wide expanse of perfectly flat black sand. Wading into the ocean, the ground remained consistent for as far as my atrocious swimming skills allowed me to go. Surfers had their own corner where the waves were powerful. I was where my people belong—people who enjoy flailing themselves at big waves with the relative assurance that the ground is neither painful nor going to sweep you away. It was also on these sands that I had a bit of a religious experience. I cannot say for certain if it was remnants of a bug bite I got in Suchitoto that left me ill for one evening or something I ate, but I suddenly felt a bomb in my colon ready to blow.

Oh, God, please. Oh, God, please. Oh, God, please, I chanted to myself, like a Buddhist mantra praying desperately to avoid unspeakable embarrassment.

I needed a solution—fast. But beaches are notoriously the worst place to be for an emergency. Unless you're near your hotel, all the bathrooms are for guests only. We were about a half-mile or more from our hotel, a distance my rumbling digestive system would not allow.

Desperate, I approached a group who appeared to be offering surf lessons. I cut them off before they could give me the pitch.

"Do you know where there's a bathroom?" I asked, flexing every muscle in my trembling body.

They pointed behind them, to another hotel.

Oh, God, please. Oh, God, please. Oh, God, please, I repeated as I darted by the sandy steps up to the hotel patio bar and over to the bathroom, praying that the Gods would answer my call for porcelain.

Success. Travesty averted.

I don't often discuss my appearance, but it saved me from turning my shorts into a Jackson Pollock. When being fitted for my wedding tux, I was told I had the exact dimensions of the store mannequin. I could sneak into a J.C. Penney catalogue unnoticed thanks to my blonde hair, blue eyes, slender frame, and pasty white complexion. This is all to say I'm built in a very non-threatening way. Nobody sees me and trembles in fear. I barely register on anyone's radar, allowing me the opportunity to, say, sneak into a hotel bathroom for emergencies without suspicion, as I did in El Tunco.

After a day at the beach, we rewarded ourselves with some sloth mimicry and a bit of gluttony thrown in for good measure— just to cross off a couple deadly sins within a few hours. This led us to Sweet Garden Café & Crepas, a small eatery perched on the second floor with an enjoyable overlook of passersby where we were consumed a delicious crepe concoction of chicken and cheese. Perhaps it was the sun rendering me useless and hungry, thus truly excited to eat just about anything, but dammit if that wasn't one of the best lunches I've ever had, topped off with a strawberry fresca natural.

On our final day, Laura hooked us up with her husband's cousin Luis for a hike to a series of waterfalls. She sold us on the hike over a Greek dinner as we sat on wooden swings that surrounded our high-top wooden table on the restaurant's front patio with the Ohio State college football national championship game on in the background. A drunken German tourist had followed us briefly, apparently mistaking Laura's ability to speak German as an invitation to bother us.

Talk about a cultural explosion.

We met Luis a little after eight in the morning. He was dressed in a light long-sleeve shirt and shorts with long black hair coming out from underneath his mesh ball cap. The drive was about twenty minutes to what we were warned would be a somewhat rigorous hike. But after noting we had just done the hike to the crater of Santa Ana, we were assured it wouldn't be too challenging.

Unlike the Santa Ana trail, this was nothing official. When I asked Luis for the name, he shrugged his shoulders and said, "Caminata Cascada" or "Waterfall Hike." It was something Luis said he remembered using twenty years ago when he was a little kid before moving to Maryland with his parents. It hadn't changed a bit since, he told us.

The hike was more technical than difficult. The entire hike to the collection of waterfalls was moderate, but the rocks were as sturdy as if they were natural rock climbing walls. Twenty or thirty minutes later we had arrived to the waterfalls. Luis suggested jumping off one that dropped fifteen feet below, but I wasn't going to do a damn thing until I saw him do it first. Admittedly nervous, Luis waded into the pool of water between waterfalls to get a sense of where the rocks were. Then he jumped in from a spot around ten feet high before finally taking on the highest point.

Ten feet seemed manageable for me. Surely I wouldn't paralyze myself, I thought, even though I'm not typically one for jumping off the safe ground to the unknown. The nerves kicked up a bit, but I climbed up, convinced I was only going down one way. Needless to say it wasn't nearly as bad as my mind had made it out to be. It never is.

This conjured up an obvious metaphor for El Salvador. You hear all these stories about the country that either make you nervous or completely disinterested in visiting. I'll admit that I let the uneducated warnings and documentaries rattle me in spats.

Maybe you make the decision to visit anyway, but you're still nervous as your trip nears. Finally, you go and see the reality of El Salvador is not black and white, just as you would find in any country. You see the indisputable fact that this a fascinating country full of kind, hard-working, curious and welcoming people.

Then you realize characterizing an entire country's people based on a handful encounters is a bit cliché, but it somehow feels okay for tiny El Salvador. And so you jump in. By the time you land, you're glad you did it and you're looking to climb back up and do it all over again.

On our way back, we passed by a group of school kids playing in the river with a handful of older chaperones looking on. They laughed, shrieked and squealed like any kid does around the world when playing outside. This is when it hit me. I thought of all the people who blow off entire countries and groups of people as *too dangerous*. I thought about how this is almost always based on ignorance and prejudice. I thought, well, *fuck 'em*. Seriously. Fuck anyone who can look at a group of kids playing outside, like you and I did growing up, and dismissively deem their entire country not worth seeing or their culture not worth experiencing because of something they may have seen on the news a few years ago. Anyone that bullheaded doesn't deserve to travel.

But I suspect most aren't like that. I suspect there's wiggle room to change minds and perceptions—to scrub away the stereotypes and show the true character of people around the world. That's something I can work with. Just give me some wiggle room.

I left El Salvador with a new preference for traveling to and documenting places that would raise eyebrows among the average North American traveler. I don't want the perceived safety of distance, I want to get up close. I want to meet people, hear their stories, see their country, learn about their culture and share it with anyone who will listen.

Maybe if we knew a bit more about each other, we'd be a little less okay with killing each other. Maybe we'd even get along. Maybe the world would suck that much less.

A Tale Of Two Antiguas

I felt bad for our driver, a Guatemalan if I had to guess. He picked us up in a shuttle for Antigua, right on time, before moving on to a hostel to pick up the rest of the crowd. They were all Americans, it sounded like. Their thin tank tops, shorts, sandals and backpacks half their size suggested to me that they were hostel-hopping around Central America. If only their timeliness matched their apparent curiosity for the world, we all would have sweated a little less, and the driver could have enjoyed the air conditioning a bit more rather than camping out on the roof of the shuttle while he waited for everyone to hand him their bags to tie to the roof. By the time he returned to the driver's seat, his shirt was an entirely different color.

Neither Melanie nor myself are the most sociable people. I was happy to put my headphones on for the entirety of the ride between El Tunco and Antigua, taking them out only for the uneventful border crossing and our drop off. Melanie had to snuggle close to me due to one of the backpackers seated on her right taking up as much space as possible, spreading his arms out across the back of the seat like he was sitting alone. I'm all for the arm-stretch when it comes to relaxing, but I had always thought it an unspoken rule that you keep your arms within your personal box when traveling with strangers, much like all men know to leave a urinal in between whenever possible.

The ride took about five hours, including the obligatory bureaucratic stop at the border. Melanie and I were dropped off last as we bounced around the Antiguan cobblestones into the late evening. Some of our fellow travelers hadn't bothered to book lodging in advance, leaving Melanie cursing them silently as they repeatedly shouted at the driver to stop whenever they saw a hostel so that they could pop out quickly and inquire as to their availability. I'm all for a carpe diem spirit, but not when it impacts my eating schedule.

Minor inconveniences aside, our excitement to be in Antigua far outmatched our grievances once we were left at our hotel. We were floored the moment we stepped off the quiet street and through the wooden gate into the hotel lobby. Our stomachs demanded sustenance, however, so we paused our admiration to head out for a quick meal. A friendly gentleman at the front desk recommended that we take a cab, a general precaution in line with all the other general precautions we had seen throughout Central America. The hotel was just a kilometer away from the central plaza, but experience had told us that locals always prefer their guests play it safe among new surroundings. We obliged his offer to take a cab. (By the next day we would be walking around at night without the slightest concern for our safety.)

Antigua is a living relic of colonial America. The living aspect is that not everyone is there to be romanticized by the architecture and charm. Some, Guatemalans for example, are there to party—loud and all through the night. They're exhausted after working their jobs in Guatemala City an hour away and are looking for their own escape. We saw that juxtaposition our first night in an establishment that surely plays as a modest pizzeria by day; by the late hour it had turned into a club, its heavy bass music ricocheting down the block. Great to blow off steam, but decidedly not my scene. That's not meant to be a snobby jab. To the contrary, we were doing everyone a favor, as our presence would have brought down the *cool* factor an appreciable amount.

Instead, we found our way to a perfectly agreeable restaurant for a quick bite and called it an early night. After all, we knew we'd be walking day and night for our next few days in Antigua.

Breakfast was at our hotel's open-air dining space overlooking their impressively maintained garden. With no clouds to mar the view, we could easily see the surrounding volcanoes—namely Volcán de Agua. It's a treat to see now, but half a millennium ago it destroyed Antigua, then the capital of Guatemala. The conquistadors worked from scratch by moving Antigua five miles further away and settled the present-day city in 1543. Earthquakes then had their turn with Antigua during the eighteenth century, creating many of the ruins that now draw tourists from all over the globe and made it a UNESCO Heritage Site.

We were joined at breakfast by the hotel's owner, Claudia—a Guatemalan, mid-fifties I'd guess, with dark, frizzy hair. Melanie, knowing the top fashion brands better than I, noted her name-brand attire as if she was wearing her status in the community. The hotel had been passed down for generations within her family, so it wasn't a stretch to assume she came from money.

Claudia pulled a chair and sat down, armed with a black pen and matching notebook. Her smile was radiant and welcoming, as one might expect from someone in tourism wanting their guests to have a good time. Our initial friendly smalltalk—where are you from? How do you like it here?—slowly slipped into something more sinister; a mixture of classism and something else I couldn't quite put my finger on. Definitely an "-ism," I know that much.

"We need more people like *you* to come here," she said. "Those people from Guatemala City come on the weekend and are *so* loud. They stay up all night partying."

Ah, yes. The dreaded *those people.*

It got worse as she turned her attention to world affairs, namely the recent Charlie Hebdo terrorist attacks in France.

"I probably shouldn't say this," she started where she probably —no, definitely—should have stopped. "But those French had it coming." Her once warm presence took a harsh, frigid turn, like an impatient father dangerously jerking the wheel rather than miss his exit. Except this lady's exit was somewhere in Looney Tunes land.

"They're snooty. It's terrible, but this will take them down a peg."

It will never cease to amaze me how quickly people will reveal their slimy character without provocation as long as you let them keep talking. But it does surprise me how often it's happened to me while working in travel and tourism. You'd think these folks would especially want to put their best foot forward and keep it that way. That's how it starts, but then they unleash their racist rants—like the Frenchman in Orosi, classist qualifications, xenophobic word vomits, and they'll only pause to send an important text while driving on the highway. (Seriously—stop texting and driving, tourism people/everyone.)

Not wanting to start our first day in Antigua with a *thing*, Melanie and I were left uncomfortably gritting our teeth until we could somehow seamlessly squeeze our way out of the conversation. Luckily, travel always gives you an out from an unwanted conversation, because anyone—even the kind of human being who could endorse a terrorist attack as payback for supposed snobbery—can understand that travelers need to keep moving and explore their new destination. We managed to escape our unfortunate breakfast encounter and start our meandering around Antigua.

There are more buildings, churches and ruins to see in

Antigua than craters on the moon. To see them all would resemble a shopping list of artifacts and I don't enjoy traveling with a checklist. The first handful are mesmerizing. The attention to detail, the intensive care it must take to preserve these wonders, and the history that took place within these walls made my imagination run wild. I wondered how enchanting it must be to live in a place like this. But before long, they all quickly blurred together into one historic blob. The seventeenth century architecture barely raised an eyebrow after a full day of walking. Only after returning to the States, where so much of our best architecture has been destroyed to ensure everyone and their two kids will have a space to park, could I truly appreciate the efforts that have gone into maintaining Antigua. Antigüeños rightfully take great pride in their accomplishment.

The churches stand in various states of functionality and repair. La Merced is an especially popular church with worshippers attending service throughout the day and tourists flocking to quietly take in the moment for themselves. I personally enjoyed gallivanting through the church and the Convent of Capuchins and sneaking into the Santo Domingo Monastery, the latter of which also serves as one of the more popular hotels in the region nowadays.

More than the buildings, Antigua is Antigua because of the tapestry of Mayan colors that permeate the city. Magentas, yellows, browns, blues, pinks, oranges and violets of every shade. Miniature Costco-sized market places, like El Mercadito, feature an astonishing amount of Mayan fabrics, music and artifacts. A shopper could get lost for hours.

After a while, I began to wonder how much the Mayan people have been relegated to serving the tourist economy. Do they truly love what they do or is this all they can do? Lest we forget, Guatemala's brutal thirty-six-year Civil War that saw Mayan genocide is still a fresh event having only officially ended in

1996. Like in El Salvador, this was one of the last satellite wars of the Cold War that saw the U.S. propping up yet another brutal anti-Communist power against the leftist guerrillas supported by the Soviet Union. And lest we forget, we purposefully gave them freakin' syphilis.

Guatemalans are still fighting to ensure some combatants from the Civil War see a trial. Former president Efraín Ríos Montt is currently facing genocide charges, the first former head of state to be prosecuted for such charges by his own judicial system. He had previously been found guilty, but the sentence was reversed and a new trial ordered due to alleged judicial anomalies. This is all on the heels of Otto Pérez Molina's sudden resignation from the presidency and subsequent arrest following allegations of corruption. (Indigenous groups have accused Pérez of participating in the genocide during the civil war.)

With all that history under their belt, it's almost no surprise a comedian by the name of Jimmy Morales ascended to the presidency in 2015.

In the midst of Guatemalan's bloody modern history, there was a satirical voice that shed a different light on the country's harsh realities. Miguel Ángel Asturias was a Guatemalan author who penned *El Señor Presidente*, a fictional account of life under a ruthless dictator not unlike what Guatemala has seen. The 1946 novel won Asturias the Nobel Prize and helped establish the foundation of Latin American literature.

A modestly sized museum at nearby Santo Domingo Del Cerro pays homage to the author's prolific career. Casa Santo Domingo, the monastery turned hotel, offers rides up to the scenic hill surrounded by contemporary art and fantastic views of Antigua below. The aptly named El Tenedor Del Cerro allows for a more open and remote dining experience than anything else available throughout Antigua. Not that Antigua is hurting for fine dining; the city of just 35,000 could rival any of the cosmopolitan capitals of the world.

I was left with conflicted feelings when it was time to leave Antigua. Whereas my first days were filled with fantasies of relocation and making this walkable museum our next Latin American home, I left wondering if there's just too much tourism in Antigua.

Besides being popular to tourists, Antigua has become an international capital for budding linguists looking to perfect their Spanish abroad. It's gained such a reputation that many now jokingly wonder if one can even perfect their Spanish in Antigua with so much English being spoken. Not to mention there seems to be a clear divide between tourism and locals, and I have to believe more could be done to offer Mayans other opportunities besides constantly competing with one another to sell the same thing for already meager prices.

Despite what issues remain in Antigua and throughout Guatemala, I ultimately felt it was impossible not to love this city. So few cities in this world are permitted to maintain their historic aesthetic. Antigua stands out as a city that has maintained its historic charm and locals fight to keep it that way. In fact, putting a fresh coat of paint on the famous Arco de Catalina—the postcard image of Antigua—was one of the hotter issues of the day during our visit. Not to belittle that debate, but at least they're arguing over paint and not a wrecking ball.

I now worry that perhaps I didn't appreciate Antigua enough while I was there. If so, then that's a regrettable mistake on my part. But hey! At least I didn't give anyone syphilis.

An Atitlán Lake and a Chichi Market

Following our three days in Antigua, we boarded yet another shuttle for a two to three-hour drive west over to Panajachel on the northeastern shore of Lake Atitlan. The ride was nauseating even for the strongest of stomachs thanks to an unfortunate cocktail of winding roads and fumes pouring out of every passing muffler. The rising black clouds conjured images of some kind of religiously-tinged apocalyptic scene. My generally euphoric attitude after three tremendous days in Antigua had pulled a one eighty. I was left wondering how humanity could accept a world where vehicles are able to spew such unhealthy substances into fresh air while innocent passersby suffer the consequences.

Things vastly improved once we pulled into the Panajachel exit off the highway, where the road immediately descends steeply to the lakeside town. Finally we could see clear skies, the sparkling lake and those precious volcanoes that we hoped would make the excursion worthwhile.

The town itself first reminded me of my summer in Dharamsala, India. This felt like a similarly-sized town developed by narrow streets mostly populated by tuk tuks, motorcycles, and pedestrians trying not to get hit. Shops, run mostly by Mayan women, lined the main street with all their offerings in plain sight. A number of restaurants and hostels, too, were ready to serve.

We were advised to take a tuk tuk over to our hotel, though the ride showed us that it was a perfectly manageable distance by foot. A hostess briefly met with us, giving our key to the room. The room itself looked and felt like a tool shed. There was plenty of space and the beds were perfectly fine, but the walls were of that bulletin board material, complete with some newspaper clippings posted to them. It was nothing gross, inhospitable or anything at all that would impact our sleeping. It was just… strange. We were sleeping in a tool shed.

After dropping our bags off, we decided to walk back into town with hopes for a better impression of Panajachel.

Unfortunately our initial disappointment remained. We imagined that this area, which eighteenth century German explorer Alexander von Humboldt described as "the most beautiful lake in the world," probably fared better before industrial man showed up. As history has shown us, we humans are pretty good at fucking up nature.

Luckily the beauty of the lake itself and its surrounding natural charms remained. Once we worked our way through Panajachel and onto the lakeside paths, our experience improved immeasurably. With vehicles unable to travel here, the air was finally fresh, and a mixture of tourists and locals seemed to be enjoying the setting sun. This was the magical Lake Atitlán we had heard about and were glad to finally be experiencing.

Once the sun set, we went through town again looking for something to eat. Nothing grabbed us, but we opted for what looked to be a family establishment with live xylophone music. Talking with the owner, we learned this truly was a family establishment with his wife in the kitchen and a combination of daughters and nieces entertaining with traditional Mayan music. The owner, who had walked from table to table to introduce himself, grabbed the microphone in between performances to personally welcome everyone by announcing what country all of his guests had come from. There were U.S. Americans, Mexicans, Guatemalans, and we got credit for Costa Rica.

After dinner we meandered around for a bit, ending up at a convenience store to buy jugs of water for the next day's hiking. In our small transaction, we were chatted up a bit by the clerk, and what appeared to be his younger brother sitting next to the counter. Initiating conversations in Spanish often opened the door to brief conversations across Central America. If you're silent, they'll usually just assume you don't speak Spanish. Usually I would be thrilled to be left alone by strangers, but traveling in Central America made me inquisitive and wanting to learn as much as possible about everything, even if it wasn't particularly interesting.

"We don't need a bag," I said. Even that small phrase can be enough to open the door for a conversation.

"Okay." There was a pause as, I'm guessing, the young man across from me wondered if I spoke enough Spanish to keep this going.

"Are you guys married?" he asked.

"Yep! We live in Costa Rica. Moved there back in August," I replied in what was a familiar script by this point.

"That's great! Do you have kids?"

A look of disgust and horror instinctively crawled across mine and Melanie's faces.

"No, no, no," I laughed. "No kids."

This appeared to catch the clerk and his companion off guard.

"Why not?" the younger man sitting asked.

"I'm married and I have kids," the other added.

Suddenly I could feel the cultural difference, that it might be less common to get married and not have kids right away in Guatemala. Even in much of the United States, young married couples still start spewing out kids within the first year of marriage.

"Well, we don't want kids. At least definitely not right now," I tried to explain.

"Why not?"

I started to wonder if they thought I was sterile or something.

"Well, we like to travel and…" I drifted off, the translation for "turd-filled diapers terrify me" not immediately springing to mind.

"Hmmm," the clerk pondered.

I grabbed whatever it was we bought and ended the awkward exchange.

"Thanks! Have a great night!" and we continued our walk back to the hotel.

Our first impression of Panajachel was not entirely kind. The lake appeared to be as magnificent as promised, but the town itself was rather dirty and reeked of diesel fumes left by the armies of tuk tuks. To be fair, Panajachel has never been used as the selling point for Lake Atitlán.

We awoke around a quarter to six for a quick breakfast and were lucky to catch a Mayan ceremony at the hotel scheduled for some other guests. Usually I'm leery of tourists having indigenous peoples perform traditions for them, but the old Mayan woman seemed happy to share her culture with us—or at least knew how to put on a smile. Unfortunately we had to leave midway through in order to meet our guide for the hike up Volcán San Pedro.

Arriving at the docks by seven, we met with our Casa Alegre guide, Antonio. His younger companion barely spoke, but Antonio was pleasantly chatty enough to compensate.

First we took a speedboat holding about twenty or so other hikers for a thirty-minute ride across Lake Atitlán to the town of San Pedro, which had a similar layout to Panajachel without the cacophony of tuk tuks.

After picking up some fruit snacks—actual fruit, mind you, not cavities in a plastic bag—we hailed a ride up to the Volcán San Pedro entrance. I'm still amazed how our little tuk tuk was able to climb the steep roads with the weight of four people inside.

San Pedro was without question one of the most difficult hikes I've ever done. It was straight up the volcano's beaten switchback path for three to four hours. A Guatemalan family we passed had started much earlier at half past six in the morning, planning for a six-hour ascent. This was just one of those athletic feats that nobody, regardless of their condition, can do with complete ease.

Of course Antonio seemingly had little problem with it, considering he is, after all, a guide who has done the climb more times than he could count. I like to think we were hiking at an equal pace, but he very well could have just been allowing us to set the pace, as I suppose it wouldn't be very guide-like to blow by us.

As we neared the summit, the terrain turned rocky and required a bit of light climbing. Once the lake some 5,000 feet below came into view, it was without question worth the effort. This was admittedly difficult to convey to the passersby on the trek back down who seemed desperate for any sign that the summit was near. Luckily for us, the rest of our day would consist of nothing more than a relaxing jaunt around the surrounding Mayan villages.

Back at the hotel, the owner, Carl, asked us to join him for a drink inside. It quickly became clear that he wanted to talk about himself. To be fair, he did have an interesting story. He was in the military for twenty-some years, spending time in Vietnam and Germany. His time freezing in Germany is what helped him follow his dream of living in warmer Latin America. He landed on Guatemala because he heard it was one of the best countries to learn Spanish and the cost of living was more favorable for his military retirement.

The chat then moved over to the communal table outside for more drinks and conversation with other guests. Besides our host, there was a U.S. military couple and an older pair from Israel.

The conversation was as boring and awkward as one could expect among strangers forced to share a table, some of whom evidently feared any moments of silence. Our host uncomfortably discussed his career in the military and how they had a motto of, "Join the military! You get to meet people across the world... And then kill them!" The military couple sitting across from him politely remained silent, though I can only assume they were mentally pummeling him.

At one point there was a painful-to-endure conversation about non-acidic nuts. Yes, *non-acidic nuts.*

Then, another asked the Israeli gentleman about his experience in the military. He worked on a tank.

"Did you do repairs?"

"No," he responded tersely, his strong gaze anchored on his drink.

No follow up questions were necessary.

Sunday was yet another early morning with a ninety-minute shuttle ride out to Chichicastenango—an indigenous town home to Central America's largest public market, open only on Thursdays and Sundays. The scene starts relatively calm, but blink and you'll find yourself enveloped in a delightful display of colorful chaos. Tourists come to click their cameras. Others come for crafts, flowers, pottery, candles, and a plethora of the impressive textiles that the Mayan are known for.

Some had warned me about pickpocketing in Chichi, insisting that I wear my backpack on the front of my body, but I just couldn't do it. I would rather be pickpocketed than walk around like some Gringo buffoon overly cautious of the locals. Besides, I had Melanie with me to help keep an eye on my backpack, and my camera was secured out around my neck. If anyone went digging into my pack, they would have been sorely disappointed and at best snagged an old foreign coin I forgot to take out.

The streets and alleyways lined with shops and makeshift stands had become as crowded as an American Black Friday, but without the Walmart-induced murder and mayhem. Most impressive was the Church of Santo Tomás—a Roman Catholic church built atop a Pre-Columbian temple platform around 1545. The eighteen steps representing the Mayan calendar originally led to a temple of the pre-Hispanic Maya civilization and remain venerated to this day in their Mayan-tinged take on Catholicism.

The steps were covered in an assortment of vivid bouquets leading to worshippers reciting prayers in front of the main doors on their knees. Inside we sat quietly in the sparsely populated pews as Mayan men and women crawled on their knees toward candle displays. Sweet incense from blessings outside and within filled the church. This alone was worth the trip to Chichi.

We decided to give Panajachel another chance. On a quiet weekday evening, the fog of tuk tuk exhaust had mostly dissipated. We could finally see some of Panajachel's charm as we sat outside with a cup of coffee at a local café, talking briefly with the shop owners, and discovering a different area along the Atitlán coast brimming with restaurants—both large and modest. We took in one last sunset before hailing a brightly colored tuk tuk with electrified lights that could've made a cameo on *Pimp My Ride*.

In the end, I found much of Guatemala's world renowned lake and the surrounding area to be a study in stark contrasts. Vistas of this dazzling body of water surrounded by equally arresting rolling hills and three volcanoes are only achieved after trudging through clouds of black exhaust leftover from buses, shuttles, cars, motorcycles, and the army of tuk tuks that run across Panajachel like moths devouring a piece of fabric. The bright mosaic of Mayan colors that give the region a feel of life are set against a historic backdrop of government-sponsored genocide.

Our last in a series of shuttles between our two weeks in El Salvador and Guatemala took us from Panajachel directly to Guatemala's international airport. Poor Melanie was left nauseated by the time we hit Chimaltenango halfway to our destination. The heat wasn't the problem. It was, again, the exhaust. Both of us felt like we had been making out with mufflers.

But neither of us deserve an ounce of sympathy, because there were people walking alongside this bottlenecked thoroughfare with God knows what poison pouring into their innocent lungs every day of the week. Many of them were carrying heavy objects, meaning their hearts were pounding that much more, and they needed to breathe harder to get more oxygen flowing through their bodies. The icing on this miserable cake? No sidewalks.

I loathed that we were contributing to what was already a pretty dismal scene. It was hardly the cheeriest way to end the two weeks, rushing Melanie into the airport where she could sit still for a moment and breathe something relatively clean. But it's something that has left a lasting impression on me. Because of the poisonous plumes of Guatemala's Pan-American highway, I'll forever remain cognizant of my own carbon footprint and how my existence is in many ways destroying the planet.

Unfortunately this renewed commitment to environmentalism started with having to catch a flight home to Costa Rica.

pura vida (*poo·*ra·*vee·*da)
adjective

1. "Pure life" is a mentality or state of being in Costa Rica with many uses.
2. "¿Pura vida?" = "Everything okay?" "Sí, pura vida." = Yes, everything's fine.
3. Used as a salutation after a phone or face-to-face conversation.
4. The only phrase many immigrated Gringos will ever bother learning.

Example:

Tico: Hola! Como estás?

Gringo: Uh, sorry. Even though I've lived here for the better part of a decade and have had plenty of opportunities to learn Spanish, I only know how to say one thing, because it's on tee shirts and hats at all the gift shops. So, uh, pura vida!

The Messiah Of Moose Country

When National Geographic first acknowledged Atenas for having the best weather in the world (or *el mejor clima del mundo* as you'll see plastered across buses passing by) they—perhaps inadvertently—opened the floodgates to shivering North Americans. Today Atenas holds the distinction as the second-most Gringo-populated city in Costa Rica behind San José suburb Escazú, and it's easily apparent during a walk through town.

Coming from Ciudad Colón, Atenas struck me as an easy overnight destination, not to mention it was in line with my desire to see as much of Costa Rica as possible. What admittedly little reading I did won me over. It seemed nice enough for a weekend getaway.

Historically speaking, Atenas is off the *camino de carretas* (oxcart trail)—a route created in 1843 to carry coffee beans out of the central valley to Puntarenas and Limón. The name, which some might recognize as "Athens" in English, allegedly comes from José Rafael Gallegos Alvarado, the region's chief of state in 1833, and his admiration of Greek culture. Historians, in their pesky attachment to the truth, aren't so sure about that story.

Our bed and breakfast for the night was off a gravel-covered road just a couple of kilometers outside of the town center. Despite the overwhelming presence of North Americans, Atenas is not overrun with hotels and hostels. This still very much has the feel of a Tico town, with an impressive public park anchored by an architecturally interesting church, and surrounded by a variety of restaurants and shops.

The history of our lodging stretches back to 2001 when owner Carol first arrived with her then-husband and two girls to start working on the property. She rented out the property while she returned to her native Canada in 2005. In 2011, Carol came back for a three-month visit to the property with a new romantic partner and eventually reopened the bed and breakfast. She met us at the driveway with two lovable German Shepherds behind what looked to be a freshly painted blue gate. Also by her side was the aforementioned romantic partner.

With respect to Carol's romantic partner, this is an example of where I am obviously changing the name of the individual. I'm doing this because I am both benevolent and wanting to avoid angry, misspelled emails. I can share, however, that the name he goes by (not his birth name, mind you) was allegedly given to him by an Indian guru. This name, he said, means "incarnation of God."

How humble, I thought.

This guy was an ass. Pure and simple. He was smug, boastful, and every thought or opinion that escaped the clenches of his weasely smirk—a smirk that any reasonable person would want to remove with a swift smack—was oozing with a holier-than-thou superiority complex unlike anything I had ever seen. A truly sanctimonious bastard who transcended both mansplaining and whitesplaining. Street corner evangelists would tell this guy to tone it down a notch.

I could feel Melanie's eyes rolling, too, as Mr. Incarnation of God explained the origins of his new name. We later compared his appearance as some kind of hybrid of Wolf Blitzer and Bob Ross, the once upon a time famous television painter.

Before starting the tour of their property, he led us to our room, which he classily referred to as the "titty room" thanks to a painting hanging in front of the bed of two women whose breasts were exposed.

Clever.

As his horticultural tour of the property began, he first offered an explanation of Atenas' reputation of having the best climate in the world.

"You're probably going to think this is bullshit," he admitted, "But if you follow the wind currents, it points to a large palm tree on our property."

He pointed over to the tree in question.

"That's the epicenter of the world's best climate."

He was right. I smelled bullshit.

This humble servant of the Almighty then began to lead us around the sprawling property, following a mixture of dirt, gravel and paved paths. Royal cuban palm trees, ginger, bananas, pineapples, cas, tangerines, papayas, and cumquats are just a small sampling of the botanical garden surrounding the B&B.

To their credit, maintaining this work was no easy feat. When our Canadian couple moved down from the Great White North, the property was a modest farm. What we were looking at was twelve years in the making, with various buildings and rooms added on over time. They also explained that for five months out of the year, the B&B serves as an "experimental community." Imagine a heavy dose of spirituality, drum circles and loose boundaries, and you've got a pretty good idea of what's going on.

Again, I could sense Melanie's grimace as we regrettably imagined throngs of sixty-year-olds frolicking naked around the gardens, longing for a return to the '60s.

Back at the building, we met a couple from Australia who shared that they just finished a twenty-one-day water fast in

Guanacaste.

Another eye roll.

"We wanted to get healthy the healthy way," one explained, whose thin frame reminded me of the American musician Moby. His experience sounded truly awful, but their spirits were to the contrary. It was a perfect example of, "to each their own."

We were hungry, so Carol was kind enough to offer us a ride into town. During the short lift she explained that she selected Costa Rica for "a better climate and a place with Canadian values." We were then treated to an unwanted lecture of how awful U.S. Americans are—all of them, apparently—compared to the great and glorious people of Canada. She lamented how "Americanized" Atenas had become as if Canadians weren't moving to Costa Rica for the exact same respite from the frozen tundra.

This was a continuing theme throughout Costa Rica, foreigners sharing their story with an air of superiority over other foreigners. Just once, *just once* I wanted to hear someone simply admit that they moved for better weather and that's it. But so many seemed to feel the need to overly justify their international move by either putting down other foreigners or bizarrely enough, Ticos themselves.

Carol left us just a couple blocks away from Balcón del Café, an enjoyable lunch spot with—as the name suggests—balcony seating. The menu featured a mixture of traditional Tico cuisine, though no casados, and German food. My German breakfast with sunny side up eggs, cheese and toast hit the spot. Melanie opted for a chicken sandwich "sin mayonesa," but as we've learned over the past six months, mayonnaise still had a solid eighty percent chance of making an appearance anyway. This was no exception, but the mora fresca natural more than compensated for the error.

Following lunch, we went for a brief jaunt around the town square. A young Tico was intrigued by my camera, chasing behind with a beaming smile and dance moves reminiscent of Chris Farley's "I'm a maniac!" performance in *Tommy Boy*. A woman, perhaps his mother, followed behind laughing as we joked about him growing up to be either a professional dancer or model. After corralling the little boy, an older man sitting at a nearby bench called me over. He looked like a shopping mall Santa Claus dressed up as a southern plantation owner.

"Hombre! Habla inglés?" he hollered in a distinctly North American accent. It was the most American interpretation of Spanish I had yet heard in Costa Rica.

"¿Cómo?" I jokingly replied as if I didn't understand.

He waved me over again.

"You know, there a lot of people here who would like to take that camera out from under you."

Now my eyes were beginning to roll.

"Oh, thanks," I replied. "But we live here, we've been around the country and Central America. Everything's been fine."

"Okay, just letting you know. Someone was killed over one of those a week ago, and I've been pickpocketed myself." His Canadian friend sitting on the other end of the bench nodded along in agreement.

Perhaps I read it wrong, but it felt more like a "beware of *those people* who look different" warning than anything backed up by reality.

Wishing them a good day, I walked back to Melanie, who overheard the guy mumble to his friend, "That's what I get for being a good Samaritan."

This interaction epitomized the ugly Gringo stereotype that seemed more visible in Atenas than anywhere else. There was definitely an inherent suspicion of Ticos, as if they should have to present themselves and behave like the North Americans who decided to relocate here. Then again, history is full of people relocating only to tell the locals they're doing it wrong. I guess Atenas is just another chapter in *Encyclopedia Intolerant.*

Atenas itself struck us as perfectly lovely. It was very easy to see why people live there. Despite Colonel Claus' fears, our encounters with Ticos in the area were very pleasant. Two we chatted with over breakfast at the B&B were visiting from Heredia and, as most Ticos had, offered their favorite corners of Costa Rica. I had previously helped them with directions to the property over the phone when His Holiness of Canada couldn't give directions in Spanish.

(How one owns a lodging establishment in Costa Rica for several years and makes no attempt at learning Spanish was beyond me, but ultimately seemed unsurprising given everything else we had learned about him.)

Our afternoon was spent meticulously studying this "best climate in the world" reputation by using a method I learned back in Bocas Del Toro—the hammock. Drifting in and out of consciousness over a couple of hours as a light breeze brushed past me every so often, I could comfortably report that Atenas made a strong case.

Eventually we decided to make our way down past the pool and over to the patio with an outdoor kitchen and seating area overlooking the impressive gardens. Our hosts had already been savoring the view when we joined the conversation.

This is when things took yet another uncomfortable turn. When launching into a story, the Messiah of Moose Country started with a "This might be racist..." and proceeded to catch himself, realizing that a racist statement almost always follows such a declaration. He continued with a different story, for context I suppose, about joking with his American mother that she probably let her black maid in from the back door.

"I'm Canadian, so..." he laughed, as if that's equal with not being racist.

Evidently her response was, indeed, deplorable, saying "she preferred it that way." This somehow seemed to validate for him that all Americans are as racist as his old southern mother.

Nothing like painting with a broad brush.

Our Divine Savior from the North followed that gem of a story with the original tale he wanted to share about how he and his partner won't take Ticos for some reason that was articulated only under his breath. Unfortunately this was not the first time we've heard of reprehensible screening practices by North American or European lodging owners.

"But now we're trying again, right?" he said, looking over toward Carol for confirmation. He appeared proud of his willingness to consider taking in people of the country he was in, whom he spent a good chunk of the remaining conversation insulting.

"Yeah, I mean, we're not screening them," Carol replied, which was disappointing considering she was otherwise quite pleasant and had a very peaceful presence about her.

This was all colored by a couple of additional references from the Exalted One, who admitted that he was afraid of visiting the United States because of, "those guys wearing bandanas and tank tops in those bouncing cars."

Yikes.

He continued rambling and spilling the unfettered contents of his convoluted mind, referring back several times to not being welcomed in the United States because he supposedly helped fund Nicaraguan revolutionaries in the '80s, a claim that felt like he just wanted to believe he's on some blacklist, not necessarily a reflection of reality. The U.S. government does its fair share of crazy shit but it seemed unbelievable that they would ban some random Canadian for having a contrary opinion when millions already do it back home.

He also shared that a Chinese guest once asked why he hasn't visited China.

"Because you fucking raped my planet!" he told us.

On top of everything else, it became clear that this gentleman was one of those self-important individuals who could not possibly do wrong. Everyone else in the world, however, were directly responsible for the actions of their government. Only Canadians escaped his judgmental wrath. All night we heard about wonderful Canadian values. They take care of the poor, they have excellent health care, and they supported the poor revolutionaries throughout Latin America. It took everything within me to refrain from mentioning Canadian mines, oil drilling, or First Nations cultural genocide. But my wanting to sleep peacefully and not be poisoned in the following morning's breakfast trumped my desire to show him he was being an exceptional twit.

(This interaction was doubly sad for me, because I love Canada. My first travel writing gig was to northern Lake Superior with a group of Canadians traveling on a seventeenth century-style voyageur canoe to a music festival in Red Rock, Ontario. I've been fortunate to travel across the Americas, Europe, and a bit of Asia and the Middle East, yet that trip remains a personal favorite.)

As if this guy wasn't already mentally draining enough, a solid thirty minutes of conversation were devoted to his passion for Nicaragua. Sure they have drug lords ruling the eastern half of the country and the government is rife with corruption, as he admitted, but Nicaraguans seemed free of his previous "guilt by passport" belief. Why?

"They're just so genuine. I'm always in tears when I'm there. I can feel them now."

God, how painful it was to listen to him seemingly romanticize the plight of Nicaraguans—because they smile?—while trashing just about everyone else, especially Ticos.

Our illustrious blockhead continued, describing his alleged travels to Nicaragua during a time of a famous Catholic priest who stood up to the government. I say, "alleged," because it dawned on me that he had confused his history. He was describing Óscar Romero of El Salvador, not Nicaragua. Admittedly I only knew this because I had just traveled there and recently studied the topic, but I most certainly knew whom he was talking about.

When I politely offered the correction, he was defiant.

"No, no, no. It was definitely Nicaragua."

I couldn't let it pass, even though Melanie's look insisted I drop it. I looked it up on my phone and showed him. He still refused to believe it.

"No, that can't be right. It absolutely can't be right."

Seemingly distressed, he turned his gaze back toward criticizing the world. Even the Swiss were invoked, who are apparently "bastards," but the geographically adjacent Germans are "cool." Of course he had German ancestry, had lived in Munich and spoke German, thus purifying all of the Fatherland. Plus it's just one of those rare western powers without a troubling history, right? However, he was living in Costa Rica, not Germany, and had in some form for over ten years. He and his partner were also happy to continue living on the tourist visa, thus avoiding certain taxes. Yet Ticos are the shady ones?

Getting a passport, he said, "just says something I'm not prepared to say. I'll leave it at that."

That you're willing to contribute to the roads and services you and your business benefit from by paying taxes? What a terrible thing! Thank you, Your Benevolence, for taking a stand and gaming the system.

It had been a long time since I have sensed this much bullshit from a single individual. When silence finally came, and believe me he battled like hell to prevent it from coming, we used it to excuse ourselves. At least he provided plenty of fodder for Melanie and I to riff off of for the rest of the evening. That's about the only purpose he should serve in society, we decided.

The night ended with a couple of beers and plates of arroz con pollo at El Tronco, an open-air restaurant on the outskirts of Atenas. We chatted briefly with our waiter, who had the smile of a guy who just won the lottery. He offered some basic small talk —where are you from, what are you doing here, how do you like it in Costa Rica?—as most Tico waiters do outside of the tourist towns.

It all felt familiar and comfortable, probably because this was a routine we had come to know quite well over the past six months. The restaurants, the decor, the food, the verbal exchanges, the mannerisms—all of it. I loved eating out in Costa Rica and around Central America (again, outside of the tourist towns), because we were almost always met with a hearty smile and a short story with chattier waiters sharing where they're from and what they love about their country.

Despite its large population of Gringo expatriates, Atenas, in the end, still had all of that. It still felt like a Tico town. Our Celestial Canadian and Southern Santa can eat it.

The God Of Fire

It was about half past seven in the morning when Volcán
Arenal's alarm clock went off on Monday July 29, 1968,
blanketing a region of fifteen square kilometers in volcanic rock,
lava and ash. A whopping 232 square kilometers were damaged,
including crops and surrounding forests. Eighty-two people in
Arenal's path lost their lives as rocks spewed as far as a mile
away. These rocks reportedly hit speeds of 600 meters per
second—a geological fastball more terrifying than most of what
Mother Nature can cook up.

In the aftermath, the villages of Tabacon, Pueblo Nuevo and
San Luis were gone. La Fortuna, appropriately named "The
Fortune" given the circumstances, survived to become the heart
of the region. Today, Volcán Arenal remains closely monitored
as one of the most active volcanos in the world as tourists
continue to flock in record numbers to what the local indigenous
populations once knew as the God of Fire.

The rain was constant from the moment Melanie, myself, and
my visiting Aunt Bea arrived in La Fortuna. Aunt Bea was not a
frequent international traveler, but hardly a novice. She
generally knows what she wants to do and finds a way to do it,
something I've always admired about her. Perhaps that's why
she helped make our Costa Rican dream a reality when she
awarded me the "Aunt Bea's favorite twenty-seven-year-old

nephew" scholarship to help with UPEACE tuition. In exchange, she'd get to visit whenever the hell she wanted and we'd have to do the planning. Not a bad deal.

We were grateful to have made it in one piece, having made the mistake of hiring Ramiro to drive us the three hours up to La Fortuna. During a particularly foggy and windy portion of the route, we all noticed he was starting to nod off behind the wheel. There's not much leeway for error on the narrow roads in Costa Rican mountains, so it was a particularly terrifying experience. And driving is one of those things in life where you're never allowed to comment on a person's performance no matter how warranted a "slow down" or "WAKE UP, YOU MANIAC!" might be. It's like sex to people. Everyone thinks they're the best and couldn't possibly have room for improvement.

Then as we made it into town, there was the issue of actually getting to our hotel. The owner, Alan, left us with vague directions. A bus would have actually been our preferred method of transport, but he insisted there was no way to arrive by bus. I found that highly unlikely; Costa Rica was well connected by bus, even if it was difficult to find reliable information on the system.

Eventually we had to call in and we discovered that the directions were confusing because they led to his travel business, not the hotel. Luckily La Fortuna is a small town and was easy to navigate once we were given some points of interest to look for. In any event, it didn't leave a great early impression of our host. Aunt Bea and Melanie were similarly annoyed by the apparent sales tactic.

"At least let us get our bags in the damn door before you give us the sales pitch," we all agreed.

We compromised on his dropping by later to talk about what tours he could offer in the area.

After setting down our bags, we made our way to the nearest

establishment serving any kind of food. Fortunately for us, our first find was Soda El Rio. It was not unlike that obligatory scene in romantic comedy films where the woman declares she has given up on relationships and will sleep with the next guy who walks in and it's either Danny DeVito or Hugh Jackman. Soda El Rio was our Casado con Hugh Jackman.

The rain kept us relatively hunkered in for the rest of the day, a blessing in disguise that allowed us enough time to plan whatever outdoor activities we'd take on during our time in La Fortuna. Cerro Chato immediately caught our eye as the most difficult hiking option in the area but Alan cautioned against taking it on owing to nonstop rain over the past three weeks. Evidently he had heard of people having to give up due to muddy trails that were impassable and impossible to climb. This was a hands and knees hike on a dry day, after all.

While initially disappointed, this saved us from what probably would have been an awful and/or embarrassing venture, yet our pride remained intact, because we had every intention of doing it.

To finalize our plans, Alan stopped over to our room. Within a moment of walking into the door, his jacket was off and his arms in full display from his tank top. Just as quickly, he made it known that he had come from the gym. It felt like he *really* wanted us to know that he goes to the gym.

Alan spoke like he just chugged three cups of coffee. He was very energetic and excited about everything, like a puppy left in a room made of chewable treats and rag toys. He delivered the same sales pitch he had given us online and over the phone about wanting to make sure guests are left with a great experience of the area and Costa Rica. A transplant from Canada, he had fully embraced the tourism side of "Pura Vida." In fact, he had the phrase tattooed on his arm and I wasn't the least bit surprised to find it there.

Has a Tico ever tattooed "Pura Vida" onto their body? I wondered.

While selling us on a combination of an easy hike around the Arenal Observatory Lodge and the intermediate hike up the lava fields of Volcán Arenal, Alan dove right into his observations of Costa Rica over the past fourteen years of his time abroad. The gist was essentially that Costa Ricans used to work for themselves on their farms and were happy simpletons, but now work for other people as their *pura vida* culture gets exported.

"These people are losing their culture everyday and they don't even know it," he said.

It was astonishingly patronizing stuff, like every adult Tico is really a kid trapped in an oddly sized body.

He continued, describing how so many have come from abroad to take advantage of the Ticos. Not him, of course. Why, to the contrary! He was there to save the Ticos.

"That's where I come in," he said without a hint of irony. The man was shimmering with the glow of white savior's complex. Pura vida was in jeopardy, and random Canada-man was here to save the day. I feared we had another "Incarnate of God" on our hands.

But that's Costa Rica for you, a country full of foreigners on opposite ends of the spectrum. One side being those who either question how Ticos generally live or have outright racist opinions, like the French hotelier in Orosi who now refuses to hire Costa Ricans for demanding, gasp, health insurance, or the Canadian couple from the week before who admitted to screening Tico customers. The other is where Alan lives, having completely bought into "tourism pura vida," armed with good intentions that in practice looked like another white hero putting on a cape. I imagined the *Indiana Jones* theme song playing on endless loop in his head.

That aside, Alan was helpful in getting us a good deal on the next day's hike while recommending Las Termalitas as an option for spending a raining day in La Fortuna. Most tourists, he said, head to Baldi for a hefty price of about $40 while Termalitas costs a mere $8. Plus on a Monday afternoon, the joint was practically empty save one other family and a couple of German travelers.

The concept behind Termalitas was completely foreign to me. Water heated by the volcano gets piped from underground and delivered into man-made pools. They say the water is supposed to be especially good for the skin with its minerals and whatnot, but that part felt like a piece of the sales pitch. Regardless, it was a gratifying way to kill a rainy and lethargic afternoon.

Back in town, we stopped for a coffee at the aptly-named My Coffee as the rain finally took a break. We used the opportunity to take a jaunt around the town square, easily the most appealing of town squares in Costa Rica I had seen. Tall bushes, lilies, palm trees, and monkey grass (yes, that's a thing) surrounded an impressive fountain right in line with the town church. Small towns across the globe could learn from Costa Rica's squares, most of all from La Fortuna.

Peeking into the church, we were reminded of all the churches we had seen throughout our Central American travels. Not merely the construction, but the use of a Christ model lying in a see-through casket. Or as I like to call him, Creepy Christ—vastly different from, "Wink and Gun Jesus." Now that's a Jesus I can hang out with.

Our visit to Arenal Volcano National Park came with the ironic and tragic timing of Álvaro Ugalde's passing from a heart attack in his Heredia home just a day before his sixty-ninth birthday. Mr. Ugalde was a founding father of Costa Rica's world renowned national parks system along with Mario Boza. Despite being in retirement, Ugalde continued to work tirelessly throughout his final days to ensure the long-term integrity of the nation's twenty-six national parks and 166 public and private protected areas.

Ugalde first gained traction with his and Boza's idea to preserve pockets of Costa Rica as national parks in the 1970s. The dream inched closer to reality when President Daniel Oduber and Karen Olsen, former First Lady during José "Pepe" Figueres' three terms, supported Ugalde's vision. With that, Poás Volcano became Costa Rica's first national park in 1970.

Of course political declarations and legislation meant little to those who couldn't fathom the benefit of a national parks system. Exploitation continued at the hands of business interests. By the '80s, Ugalde warned that the parks were in danger due to surrounding deforestation, saying they would be lucky to be left with islands surrounded by barren lands—not exactly the stuff of modern day Costa Rican postcards. Thankfully, the gloomy fate of the parks system changed with the election of President Óscar Arias, who saw value in the national parks for attracting tourists. (He also saw the value in peace, winning a Noble Peace Prize in 1987 for his role in designing a plan to end the civil wars of Central America and resisting U.S. attempts to alter the plan.)

Unsurprisingly, Ugalde continued to see encroaching threats, such as the Instituto Costarricense de Electricidad (ICE) and their desires to exploit geothermal energy from Rincón de la Vieja and a combination of gold miners and developers tarnishing Corcovado in the Osa Peninsula—Ugalde's most beloved national park. The fight will assuredly rage on, but the millions of annual park tourists and Costa Ricans themselves largely have Ugalde to thank for leaving something worth fighting for.

Tuesday morning, the clouds had finally parted. We could see the volcano clear as day right outside our living room window.

Apparently it had been there the whole time!

We started off with a bumpy drive over to the Arenal Observatory Lodge and lava fields. Our driver seemed excited to have passengers he could actually communicate with, although my Spanish brain had a difficult time keeping up. We got enough to know that everyone in the town thought Will Smith was a kind man during his time in La Fortuna filming *After Earth*.

"That movie was very bad," he said shaking his head. "But Will Smith was super nice, always waving to people."

The hiking around the observatory was a mixture of what felt like remote trail and easy walking around impressive gardens with panoramic views of the volcano. We left my Aunt Bea, content with her trek around the observatory, at the lodge while we continued onward to the more strenuous lava fields.

Like Orosi (and unlike Poás), the trail was left mostly wild. There was a mixture of primitive trail that felt like it hadn't been maintained recently due to the longer than usual winter rains. This eventually led to the lava fields, which sat over a dry river. The trail here was less confined and more about going up however one could. We paused for a moment at one point to watch a small pack of spider monkeys swinging from tree to tree. Our guide admitted to spotting them only because he noticed a little monkey poo underneath a tree in our path. Without dwelling too long on it, it was indeed quite strange looking, even by poo standards. Orange, white, and let's say, gooey.

The fields eventually widened before narrowing once again to a line of rocks and dirt trail. Much of the latter portion of the hike was spent minding our footing, avoiding holes in between the rocks where snakes were supposedly sleeping. I only ended up having to catch myself once, which at the time felt like an impressive athletic feat that in reality probably looked clumsy to a third party.

There's no definitive end point on this hike. Our guide, who blew our minds when he said he does this hike sometimes twice a day and can converse in four languages, informed us during the return that they take you up as high as the weather will allow and however fit they think you are. We, evidently, were awarded the highest viewpoint of this hike, though maybe he just wanted to let us think that.

After collecting Aunt Bea, we continued back down the park for a brief stop at a warm river heated by the volcano. This was interesting for about ten minutes, though still an enjoyable addition to the day. We waded around a bit in the two-foot deep river, wondering if it was such a good idea to be floating around in warm water where, at least I thought, bacteria could flourish. After getting pulled over a rapid by a strong current (my fault, I was being an idiot and dangling myself over the edge) and scraping up the side of my chest, we called it quits.

People, tourists and locals alike come here with coolers and drinks to make a day out of it. There was also a story of a private resort taking advantage of the area before there were stricter environmental laws. The resort is gone now and entrance to the river is free.

That's the way it should be, I thought.

Yet another challenging hike behind us, I was ready to throw my face into another casado.

Catarata La Fortuna is the other postcard staple for the area with a gorgeous seventy-five-meter waterfall drop fed by the Tenorio River. Most drive here as it's perfectly accessible by road, but as always, we wanted to feel like we earned the view. So Melanie and I worked up a sweat over the five-plus kilometer hike from town to the entrance of the waterfall, paid our eleven bucks, and proceeded down a winding staircase of about a half-mile in length to the bottom of the waterfall. This was one of those natural attractions you're glad you made the effort to visit, but are ready to leave after about twenty minutes.

We enjoyed various views of the waterfall, took pictures for ourselves and others (a Colombian group chanted "gracias!" after I took several photos with several devices, making me feel as if I really did accomplish something phenomenal), let the pounding water spray on us a bit, and declined hopping in for a swim after I felt how icy cold the water was. I wasn't mentally prepared for the discomfort that the initial leap does to certain nether regions of the body.

Now a theme for my travels in Costa Rica, I imagined what the falls would have been like before the development. Much more rewarding, I suppose, but still worth the visit in any event. I left wondering what Ugalde would've thought about it all. Was it wise to make it more accessible for various travelers to admire or should they have left it all alone? At least it wasn't a mini-amusement park with trapped animals like the La Paz Waterfall Gardens. The only animals who could be trapped here were some of the more portly demographics visiting. Descriptions of the walkway down to the falls and back up depict it as some kind of athletic feat, budgeting something like forty-five minutes to make the trek. It took us just ten or fifteen. (I know, I know... "Look at me, Mom!")

Either way, I think we can all agree that La Fortuna doesn't need to see any more development for the purposes of tourism. It already appeared to be on the brink of going too far. What I loved about Ciudad Colón was how easy it was to blend in. It's not a tourist town, so nobody treated me as such. But in La Fortuna, the representatives of various tour companies would shout at us as we passed by, insisting we sign up for x, y, and then z for a discount. A number of restaurants also seemed especially catered toward the tourist crowd, but I reminded myself that tourists are more likely to go out to eat on a random weekday night than locals. It ultimately shouldn't have been too surprising to see tourists outnumber Ticos at the various eateries in the heart of town.

I'm sure Alan would have plenty opinions on the topic, but I didn't bother asking because he lied about the damn bus. There was indeed a station just a few blocks away from the hotel that we used to get back rather than put ourselves (and Ramiro, for that matter, with his Mr. Magoo glasses) through another dangerous drive.

Adelante on the Río Sarapiquí

There's something objectively odd about the sport of whitewater rafting. At its most basic level, you're sitting in a large floating thing with the current pulling you over boulders larger than your body. Not to mention the only way to put on a "seat belt" is to wedge your feet into crevices on the bottom edges of the boat. It all sounds a little nuts. But in Costa Rica, it's one of the things you do.

Going a year without whitewater rafting in Costa Rica would be like a year in Paris without seeing the Eiffel Tower. Sure it can be done, but you might as well, right? Fortunately Melanie and I were invited by Outward Bound Costa Rica to join a group of travel writers on an excursion up to the Sarapiquí River a couple hours' drive northeast of San José.

Outward Bound was founded in 1941 during World War II in Europe's North Sea under a mission to build leaders through the outdoors. The Costa Rica iteration came about some twenty years ago and has been working with high school, college, and gap-year students throughout the tropical reefs, rivers, and rainforests between Costa Rica and Panama. A two-hour paddle through the Sarapiquí is hardly the toughest or longest program they offer students, but it was plenty for us journalists to get the gist and write our articles.

Melanie and I met with Lindsay and her Outward Bound Costa

Rica team in San José on a temperate and sunny March morning. After exchanging the obligatory pleasantries with the team and group of accompanying writers, we piled into the shuttle and made a beeline north to the Sarapiquí in the Heredia province.

A theme in Costa Rican travel is witnessing at least two if not several of the country's many microclimates on a single journey. So it wasn't surprising to see our sunny morning in San José turn into grey skies and rain as we traversed the hills into Heredia along Ruta 32.

"I've never seen this part dry," said Lindsay.

Historically, this area thrived off of not being dry. The Sarapiquí region is known for its biodiversity and wildlife throughout the lowland tropical forest that traces along the river. In relative modern history, this area is known for its relationship with the United Fruit Company. Far more informative books exist on the topic, but we can summarize by noting that the banana empire once shuttled plantation crops from this region to Puerto Viejo de Sarapiquí and eventually to North America. Once the United Fruit Company developed a rail line between San José and Puerto Limón in 1880, the area was largely forgotten and has never quite been able to reach its former glory. (Though the creation of La Selva Biological Station anchored in the Caribbean lowland is an internationally renowned tool in researching rainforests, especially concerning the impact of climate change.)

This region, however, is growing in fame for its tourism potential. Adventure travelers across the globe are coming to the Sarapiquí for their own whitewater rafting and kayaking adventures through the river. Anecdotally it seems that tourism has yet to dramatically alter the region. There was nothing gaudy or manufactured for foreigner's here, like some Señor Frogs of adventure sport. Our entrance to the river was no more than the side of a muddy gravel road with the fresh smell of nature in the air—not the exhaust of tourist buses filing in.

Our guide for the two-hour journey was a Tico named Julio. Jumping back and forth between English and Spanish, Julio enjoyed playing ignorant to his guiding background whenever novice paddlers were looking for some sort of reassurance.

"Is this anyone's first time?" he asked with a couple raising their hands.

"Good. Mine, too. Don't worry, we'll figure it out together," he deadpanned.

Phil, our Outward Bound leader whose slender and athletic frame hinted that he partakes in a little bit of everything in the outdoors, set up Julio by noting his experience and generally reassuring everyone that they know what they're doing. Once on the river, it was indeed clear that Julio was hardly new to the rodeo.

Paddling along the Sarapiquí was a mixture of exercise and getting to know one another in between the rapids. Our travel writing colleagues were in the raft behind us, led by our aforementioned man of the outdoors. In our raft of five we had myself, Melanie, Lindsay, an Outward Bound intern, and of course Julio guiding from the back with his paddle serving as the rudder. Julio, dropping his Costello portion of the comedy act, shared that he splits his time between Costa Rica and guiding in Colorado depending on the season. By his account, tourism is doing good things for a region that otherwise wouldn't see many visitors.

The rapids were smooth—nothing more worrisome than a Class II—and Julio was able to turn the experience into something of a carnival ride, knowing exactly how to hit the rapids to get our raft to turn just so. He'd shout "adelante!" to get us to paddle forward quickly. "Alto," like the stop signs, meant "stop."

Julio mostly reserved our paddling for the rapids themselves, allowing us to rest in between as we allowed the steady current to lazily move us along. When we did hit the rapids, it was like an aquatic trampoline. Others—definitely not me—squealed in delight every time we launched into the air and landed with a Sea World-esque splash (sans animal torture) that soaked everyone on board. We all took turns sitting in the front for the best vantage point. Also, coincidentally, the best spot to both get splashed and to get launched from the craft. (No paddlers were launched or drowned in the making of this chapter.)

We did not, however, take turns guiding the raft. Only I got the *privilege* after Julio and my so-called shipmates heckled me enough to give it a try.

"You're the writer!" they said. "You have to do it."

This was a questionable idea, throwing me at the helm with no prior training, expertise or even much time to mentally prepare. I rarely remembered to yell "alto" to give my crew a break nor did I ever get a firm grasp on the steering technique. Of course Julio was ready on standby to make last second adjustments and to shout "alto" on my behalf. Nobody drowned on my watch, so I'd call it a win, but I was happy to make Julio captain again.

Prior to setting off, Phil warned us that Outward Bound likes to see any number of obstacles that might appear during an adventure such as this as a metaphor. The situation itself was about a group of people working together to overcome obstacles presented by the Sarapiquí. Such metaphors typically strike me as overtly corny, but we admittedly weren't the typical Outward Bound audience.

Our metaphor moment with Outward Bound came after pulling our raft over for a bit of cliff jumping. We all plummeted into the river one by one without much hesitation. But then it was suggested that we hike back up to the cliff and all jump at the same time. This wasn't as much a metaphor moment as it was an opportunity for an awesome photo.

Melanie, however, was understandably nervous about jumping all at once whilst holding hands. Even I saw the potential for disaster. There was also the giant boulder jutting out from the side of the cliff down below that I had failed to notice during my first jump. Melanie was suddenly paralyzed with fear, probably because the boulder below very well could literally paralyze someone. Her eyes widened and her heart started on a drum solo as she contemplated backing out.

"I don't know about this," she said with a slight quiver in her voice. She grabbed my arm, presumably looking for some kind of husband-comfort.

"You can do it!" I reassured her, followed quickly by "But you don't have to if you don't want to." I was trying to walk the fine line between having confidence in my wife and not forcing her to do something that made her uncomfortable.

"I don't think so," she said peeking over the edge, her nerves visibly taking over.

"You've already done it before," I reminded her. "Remember when we did that Warrior Dash and you climbed the top of an obstacle, got scared and wanted to come back down?"

"Yeah..." She knew where I was going with the story.

"And the distance down on the other side was the same as the side you just climbed? So you did it and it was fine!"

"Yeah, but..." I left her unconvinced.

"Ready?" somebody shouted.

"Not yet! Need a second," I hollered back, trying to buy time. Phil came over.

"What's the problem?" he asked.

"She's just not so sure about the jump this time with the boulder there," I explained.

This gave Phil an opportunity to jump into his wheelhouse, waxing metaphorical poetry about the challenge before her and

how she can use this opportunity to overcome, succeed, triumph
—yada, yada—all that jazz. I wish I paid closer attention to his
speech, because apparently it worked. We were off the ledge a
moment later and into the river as one group linked together
hand-in-hand. (Except me. I only held onto Melanie's hand,
because there was a freakin' boulder underneath and I wasn't
about to get paralyzed or loose Melanie for a goddamn photo
op!)

After hoisting ourselves back into our respective rafts, we
finished our paddle by admiring the sights and sounds of the
dense forest surrounding us. I started to wish that I had it in me
to care more about birds. That's not to say I don't appreciate
their existence and what they do for the world, but I just have a
difficult time getting excited for something fluttering off in the
distance that I can barely see.

Birder 1: Look! See that blue body and red stripes?
Birder 2: No, that was a red body with thick blue stripes.
Birder 3: I think it was a rare Avian-American pájaro!
Me: Maybe it's just a bird.

I was, however, excited to hear and actually see for the first
time a pack of howler monkeys. Considering their position high
above in the trees, they still registered as nothing more than
rustling blurs to my eyes, but I was nonetheless excited to see
how a modest sized frame could make such a horrific sound.

We finished at a local restaurant perched alongside the river.
Unfortunately I couldn't for the life of me remember what it was
that I put into my body. This was likely due to a combination of
reaching a level of hunger where I didn't much care about what
was going in, and my excitement to recount the day with
Melanie. We paddled, we jumped, we landed, and we were on
our way home. There's probably a metaphor in there
somewhere, I thought, but I was too tired to grasp at straws.

Drugs and Reagan in Guanacaste

If Manuel Antonio is the king of Costa Rican tourism, Guanacaste is next in the line of succession. Millions travel here for the Pacific canton's prized coastline—more than 400 miles worth. White sand beaches, crystal clear blue waters, gaudy Gringo towns, sleepy beach villages and name brand resorts all have a place under the punishing Guanacasteco sun.

As we all know at this point, beaches aren't really my thing. In all honesty, I was more excited to have an excuse to read about the history of the region and see it all for myself. The beach was an afterthought, something I felt obligated to see because I was living in Costa Rica and everyone says "you gotta see the beach in Guanacaste."

But before the beach tourism, open-air restaurants, hotels and early morning clubs, there were Chorotega Native Americans and political intrigue involving the infamous Iran-Contra scandal. That's right, folks, not even this dry, arid corner of Costa Rica could escape the talons of Uncle Sam.

When reading the history of Guanacaste, I found it hard to believe that a glitzy tourist town like Tamarindo is the canton's most popular destination. Chorotega Native Americans lived in this territory before the Spanish conquest, though closer to the eastern shore of the Nicoya Gulf. The mid-nineteenth century saw cattle farms and the baptizing of the province as

Guanacaste, named for its famous sprawling tree with a connection to the indigenous Nahuatl language.

Some of the land that constitutes the present-day province (then called Partido de Nicoya) was originally allied with Nicaragua following the Spanish exit, but the territory's leaders accepted annexation to Costa Rica on June 25, 1824. Guanacaste followed suit, asking for the Costa Rican Federal Congress to ratify their annexation in early 1835 and confirmed their decision in 1838.

Nicaragua lamented the loss of Guanacaste, which had strong economic ties to Rivas and the Nicaraguan economy, but ongoing civil war between Granada and León threatened commercial interests and made sticking with Nicaragua less appealing. I mean, would you want to stay in the same apartment building if your neighbors were constantly shooting at each other?

Perhaps this all foreshadowed today's ongoing political boundary disputes between the squabbling national neighbors. In fact, Nicaragua's Daniel Ortega has even said he wouldn't rule out seeking an International Court ruling to get Guanacaste back (spoiler alert: That will never happen, Danny Boy).

The true twisting of the knife came when the U.S. used Guanacaste's Santa Elena peninsula as a stopping ground to arm Southern Front guerrillas in the fight against the Sandinistas during the Contra War chapter of the Nicaraguan Revolution. John McPhaul's two-part account of the recent revelations for *The Tico Times* tells the tale of how Santa Elena was tied to the notorious Iran-Contra affair that embarrassed the Reagan White House.

In short, a former CIA contract pilot by the name of Robert "Tosh" Plumlee claimed that drug smugglers had for years used a secret airstrip in Potrero Grande. Infamous U.S. Lieutenant Colonel Oliver North later got wind of the area by way of North

Carolinian Joe Hamilton, who represented the Santa Elena Development Corporation. After taking out $5 million mortgage on the property, Costa Rican President Luis Alberto Monge was approached about constructing an airbase at Portero Grande in the event of a Sandinista invasion. Monge later admitted he thought these clandestine men were U.S. officials, so he agreed. Equally shady deals and a phantom company followed, leading to the extension of the airstrip in 1984 to accommodate C-130 transport aircraft.

Plumlee began flying to the concealed airstrip in 1983 and trafficked upwards of 30,000 kilograms of cocaine from Colombia. (He used a smaller C-123 transport plane, like the one on display at El Avión in Manuel Antonio.) Costa Rican President Óscar Arias assumed office in May 1986 and ordered the U.S. ambassador to shutdown the site. Apparently the Americans didn't move fast enough, because Costa Rican officials took it upon themselves a few months later and seized the airstrip. Arias then expropriated Portero Grande for the surrounding Santa Rosa National Park, paying about $13 million for the land, but only after a lengthy legal battle between the airstrip owners and direct intervention from U.S. President George H. W. Bush.

Oh, beautiful, for spacious skies...

These days, Guanacasteco politicians quibble more with their own government in San José; some even discuss separation from Costa Rica due to what they claim is unfair treatment from the capital, pointing to the tourism dollars the province brings to the nation with little return (they allege). It appears to be an empty threat, but it did bring the issue to the forefront. Politics aside, all 6,000-some square miles of mostly dusty land and its celebrated coastline continue to remain with Costa Rica. And despite all appearances to the contrary, Tamarindo, too, is Costa Rican territory.

Tamagringo, Booze Snorkeling, and Tempting Darwin

Bland modern stylings, restaurants with a global touch and cookie cutter plazas covered the Guanacasteco beach town. This did not feel like Costa Rica in the least, but that in and of itself was not necessarily good or bad. It was just different—an island of Gringos and the occasional Costa Rican family enjoying the wide expanses of white sand and ubiquitous sun. (Locals and Gringo transplants alike call it, "Tamagringo.") The only reminder that this was, indeed, Costa Rica was the occasional flag and casado or arroz con pollo on the menu—a need we were able to satisfy at Gallo Fino where they humorously boasted a TripAdvisor review from susanallen531 of Chesterfield, Virginia. Suffice it to say that Susan was spot on.

Tamarindo made me irrationally frustrated. I awoke early and took care of some work before eating a quick breakfast and heading off to the beach with Melanie. We went for a long walk north along the sand toward a nearby national park whose sole purpose was to protect incoming turtles.

I struggled to pinpoint my frustration. Was I preoccupied with work and pending projects? Was I feeling guilt for not being entirely enthralled with beaches like normal people are? This felt different than my usual neutrality, or at worst, disinterest in beaches.

You're seeing so much more than what most get to in a lifetime. Be happy, damnit! I told myself in an obscenity-laden mantra.

Perhaps my issue is that I can barely tell the difference between the beaches of Tamarindo, Santa Teresa, Puerto Viejo, El Tunco or the others I've been fortunate enough to see in my life. The surrounding view may be different, which I can appreciate over a long walk, but the ingredients of the beach itself are always the same. There's sand, water and various amounts of rock. Sure, the towns are different and I can get on board with a good beach town, like El Tunco. But the beach itself, plopping myself onto a towel and melting underneath the sparkling sun for hours on end like a baking slug... Meh. I'd rather get lost in whatever greenery is nearby. Otherwise, I'll be at the bar.

Besides, there's only so much one can do in a town like Tamarindo beyond the beach. If you are of age, you will gladly partake in the obnoxiously loud beats of clubs named after ocean animals. Otherwise you're on a retirement vacation, paying the extra bucks to stay someplace a bit fancier and away from the noise.

Guanacaste, however, is a massive swath of land. And in its vastness, there was plenty to see and do all within a short vehicular ramble away.

We took a cab just twenty-five minutes or so north to the rustic beach town of Brasilito, known for having the adjacent beaches of Playa Brasilito, covered in dark sand, and the more popular Playa Conchal. Our hosts were Paul and his Venezuelan wife, Matilda, at Hotel Conchal, a comfortable walk away from the beach even if the sun was downright oppressive. This was a twelve-room boutique style hotel with a pool greeting us at the entrance. Bright red paint decorated the hotel over stucco walls.

Matilda's English was vastly superior to our Spanish as we discussed our plans for the area. Paul joined us, dressed in a beach-y tank top, shorts and sandals. For some reason I was initially surprised to hear a British accent coming out of his six foot six frame. American, German, Spanish, and various Latino accents were commonplace in Costa Rica, but I couldn't recall ever hearing a British accent outside of UPEACE.

After exchanging pleasantries and getting a better look, it was clear he was in the right place in the world with his light stubble for a beard, single earring, and a voice that blended the best of a soothing radio host and a beach bum. They were both easily some of the more accommodating hosts we had met in Costa Rica. Within mere minutes of our arrival, Paul and Matilda (who coincidentally met while studying abroad in Ohio) had our next days planned.

First we had about thirty minutes to get ready for catamaran sailing. All we knew was that a sunset was involved. We soon discovered that booze and snorkeling was also involved over a few hours.

En route our hosts at Lazy Lizard treated us to a selection of alcoholic beverages. Had I known we were in for snorkeling, I might have passed on the second (or third?) glass of rum. Thankfully for atrocious swimmers such as myself, we were each given our own little noodle to help us float about like children in a never-ending swimming pool.

So there we were, floating around with our heads underwater —our group of about twenty assorted strangers, mostly Americans. Highlights included seeing a porcupine fish (the kind that blows up and once almost killed Homer Simpson) and an eel. Eventually we waded back into the catamaran, warmed ourselves under the setting sun, and filled ourselves with sandwiches, refried beans, fruit, and of course, more booze.

This was not how I would typically spend my time away from home, much less in a foreign country. At this point, though, we were about seven months into our year in Costa Rica. One little touristy excursion wouldn't kill us, so we embraced Paul and Matilda's plans for us—fake tattoos of the company on our shoulders and all. Plus we got to hear all afternoon about just how gosh darn incredible everyone thought we were for moving abroad.

"That's terrific! Wow, good for you. This is the time to do it. You know, while you're young. Before you have kids."

It amuses me how strangers in my culture find it perfectly acceptable to presume having kids is a no-brainer. This "before you have kids" business comes up most every time Melanie and I have this conversation. It doesn't exactly make having kids sound appealing. What happens after kids? We can't travel or live overseas? That doesn't sound fun. Maybe we'll get a dog instead. (We got a dog a year later.)

A jazz tune right out of the '30s woke us up the next morning. It was the soundtrack at the restaurant upstairs where breakfast and coffee awaited. Sufficiently satiated, we made our way to Playa Brasilito, which was as empty as advertised. This was nothing against the beach. Conchal is just better. Scottie Pippen was great, but most people are going to want to talk to Jordan when they're in the same room. Anywhere else in the world, Brasilito would do just fine (as I'm sure Scottie Pippen does).

The beaches are, indeed, quite different, separated only by a large rock formation. As soon as we walked onto Conchal, we could see where the name came from. Concha means "shell," and there were millions of them crushed to makeup the sand—an immediate and stark contrast to black Brasilito. There were more people as well, in that there were any at all. But shuffle a kilometer or so down the shore, and we were completely isolated. I was starting to see how people get pulled into this "doing nothing" concept on the beach.

When the evening hours came, the second level of Hotel Conchal turned into Papaya Restaurant with relaxing, dim lighting that meshed perfectly with the Middle Eastern soundtrack. The music only paused for the arrival of The Screaming Vagabonds, a three-man mariachi band who roam the streets of Brasilito, entertaining restaurant crowds for fun (and a tip).

Melanie found her chicken curry thai dish to be one of her best meals in Costa Rica. And with the clear night sky, we were able to stargaze throughout our meal, most notably toward Uranus, which led to no shortage of immature comments that fifth graders would've found hilarious. I admit I felt a bit ashamed in retrospect for reverting to such childlike tendencies. That is until I heard renowned astrophysicist and current cool scientist Neil DeGrasse Tyson himself on a podcast giggling over the more inappropriate pronunciation of the planet.

I'm in good company.

Early the next morning we were off to Palo Verde for some river boating with Jacamar. Two Ticos picked us up and, despite knowing we could speak Spanish, they didn't hold back their comments of other passersby. One with Imperial swim shorts met their scorn.

"Ugly, right?"

Keylor was fine with the plethora of Pura Vida material out there, because it's a "slogan of the country." But Imperial? A beer manufacturer? This escaped him.

"This isn't a country of drunks, right?" I offered.

"Right!"

Our host continued searching for additional guests.

"No la veo. No la veo a yanqui." *I don't see her. I don't see a Yankee.*

"Rubio, delgada." Blonde, thin.

And so it continued until our fellow travelers joined and we switched to English.

The road to Palo Verde was less of a road and more of a generously carved dirt path. This did not mesh well with Melanie, who was battling carsickness and various breakfast beverages bouncing around in her stomach.

We arrived to a small entry point of the Río Tempisque where a green boat (something of a large johnboat that looked customized to carry thirty passengers with a roof offering shade) was waiting to take us on our tour. The tour itself entailed a slow, motorized excursion along the river in hopes of catching some wildlife. Indeed, seeing wildlife was hardly an issue. Scarlet macaws, crocodiles, bats, white-faced monkeys, and no shortage of other birds and lizards could be easily found going through their daily routine along the river.

"See that?" said Keylor, pointing up to some tall grass above our boat. After some squinting, I saw the crocodile sitting as still as a rock. Was it asleep or waiting to strike? It was impossible for an amateur to tell.

"Want to take a picture of it? You can get closer if you climb on the roof of the boat."

The suggestion surprised me. Was it safe? I wondered. Yet somehow not wanting to look like a coward outranked rational decision-making.

"Sure, why not?" I responded quickly in a half-hearted attempt to seem cool and fearless.

At the same time, I couldn't help but think that crawling on top of a river boat and leaning in toward a crocodile is exactly how I'd get myself into the Darwin Awards, removing my unique brand of stupidity from the human gene pool by hilarious means of fatality. (I later read that males make up about eighty-eight percent of Darwin Awards entries, which makes you wonder why we're still allowed to lead countries and control arsenals of weapons.) I could see my obituary as I leaned forward camera-first, capturing the camouflaged beast with my lens.

Obituary: Joe, in facing the world's strongest animal bite, succumbed to 3,700 pounds per square inch of pointy pressure.

Thankfully the croc was either sleeping or not interested in making a lunge for me, and I happily scurried off the roof as we moved onto less threatening creatures.

Ahead, Keylor pointed out a few "Jesus lizards." The little guys were named for their ability to scamper across water, not because they've amassed a following of other lizards who inevitably thank them at lizard award shows and sporting events, as I imagined.

Following our tour, we drove through rural Guanacasteco towns where streets resembled recreational running paths and people hooked up their horses when running to the store. Our final stop of the day came at Rancho Los Coyotes, an outdoor restaurant with smoked, traditional Guanacasteco cooking. Chicken drumsticks, beans, rice, tortillas, squash, and the obligatory side salad—an ideal way to end a humid day baking in the Guanacasteco sun.

Sickness had gotten the best of Melanie at this point. Keylor joked more than I would have liked about the possibility of her being pregnant as he hurried us back to the hotel.

By the following morning, Melanie felt significantly better. We saw Keylor return to the hotel from our breakfast table and I ran down to thank him for the prior day's tour.

"How's she feeling?" he asked. "Am I going to be an uncle?"

buena nota (*bwe*·na *no*·ta)
adjective

1. Literally "good grade."
2. Used to compliment someone for being a nice or cool person; essentially giving them a "good grade."

Example: "That Gringo with the blonde hair, blue eyes, about five feet nine inches, 167 pounds, adventurous spirit, worldly knowledge, charming personality, talents that cannot compare, bravery of a jungle cat, joyous and relaxed disposition of a sloth… He's buena nota."

Cerveza Artesanal

I want to take a moment to talk about the beer, because, well, I very much enjoy beer. Every country has its national preferences judged so purely by its availability and affordability. In the States, we have Budweiser, Coors and Miller. In Costa Rica, it's mainly Imperial and Pilsen. Guatemala has Gallo, Panama Balboa, Nicaragua Toña and El Salvador Pilsener. They all taste unremarkably the same with the exception of Toña. Something especially funky is going on there.

I love craft beer, especially when it hits that trifecta of supporting local businesses and neighborhoods, and, y'know, it tastes good. Some people get excited about fancy foods, wines, comics, sports—you name it. For me, I get excited about craft beer and visiting craft breweries. A lot of people can take it to a pretentious level. I try to stay cognizant of that. I try to remember that not everyone can afford to shell out six bucks for one beer, or maybe just don't want to. I don't blame them. Sometimes in the States, I'd kill to put a dollar on the bar and get an Imperial in return. You love what you miss.

I knew in going to Costa Rica that my fix of craft beer would suffer, and I came to terms with that early on. Yet there is something of a fledgling craft beer scene booming in Costa Rica.

If I haven't already said this (I have), Ciudad Colón is tiny. Keylor Navas could probably boot a soccer ball across town.

(Yes, pandering to the Tico readers with that reference.) There's not much of a restaurant scene, but there are a number of excellent options. The preferred UPEACE hangout came to be Maya's, a German-Latino concoction. Lest the concept sound too sophisticated, the Latino part was mostly nachos with some of the tastiest salsa de carne I ever had. I can't recall how many times I burnt my mouth just to have the first bite over a shared plate of nachos, but I do know it was worth it every time.

We spent many nights at Maya's. It was the only place in town where we could have a beer and just chat. They also had a selection of craft beers from the Costa Rica Craft Brewing Company, Treintaycinco and Domingo 7, all of which had something that could hold up to my favorites back home. I was later warned, however, that Domingo 7 is a mere infiltration into the craft beer market by Imperial. Esteban's cousin, also the mayor of Colón's Mora canton, revealed one night over dinner at Maya's why he won't drink Domingo 7.

"They're owned by Imperial, but sell this stuff just to take away from the little guys," he said bitterly. "They also own Magic Hat, which is why the logos for the beers look the same."

He was right. There certainly was a resemblance, though I was too busy enjoying my Latino Burger with jalapeños and cuts of chorizo sausage on top to make too much of a stink.

Costa Rica Craft Brewing, however, is the real deal, and it was incredible luck that they were in the process of relocating from Cartago to just outside Ciudad Colón in Brasil de Mora. Typical bureaucracy cruelly pushed their grand opening back month after month, but they were kind enough to give us a tour of the facility in time for my brother Dave and sister-in-law Holly's visit. Andrea, hearing of the tour, happily invited herself along.

Having covered craft beer in the States, the brewery tour was familiar to me. Costa Rica Craft Brewing Company, however, had a particularly sizable facility. Diego, a young employee of the brewery, guided us around the facility, pointing out that the head brewer came from Portland, Oregon looking for warmer weather. The Pacific Northwest origins helped explain the quality of the beer. I enjoyed watching him, lanky, bald with thick glasses wearing a tee shirt and heavy-duty boots, barking orders in Spanish.

Diego, speaking in flawless English, was also happy to share that the name of every beer holds a connection to Costa Rica. For Diego, it was important not only to sell good beer, but to link the beer with Costa Rica through their branding. One example is the Segua Red Ale, which alludes to the legend of an attractive woman who lured married men away from the straight and narrow path. Should they succumb to her seduction, her face would transform into the head of a horse.

For my money, I happily endorse the Libertas Golden Ale. Its light body with a little fruity flavor that wasn't overpowering was perfectly refreshing for those Costa Rican evenings when I missed craft beer the most. Imperials always had the habit of disappearing on me. The stuff went down like water, so finding something I could savor was appreciated.

Besides, after over half a year of learning about how much havoc my people have wreaked in Latin America, it was nice to come across a welcomed blending of cultures.

Down to the Osa Peninsula

The return of Melanie's parents was originally planned to be a longer vacation, seeing more of the popular sights of Costa Rica than on their first impromptu weekend visit back in November. That was still the case with their March return, but there was something new to celebrate—Melanie had accepted her dream job (for that stage in her career) back in Cleveland.

Of course the celebration was also bittersweet. My program at UPEACE would not finish for another two months after her scheduled departure in the first week of that coming April. Neither of us wanted to be apart, but we felt profoundly lame complaining considering how otherwise fortunate we have been in our lives.

What pain and cruel sorrow to be separated from my kindred spirit! My apple of love! The weird to my strange!

We insisted we would not be that couple... at least not publicly.

Ultimately, two months would be little in the grand scheme of things, but it was still an unwelcome change in our relationship. No more sipping coffee on our Costa Rican balcony together, planning trips across Central America. Melanie, a city woman at heart, would have to move back to her parents in the suburbs until my return. Obviously, she was grateful for the free lodging, but nobody likes to say they're moving back into their parents' place, regardless of how justifiable circumstances make that decision or how great her parents truly are. (Hola, suegros.)

Thankfully, Melanie's new employer proved flexible in pushing back her start date. The interview process had begun back in December and they set an original start date for mid-March that would have taken her away before her parents visited. The latest they could allow her to start was the second week of April, which kept her in the area for both her parents' visit and for a six-day trip to Panama City we had planned before finding out about the job.

Missing Panama City may have been a deal breaker for Melanie. It had always been a dream of her's to see the Panama Canal firsthand. The story encapsulated everything she's interested in (and, not coincidentally, what ultimately got her the job): politics, geopolitical intrigue, and inarguably exciting history. There was no way Melanie would miss seeing the Panama Canal, the last of her Central American adventures.

But first, there was Costa Rica's Osa Peninsula.

The Osa Peninsula is one of the least-traveled corners of the country. It's probably a good idea in the grand scheme of things that the Osa Peninsula remains fairly untraveled, because it's one of the most biologically diverse places in the world; half of Costa Rica's living species call it home. This is on top of the fact that Costa Rica itself is one of the most biologically active countries in the world. Some 500,000 species live over the country's 51,000 square kilometers. Estimates say four percent of the world's living species are in Costa Rica, some of which are endemic to the country.

Think about that for a moment. *Five hundred thousand*. It's impossible for a novice on the topic, such as myself, to truly comprehend such a large number in terms of living species.

I should clarify that not all of Costa Rica's species are all that exciting. Most think of the various monkeys, whales, and reptilian predators when hearing the word "species," but it's a term that accounts for just about everything—700 species of trees, more than 365 species of birds (you'll find your endemic crowd here), 117 reptiles, and here's where some may need a wastebasket—over 10,000 species of insects.

Not all that sexy, I grant you, but biodiversity accounts for all living things from microorganisms to their ecosystems. In this crazy circle of life, the less exciting trees and nightmarish insects make the more attractive elements of life possible. In other words, you don't get that cute picture of the monkey without everything else coming together just right. And that's why people have been, in increasingly greater numbers, finding their way to the southwestern peninsula several hours drive or bus from San José.

Melanie and I, however, found our way to Osa using a combination of bus and car. Helen and Patrick landed in San José, rented a car, and went directly to Manuel Antonio. We offered to catch up, because we didn't necessarily feel like we needed another overnight at Manuel Antonio.

Since we just visited two months prior, the return to Manuel Antonio was my first time traveling in years where I didn't feel the incessant need to constantly click away on my camera and turn the trip into work.

Tourist numbers had clearly increased since our first visit. The beaches were more crowded and traffic was steady, though it was hardly the likes of an MTV spring break vacation, where sons and daughters go to disappoint their parents.

We spotted Patrick on the beach enjoying the shade of an umbrella and an ice cold beer. They were happy, so we were happy. It was also the rare instance in which Melanie and I went running into the ocean waters together. Typically we would take turns, not wanting to leave my camera behind unguarded. This time we could frolic like a normal couple.

With larger crowds, more entrepreneurial Ticos were out with everything from cheap knickknacks to mindlessly entertain the four and under crowd to menus for nearby restaurants to feed hungry adults. One of the latter roped us in, delivering various lunch items to the beach for us to fill up before the drive down to Dominical where Patrick and Helen were staying.

Before making it to the hotel, we made a stop for a short walk around Dominical. Melanie and I hadn't made it down there before, and based on its reputation as a stoner-surfer party town, we knew it wasn't anyplace we'd make a significant effort to see on its own trip. Seeing it on the way to something else made sense.

Patrick and Helen had already visited the night before for dinner. Granted neither of Melanie's parents are the typical Dominical clientele, but its reputation seemed to match their initial impression.

"Not exactly the high rent district," Patrick joked.

Like Santa Teresa, Dominical was once upon a time a small fishing village before turning into a surfer mecca. The drive down is lined with African oil palm plantations that look spectacularly out of place, but it does at least change the scenery.

Dominical is tiny and easy to miss off the highway if you're not looking for it. We came in with Patrick following a mixture of GPS commands and recent memory. Again, like Santa Teresa, roads are more of a mixture of concrete and dirt here. A collection of restaurants made of wood and tin lined the road heading toward the beach where Patrick parked. Untouched trees separated civilization from the Pacific Ocean; a number of tents were planted within the woods on the edge of the sand. Some went completely minimalist, opting to camp by hammock.

It was still the afternoon, so things were rather quiet. Those among the camping crowd we did see looked exactly as you'd expect. Men and women sported equally thin frames with the kind of unkempt hair one gets after days of saltwater, sand and sun. I imagined flashing a peace symbol would be all that was required for acceptance into the crowd. They're the kind most across the political spectrum enjoy mocking—what with their free-spirited nature and complete disregard for how one is supposed to live their life. That is: graduate college, get a job, get married, vomit offspring, get a house and die. They appear to find enjoyment in experiences, not accumulated wealth and buying things to go with their things.

For as much as I feel right at home teasing the likes of this crowd, I can likely relate with them far better than I can with those who do live a "normal life." But dammit, knock it off with the drum circles!

Playa Dominical felt like more of the same in terms of Costa Rican beaches. It was flat, though notably rockier than others. Nearby, a local was selling handcrafted jewelry. Melanie purchased a bracelet, and I got to impress someone with my Gringo Spanish. Admittedly, the bar probably isn't that high in a Gringo-populated surfer town.

Ultimately, Dominical served its purpose as a way to break up the drive and allow us to stretch our legs before getting to the hotel.

Melanie and I travel a bit differently than her parents. They're okay with driving, whereas we're unlikely to visit someplace that requires us renting a car. They're also less afraid of certain price tags. That's not to say we strictly prefer cheaper lodging. We just haven't been working long enough to afford such luxuries without my heart beating out of my chest when the bill comes.

Our first hotel, for instance, a short drive outside of Dominical, practically required a vehicle to enter. There was no signage explicitly forbidding pedestrians, of course, but the driveway—possibly a quarter-mile long—was without exaggeration at least a forty-five degree grade. Driving instructions noted that a four by four vehicle would be necessary to make it up to the hotel. As we neared the top, we couldn't see over the final hill. That's how dramatic the angle was.

Once we crawled over the final hump, requiring a quick slam of the breaks and changing back to a lower gear, the hotel was right in front of us. The term "hotel" might be misleading. By appearances, it was just another property. Clearly the inhabitants had some money behind their investment, but it wasn't like there was a flickering "Vacancy" sign out front.

The room Patrick and Helen had rented out would suffice for most as an apartment. There was a bedroom, kitchen, living room, and outdoor patio with plenty of seating and dining space overlooking the ocean and jungle. Melanie and I were to stay on a pullout bed that came out of the wall into the living room. Even with that, there was still plenty of space.

The property made good use of the topography. It was a steep decline from the entrance down to our room, and even further to the pool; additional grounds with overlooks and a relaxing hammock awaited. In some respects, it felt like M.C. Escher's famous Relativity print with the staircases that defy gravity, except, y'know, in Costa Rica.

The indoor bar, where our host Gary served us up welcoming cocktails, had a rustic jungle theme. The Michigan native shared stories of the hells of constructing the property. Storms can be brutal off the coast and add unexpected costs and repairs to the budget. He also shared that he doesn't list or actively publicize the hotel. Referrals are his only business by design.

That night we followed his recommendation for dinner. It was a long drive down a dark road that required close attention to directions. It was obvious when we found it. There wasn't much else around, so it naturally stuck out, but left us wondering why the restaurateurs selected this location.

Sitting outside on the front patio, enjoying the cozy decor and dim lighting that made for a relaxing atmosphere, our French hostess came by on several occasions to check in on us, though really my only question was, "why French?" I badly wanted to ask who she was, why they were there, and why this location, but we had all but melted into individual puddles by the time our plates were empty thanks to coastal Costa Rica's infamous and punishing humidity. While I usually prefer the eco-friendly option, I was happy to slide into the rental, bask in the refreshing glow of air conditioning and drift off over the drive back to the hotel.

Content with spending most of our day relaxing, we made just one quick trip out and over to Marino Ballena National Park before heading to the Osa Peninsula. Sitting about ten miles south of Dominical, Ballena gets its name from the sandbar stretching out to the Pacific Ocean that looks exactly like a whale's tail from the sky (*ballena* means whale). It's a popular destination for whale tours, but on this day it was just a day at the beach.

Onward to the Osa Peninsula, Helen and Patrick had reserved a few days at Bosque del Cabo Rainforest Lodge on the southern tip of the peninsula. A four by four vehicle was, again, a necessity to finish the drive over rocky terrain, a rickety bridge and a couple of shallow creeks en route to the lodge after any semblance of a modern road disappeared past Puerto Jimenez.

As remote as we were, it was immediately crystal clear upon our arrival to Bosque del Cabo that we wouldn't exactly be roughing it. Though there was no air conditioning, keeping in line with the eco mission, this was an all inclusive resort that came with all the amenities and fine dining one would expect in such a place.

Usually as a rule, Melanie and I never travel to resorts for a few reasons. First, resorts are often exclusively accessible to motorists. The last thing we want to do for a relaxing vacation is get into a multi-thousand pound climate controlled weapon and navigate roads we've never seen, least of all in a foreign country. Second, there's the concern, especially in foreign countries, that the resort is exploiting or stealing land once made public to local communities for the exclusive use of tourists. Neither sit well with me. Besides, if you want a private slice of beach to drink a bunch of silly island drinks on, seriously, just go to Florida.

Bosque del Cabo, however, appeared to be a different kind of resort. There was a 765-plus acre forest reserve that promised to keep me plenty occupied, coupled with a roster of activities guests could sign up for every morning. The undisputedly gorgeous overlook of the Pacific Ocean from our room's patio never got old. Dinners were served in a communal setting under a solar-powered roof. Not too shabby, to say the least, but I personally could've done without meeting someone new at almost every dinner.

Stranger: Hey, there! I'm Blah-Blah and this is my wife, Blah-Blah. What do you do? How do you like it here?

Me: Hi. Joe. Stuff. It's nice. And since we're never going to see each other again and we've already forgotten each other's name, I'm going to pretend you're not here and just enjoy my family, if it's all the same to you. Cheers!

Point is, I like to meet people under my own terms. Familial speed dating isn't my thing.

Of all things, I started with an early morning birding tour. Admittedly it was merely an excuse to get outside with the sunrise. The trails of the forest reserve were by far what made the trip worthwhile. All told, I covered twelve miles hiking the trails. Some were easy, meandering treks in the woods. Others were long with steep climbs that had me descend to the shoreline below, admire the crashing waves that would kill any soul foolish enough to try a swim, and back up to retrace my steps.

Despite the busy schedule Bosque del Cabo could offer, I was adamant about making a return to Puerto Jimenez for kayaking. Truth be told, I had it set in my head to visit Osa's Corcovado National Park for the very simple reason that it was Ugalde's most cherished and we were right-freaking-there. Unfortunately the resort was at least a thirty-minute drive to Puerto Jimenez and the park even further on top of that. Nobody wanted to spend time in a car while in the pristine jungle and rainforest of the Osa Peninsula. Not that I of all people needed to be convinced against car travel, but it felt weird not to see Corcovado, like looking the other way when passing by Egypt's pyramids.

My consolation was to at least go kayaking. That was something we definitely couldn't do at the lodge, and I had read rave reviews of kayaking in Golfo Dulce, the body of water separating Osa from Puntarenas on the mainland. With Corcovado no longer a possibility, I decided to remind myself that a few UPEACE friends had recently told me that Corcovado was a bit of a let down and instead focused on the kayaking.

After discussing our options at dinner, I appeared to get everyone on board with kayaking. Melanie and I decided we would make her parents cash in the "Costa Rican adventure!" coupon we gave them for Christmas. With everyone in agreement, we left the dinner table and started to make our way to our respective rooms when we bumped into the chef. She had a manic smile, probably in her forties if not early fifties, and was clearly an eccentric. This lady had no problem sharing her opinions.

"So what do you guys have planned for tomorrow?"

"We're probably going kayaking in Golfo Dulce," Helen responded.

"Really? No horseback riding?" Helen had a bad experience horseback riding years ago, so I knew I didn't need to argue my way out of that one.

"No, I think we're going to start with the kayaking."

"You know, it's really not that exciting," she continued. "Besides, I just always thought it silly to leave the resort." My heart began to flutter in rage. Gee, wonder why the resort employee thinks it's silly to leave the resort.

Helen and Patrick appeared to be rethinking. I was fuming at the chef.

"I mean, I'm sure you'll have fun if you go. But you're already at the resort!" The woman just would not shut up. I tried telepathy.

Shut it! Quiet! Silencio!

Nothing worked. Instead, we endured her insistence that we stay at the resort until she finally let us go to bed. Luckily, it appeared both Patrick and Helen were also put off by the chef's overt opinions and agreed to give kayaking a shot. I must admit that I was a bit nervous, though. I stood to take all the blame should kayaking prove to be a bust.

Thankfully, kayaking the mangroves of Golfo Dulce proved to be a highlight in my rolodex of Costa Rican experiences. It was both relaxing and a bit of exercise, meandering down mangroves overflowing with wildlife (mostly birds) and dense rainforest. Plus there was the constant entertainment of listening to Melanie and Helen continuously crash into each other while navigating narrow passageways.

To cap our adventure streak, Melanie and I opted to sign up for a waterfall rappelling tour, something neither of us had ever done. So why not now?

I could sense that Costa Rica had made me bolder. Throwing on a harness and jumping off a waterfall would not typically be high on my list a year ago. After seven months of living in Costa

Rica, jumping off a waterfall absolutely made sense. Besides, I couldn't imagine that a luxurious resort would offer waterfall rappelling if they had a streak of losing customers in the fall. It had to be perfectly safe. I was sure of it.

When the moment of truth came, after a quarter-mile hike through a stream, I was surprised to discover I had no fear. That could also be because one of the gentlemen in our group appeared plenty afraid for all of us. There was an increasing tremble in his voice and reassuring whispers from his boyfriend. When I joked that he should go first, he nervously laughed and declined as he took a couple steps back. Melanie, still not a huge fan of leaping off cliffs, was happy to wait as well.

Since nobody else was eager, I opted to go first. Ever since my college trip to India, where we regularly traveled in shuttles up and down mountains out of a Looney Tunes cartoon along roads wide enough for just one vehicle but with two-way traffic and no guard rail, I've generally adhered to a philosophy that everything's going to be just fine. I won't actively try to get myself in situations that'll get me killed, but I'm not going to get in a panic at every opportunity. The Ticos leading our group were shuttling customers several times a day to go waterfall rappelling. They knew what they were doing. Ticos in tourism are by all important measures experts in making sure idiot Gringos don't off themselves on their watch. This idiot Gringo had nothing to fear.

Without hesitation, I turned my back toward the waterfall to get ready for my first leap. The guide offered quick instruction on how to safely (and with control) rappel down the waterfall using the ropes attached to my harness. With his thumbs up, I made my first bound off the cliff toward a twenty-foot drop where another guide waited. The way the cliffs worked out, I was able to get something of a practice round before making the largest and final descent down a 200-foot-plus drop.

I reached the break after just a few bounds off the waterfall. Besides some uncomfortable tightening in the groin (which we were warned about), all was well and I was eager to continue. The second leap was, of course, much more enjoyable. It was easy to slip into my cinematic imagination once I could no longer see the guide as I dipped deeper into the waterfall and the pounding water made it uncomfortable (if not impossible) to look up for an extended period of time.

After getting about halfway, the guide on the ground started shouting instructions.

"Right! Go right! Aim for that rock. Now a little left!" and so on until my feet hit solid ground.

It was a great thrill, but I wish it were longer. All of my Costa Rican adventures (if I can even call them that) had been short and sweet. Waterfall rappelling left me longing for a true jungle adventure, at least a week long, that mixes long hikes with kayaking and waterfall rappelling. What I just did was a cruel tease. Not counting the short hike to the waterfall, it was probably about five minutes of actual activity. I've now spent more time writing about it than it took to rappel down the damn thing.

Melanie followed second and worked her way down the waterfall with relative ease. She appeared to do quite well, if I (in my novice opinion) may say so, and despite my wanting more, it was an excellent cap to the Osa Peninsula.

El Clásico

I had always wanted to go to a proper soccer match full of screaming fans who live and breathe the sport. The closest I had ever come was in Ireland. In 2011, I planned an impromptu trip to the Emerald Isle with a couple of friends. It had been three years since my last overseas excursion in India and I was itching for a different culture. Ireland was the cheapest European gateway from Cleveland and thus won by default.

One of my goals in the trip was to check off seeing a proper soccer match. Ireland is in Europe and they're bonkers for the sport, I assumed.

I scoured the Irish domestic league for matches that would line up with our time in Dublin. Without much trouble, I found the Dublin Rovers playing a home match in late April. I never bothered to research where the Rovers played, but lazy internet Googling showed they were one of the top teams of their league.

On match day, we boarded a modern tram based on Google Maps' instructions, traveling through a whirl of Dublin neighborhoods most tourists probably never see. Our stop, it seemed, was near the end of the line. I was surprised to see the character of the Irish buildings, gained through centuries of wear and tear, suddenly gone. There was the stadium out in the distance, much smaller than I had expected, and a large block of new construction that looked just like new urban development back in the States.

I remained optimistic, however. Fans appeared excited and there were a number on the train marching with us to the stadium. Many wore green scarves, the team's colors, around their necks.

My disappointment grew, however, as we shuffled closer to the stadium and it managed to shrink, not grow. It was no larger than a high school football stadium in Ohio. The massive crowd of supporters drumming away throughout the game and leading chants was a scant gathering of loosely organized fans. This was not the European soccer experience I had expected.

The next day I noticed the newspaper headlines and realized, yes, the Irish do love soccer. But for professional soccer, they turn to England and its Premier League. It seemed obvious in retrospect, but I suppose I thought sensitive Irish-English history would turn Irish soccer fans away from caring about English soccer in favor of their own league out of spite if nothing else. How wrong I was.

I knew, though, that Costa Ricans were not only soccer fanatics, but cared about their own league. If there's anything that compares to European soccer fandom, it's Latino fandom. And considering Costa Rica was fresh off an impressive and historic World Cup run, I had little doubt that I could get the foreign soccer experience I had been looking for in Ireland.

Our opportunity came in an El Clásico match between Alajuelense of Alajuela and Saprissa of northern San José. The two are longtime rivals, thus garnering the distinguish of El Clásico every time they play, though they do play one another quite a bit more than the name suggests. To be fair, it's a small country so they get a small league. That means fewer teams, with championship honors generally rotating between the same three or four teams—two of which are Alajuelense and Saprissa. We were an Alajuelense household based solely on the allegiance of

Esteban and Carolina.

"Liga, Liga, Liga!" Carolina would chant with a pumped fist and smile anytime the topic of Costa Rican soccer came up.

Much like American sports allegiances, rivalries run deep in Costa Rica. The boyfriend of Carolina's daughter proudly supported Saprissa and received a thorough ribbing anytime the topic of Costa Rican soccer arose, which was often. Once over dinner, Carolina shared a video of a prank her daughter's boyfriend played on her mother during a visit. The video showed him quietly hoisting a Saprissa flag over the backyard. After the trap was set, Carolina's family called out to her mother and pointed out the flag.

"What?" the old woman murmured as she turned around. "What is that?" With that, a younger version of Carolina's mother leapt into action as she stormed towards the flag. "Get that out of here!" she shrieked, batting her cane at it like a piñata. The family could be heard off-camera choking on their laughter.

El Clásico is played at Estadio Nacional in La Sabana instead of their respective home stadiums to account for the larger attendance. Melanie and I arrived early to first tour the modest-sized Costa Rican art museum at La Sabana's eastern entrance. We were both surprised at how small the museum was for being the national museum of art, but enjoyed ourselves nonetheless. One painter was present within his own exhibit featuring his take on memorable skylines from Miami to Panama City. He chatted us up, which was fine enough, before uncomfortably insisting on our taking a picture with him.

"Do you want a picture with me?" he asked.

"Oh, no. That's okay," I said in what I thought was a polite decline.

"No, really! It's okay. Come on, I'll ask someone to take our picture."

I couldn't tell if this was some sort of a cultural difference or a marketing ploy to make it look to passersby that people were lining up to get their picture taken with the artist. In any event, we forced a smile, the picture was snapped, and we moved along through the museum without further disturbance.

We still had plenty of time until kickoff, having incorrectly budgeted our time for a larger museum. But we never needed an excuse to kill time at La Sabana, easily our most adored corner of San José. Then we started to yawn and opted to look for a coffee shop along Paseo Colón to ensure we'd make it through the game.

Paseo Colón remained as ugly as it was when we first visited back in August with its wide automobile lanes surrounded by heart-stopping fast food chains, gas stations, and car rentals. Suffice it to say we couldn't find the artisanal coffee shop we had hoped for. There was, however, a McDonald's.

Neither Melanie nor myself could remember the last time we had been through the golden arches of obesity, but I had heard the coffee is actually pretty decent. Even more relevant, I had recently listened to a Rick Steves podcast that made a compelling case for visiting McDonald's when traveling the world to see the cultural differences.

Would there be casado con Big Mac, I wondered?

Disappointingly, the menu was similar to what I imagined in the United States, except in Spanish. I was at least able to make the same observation I had previously made while walking by a Burger King in Lugano, Switzerland, that the customers were all well dressed. This contrasted strongly with my American image of McDonald's where signs are posted to remind customers they need to put on clothes before entering.

The side trip appeared to take us to an appropriate hour for walking to the stadium. I knew this because of the increased pedestrian traffic dressed in Alajuelense red and black and Saprissa *morado vino tinto* and white.

Melanie and I jumped into the march, reminding us of our walks up East Ninth Street in downtown Cleveland from our old apartment to Browns Stadium. There was increased chatter and the occasional vuvuzela—that horrific invention of the 2010 FIFA World Cup in South Africa—as we neared Estadio Nacional in La Sabana.

Inside, I was surprised by the police presence. I knew soccer games could get out of hand, but they appeared dressed to the gills for a full-fledged riot. Every corner we turned, there was another unit dressed in dark black gear with helmets, shields, and batons at the ready. What were they expecting to happen? I wondered if this tied into my theory of Central American overprotectiveness, always prepared for the worse to happen when there wasn't even a hint of trouble, causing undue suspicion and concern in the oblivious foreigner passing by.

Approaching our seats, I was thrilled to see a proper supporters section among the Alajuelense loyal. They jumped, sang, and shouted for all ninety minutes despite falling behind early and trailing Saprissa for the entire match. The Saprissa side was oddly lacking in enthusiastic support, though they certainly made themselves known with whirling towels and screams after each goal.

My greatest enjoyment, however, came in the Alajuelense fan sitting in front of me with his increasingly embarrassed girlfriend. She was embarrassed, because her boyfriend filled every moment of silence shouting some incensed gibberish at the referee, capping each rant with a visceral, "Hijo de puta!"

Just after sunset with the stadium lights gleaming over the pitch, the final whistle blew. Alajuelense had lost. I was more surprised to realize ninety minutes had already passed. It made me think of those back in the States who continue to scoff at soccer as if it's not a real sport. They're generally of an older variety.

Younger Americans, on the contrary, have taken a hard turn toward soccer and away from baseball. My suspicion has been that we no longer have the patience for a three to four hour game. Too many things demand our attention! Work, friends, family, Netflix queues—we're busy. Baseball alone demands an absurd amount of time and patience to watch. I can still enjoy an afternoon at the ballpark, but I can also admit that the game can be painfully boring.

Soccer, on the other hand, promises a swift ninety minutes with limited interruptions. The worst thing I can say about their interruptions are the dramatics some players embrace when trying to draw a penalty, but this is almost exclusive to the men's game. Watch the U.S. Women's team and you'll be hard-pressed to find a phony fall. North American sports, however, are littered with TV timeouts that help drag the games on past three hours. No can do. I gotta binge on *House Of Cards*.

Despite my faux team taking a beating, I was satisfied with the experience. I saw a proper soccer match with a (mostly) full stadium of passionate fans. And I'm happy to report, there was never a need for the standing army patrolling inside the stadium.

Splitting the Americas in Panama City

Panama City was enthusiastically at the top of Melanie's travel wish list because of the Panama Canal. Not that I had any objections or wasn't notably excited myself. It exists and seems important, so of course I want to see it, but I'm fairly certain her enthusiasm for seeing the Panama Canal *in person* managed to register on the Richter scale. Her trembling joy and excitement upon booking the trip surely sent the seismic needles into a frenzy.

We arrived on a weekday afternoon over a late March Semana Santa, the week leading up to Easter. Back in Costa Rica we had been warned that the country shuts down during this religious week. Everything is closed while Ticos flock to the coast. Panama City is an international powerhouse, though. We were assured that it would be impossible to shut it down for any single observance, much like New York City or London keep on ticking no matter what.

Suffice it to say, they were right. Panama City is many things, but dull or lifeless is certainly not one of them.

After over six months of boutique hotels and bed and breakfasts, we wanted a gargantuan, big city hotel. There's something that fires me up about staying in a skyscraper of a hotel when visiting a global city. That's how I felt during my first visit to Toronto and that's how I felt about Panama City. We ended up at the Hilton on Avenida Balboa, right in the heart of the city with the Pacific Ocean a stone's throw away. More importantly for us was our proximity to Cinta Costera, a sixty-four-acre land reclamation project along the Pacific Coast extending approximately eight kilometers. My personal travel map is still largely unexplored, as fortunate as I've been. But of what I had experienced, I could easily call Cinta Costera one of the most impressive coastal park spaces I had ever seen in a city. The sheer magnitude of it—its size, location and the rich colors of the gardens—draws people outside in a climate where if this were the armpit of Florida, people would be clinging to their AC unit and begging for a quick, merciful death.

We started with a walk along the mixed-use path shared between leisure cyclists and pedestrians. The first thing we noticed was the oppressive heat and humidity. It was as if a portal to Hell had opened in Panama City, with a vacuum sucking the atmosphere out of the underworld. Talking with locals, this was normal. At least we weren't in the rainy season, I supposed.

The humidity in Panama City deserves a novel of its own. You could cut through this stuff with a knife. It was like breathing water. I felt terrible for the city workers, trimming away at the gardens in full gear to protect themselves from the sweltering sun. They must lose several pounds a day in sweat alone.

If you walk slowly, it's manageable and actually quite pleasant. Panama City showed how a city can maintain a sense of vibrancy by offering people an excuse to brave less than ideal weather conditions with inviting public spaces, like the coastal parks or various basketball and volleyball courts placed along the path. Meanwhile, far too many cities around the globe have forfeited their coastal spaces to soulless, life-sucking (and often life-ending) highways. (That said, Avenida Balboa could certainly use some traffic calming.) The only downside of Cinta Costera came in the afternoon when low tide would unearth pungent smells that sent Melanie and myself gagging. As part of Cinta Costera, the city is pushing sewage spills further into the ocean to rid the area of its foul odor. Admittedly this doesn't sound like the most environmentally friendly solution, but was damn-near impossible to breathe at certain hours during our visit.

Melanie and I continued our little trek through Mercado del Marisco, a renowned fish market right on Cinta Costera that we first saw on an episode of Anthony Bourdain's *No Reservations*. The unmistakable, pungent smell of fish loomed in the air well before approaching the market. Platoons of modest fishing boats floated in rows along the coast and docks. Looking back toward the ultramodern Panama City skyline—something out of a Mega Man video game, I thought—offered an interesting contrast.

We continued toward the colonial neighborhood, which jumps back and forth between calling itself Casco Viejo and Casco Antiguo depending on who you're talking to. We'll go shorthand with just Casco to keep everyone happy (or to anger both crowds).

Casco is the "Old Quarter" of Panama City, hastily developed between 1671 and 1673 after the annihilation of Panama Viejo by pirates (more on that later). This fascinating colonial neighborhood has since received World Heritage Site honors and the busy sound of renovation continues throughout the red brick streets. Some of the development has even crept over into neighboring El Chorrillo, which the travel guides will generally tell you is a no-go neighborhood. Yes, there's crime and it looked a bit rough, but people in the neighborhood are understandably a bit peeved. An excessive U.S. bombing campaign that left the neighborhood in shambles during the whole Manuel Noriega fiasco of the late '80s certainly did them no favors. (You might be more familiar with the bizarre ending when U.S. forces blasted rock music at a Vatican mission where the dictator had taken refuge.)

People in the States tend to forget about that episode. Lord knows I had no idea before researching Panamanian history weeks before this trip. But yeah, we invaded Panama. And murals in El Chorrillo show that they haven't exactly forgotten about it either. One mural stretches vertically across a weathered apartment complex showing a man clutching onto the Panamanian flag with his child on his back. Above the image reads, "Yo no vendo mi patria" or "I do not sell my country." Underneath the man and child sits a bald eagle next to the phrase, "Bloqueo criminal Yanki." Methinks no translation is necessary.

Amidst omnipresent reminders of how shitty my government has been to other nations, let's awkwardly transition.

Casco immediately felt like a place we could live in. It was walkable, dressed with interesting architecture, and had no shortage of cafés that poured out onto the sidewalk. There was even a *cervecería* (brewery) in La Rana Dorada to scratch our craft beer itch. I was perfectly content spending the afternoon in a shaded corner of the centralized Plaza de la Independencia with the towering Catedral Metropolitana de Nuestra Señora de la Asunción facing me. I took note of the hollowed out buildings being remodeled alongside the freshly restored apartments, imagining myself sticking my head out through the long balcony windows for an aerial view of this seventeenth century playground.

Daydreaming fantasies aside, I knew a return visit to Casco was already in store to see how this placed ticked at night.

Now here's something about me. If there's a train in a city, I will figure out a way to ride it. Such is my love for non-vehicular transportation, specifically rail transit. Naturally I was intrigued after reading about Panama City's new rail system with Estación

Iglesia del Carmen just blocks away from our hotel. While I have no problem hopping on a train and getting off at a random stop to see what happens, I generally prefer some kind of loose plan. The plan was to get to Parque Natural Metropolitano—a 265 hectare green sanctuary just on the outskirts of urban Panama City. There was no direct train stop for the park, but we were able to piece together our own route by getting off at Albrook—a mix of transportation hub and drab-looking mall—and walking the rest of the way.

The train itself was as impressive as any other in a twenty-first century transportation system; sleek sliding doors, bright and welcoming colors, and plenty of space for traveling Panamanians wisely choosing to avoid bumper-to-bumper traffic. Though we very well could have been the first to use the train to get to Parque Natural, it was certainly better than getting into a dilapidated taxi choking on its last breath. Considering the state of taxis in Panama City, I would not have been entirely surprised if the whole of the vehicle suddenly dropped to the asphalt below, the wheels sputtering out to the sides like something out of the Saturday morning cartoons of my childhood.

Parque Natural itself proved to be an excellent retreat from urbanity, perfectly accessible from downtown and some of the western neighborhoods. Trails varied from gravel to dirt as they rolled with very modest elevation gains. This wasn't about backpacking; this was about getting a bit of fresh air within eyeshot of the city—something I appreciated about Panama City since I've never been a fan of the "either/or" choice. (I'm speaking about the prevalent false choice of cities versus suburbs in the United States that says you can either live in the middle of nowhere if you want green space or you can get the amenities of a city, but without a trail to hike.)

Something we personally enjoyed was discovering Parque Natural's faraway partner—our very own Cleveland Metroparks.

A species of bird migrates back and forth between the two park systems, plus Cleveland has its own bit of canal history (though realistically, incomparable to Panama). So, the two struck a partnership. This proved our ongoing suspicion that Cleveland truly is everywhere. (Previously in our travels we had found a Cleveland-themed bar on a remote island off Puerto Rico. Parque Natural was just the latest in growing evidence.)

Next was what Melanie had been clamoring for most (and I, a normal, reasonable amount) in our visit to Panama City—the famous canal itself.

The amount of material created about the Panama Canal—its construction, politics and aftermath—could probably stretch the length of the actual canal and then some in pages. PBS proved to have the most digestible summary with its *American Experience* documentary. Here's a short summary: The French tried it first, failed and then we did it.

U-S-A! U-S-A! U-S-A!

Nationalistic jokes aside, it was actually (and not surprisingly) a tad more complicated. A lot of people died. Racism dictated the harsh treatment of the immigrant West Indian workers to whom the canal owes its life. The French effort left 20,000 workers dead followed by another 5,600 when the Americans took over between 1904 and 1913.

Summarizing again for the sake of brevity, the French effort largely failed due to Ferdinand de Lesseps' attempt at recreating in Panama his work with Egypt's Suez Canal. See, the Suez Canal dredged the land to sea level. This was a profoundly bad idea in Panama for one simple reason: Panama is not flat. Once the French architect realized his mistake, he tried getting Gustave Eiffel, of Eiffel Tower fame, to construct locks. The venture went bankrupt in 1889 after sinking more than $260 million into the effort. Embarrassed, the French went so far as to indict both Eiffel and Lesseps for the scandal. They were sentenced to prison and fined, but the decision was overturned.

Uncle Sam, who originally wanted the canal to be in Nicaragua, got involved thanks to lobbying from the French engineer Philppe-Jean Bunau-Varilla, who had worked on the first attempt. He insisted that the U.S. should purchase France's canal assets and bury Nicaragua's hopes in the process, convincing American lawmakers that volcanoes would make a Nicaraguan venture too dangerous.

Congress authorized the purchase of French assets in 1902, but ran into a Colombian roadblock. At the time, Panama was part of Colombia and they refused to ratify the agreement with the United States. Of course, as history has shown, the U.S. generally does what it wants and the story of the Panama Canal is no exception. President Theodore Roosevelt, who was passionate about using the canal to highlight American greatness to the world when he wasn't busy wrestling bears and deflecting bullets off his chest, supported Panamanian independence. U.S. Secretary of State John Hay immediately went to work with Bunau-Varilla negotiating an agreement that gave the United States 500 square miles of canal zone for the engineering project. The Panamanians got $10 million out of the 1903 treaty, the French $40 million for their assets, and the United States would pour another $300 million into the canal itself.

(In the middle of all this, Teddy visited the project and wore a light-colored straw hat that we now call the "Panama hat." Because Teddy wore it, it was cool. Which in all honesty, I understand. The man oozed gumption. I still try to do things just because Teddy did them. So I get why these hats are still sold at any Panamanian shop that hopes to make a sale. You can't go a minute out on the modern Panama City streets without seeing someone wearing one of these things. They are, however, it should be said, of Ecuadorian origin—not Panamanian as the named would suggest. So I also understand if Ecuadorians aren't as thrilled with Teddy as I am.)

Jumping ahead, President Carter signed a treaty with President Torrijos in 1977 to hand control of the Panama Canal over to the Panamanians on December 31, 1999. Y'know, because it's Panama and not the United States. Some might remember that this was a controversial move in the '70s. Ronald Reagan even equated it to giving up Alaska or Hawaii, which hopefully seemed as preposterous then as it sounds nowadays. Internationally speaking, the move was applauded.

Today, around 13,000 to 14,000 ships use the canal annually. An expansion project completed in June of 2016 doubled its capacity (so expect to see higher ship counts in the near future). Americans use the canal most, but they're followed behind by China, Chile, Japan, Colombia and South Korea. Each ship must pay a toll based on its size and cargo. The largest payment came in around $450,000. The smallest? Thirty-six cents from Richard Halliburton in 1928 when he swam the canal.

With all that history out of the way, we can go back to our train ride on the Panama Canal Railway that took us from Panama City to Colón in just about sixty minutes, over the original French tracks used during the canal's construction. Julia, a Panamanian with Terramar Destinations, offered us some additional history and her own thoughts on life in Panama as we coasted through the narrow isthmus. She smiled sweetly as she shared her story of coming from a small village near Panama City.

"I still commute from my village," she said with a hint of pride. I admired that greatly for reasons I'm still trying to pinpoint.

What was most enjoyable during our conversation was watching her play verbal gymnastics in an attempt to avoid saying anything critical of the United States that might offend someone with more nationalistic tendencies than myself (though

I suppose it was ultimately unfortunate if she felt she could not speak candidly lest she hurt my feelings for offering verifiable history).

"During the…" she'd pause, "…incidents when the U.S. came…" These thoughts, with respect to the U.S. invasion of Panama in 1989, were shared very carefully.

After reaching Colón, we made our return for Panama City by car in order to stop at a few viewing points along the way. Tourists gathered with their guides as prerecorded announcements were made over a loudspeaker in French, English and Spanish. Melanie squealed with unfettered joy as the first ships crawled through the Gatún Locks at a snail's pace. In general the ships come in at 52,000 tons, 950 feet long and 190 feet tall, so it's no wonder they take their time navigating the narrow canal. Electric locomotives known as mulas (mules) travel alongside the ships on rail to pull them in and to ensure they stay on track while moving through the canal. (It's not entirely unlike letting go of the wheel in a car wash, except the Panama Canal is a *slightly* larger production.) That happens about thirty-five to forty times per day.

Whereas Melanie would have been overjoyed to setup camp, watch every single ship and spend the night to catch the morning ship traffic, I was satisfied with my helping of Panama Canal history and sightseeing.

Our two final stops in Panama City came at the Palacio Presidencial back in Casco and then at Panama Viejo. Palacio Presidencial sat on the northern edge of Casco, overlooking the Pacific Ocean. Its main feature, besides the splendid architecture and wondrous art that tend to come with presidential quarters, was the two herons strutting around freely in the main courtyard. Herons were first brought in 1922 and have remained a staple of the palace ever since, even giving it the name of Palacio de las Garzas or Palace of the Herons.

We fittingly ended where Panama City as we know it today technically began—at Panama Viejo where the original location of Panama City was burned to the ground in 1671 by the Englishman Henry Morgan, the notorious pirate who was far more murder-y than his rum label suggests. Reconstruction started further south in Casco as it was believed to be easier to defend. Today the area, north of downtown Panama City, shares World Heritage Site honors with Casco.

Walking the grounds of the fallen city was actually quite remarkable. Much of the original framework remained intact—dirt footpaths, stone towers and all—accompanied by the fresh air that tends to circulate in unpopulated places. Beyond the ruins, the uber-modern Panama City skyline stood perfectly visible, with scaffolds surrounding the new skyscrapers under construction. There was a palpable buzz as the city prepared to host the 2015 Summit of the Americas the following week, the first in which Cuba would participate.

While Panama's history may have been rocky—from its beginnings in Panama Viejo to the Noriega and U.S. fiasco that decimated an already severely impoverished neighborhood—it would seem that the future of the city is as bright as its nighttime sky. My only hope as we left was that the Panamanians in El Chorrillo and other similar barrios would be brought along for the ride.

orinar fuera del tarro (o·*ree*·nar

fwe·ra del *tar*·ro)
adjective

1. Breaking it down word for word, this translates to "to pee outside of the can."
2. Nothing to do with actual urination, this *tiquismo* lets someone know they're nuts, way off base, inappropriate and/or that they have no idea what they're talking about.

Example: "I'm finishing this book about some Gringo in Costa Rica and I gotta say he's orinando fuera del tarro."

Monteverde: Zip-lining Through The Quaker Cloud Forest

I left for Monteverde via a shuttle pickup from a typically unremarkable chain hotel off the highway in Santa Ana. At least I was able to take the bus there, though I'm sure I looked ridiculous lugging my roller bag behind me as I made a mad dash across Lindora Avenue to reach the hotel. (There were no crosswalks or lights for pedestrians nearby.)

The shuttle ride was much like the others I had already taken around Central America, but Melanie was notably missing having left for Cleveland to start her new job. There were a number of foreign tourists, North American and European, minding their own business for the two and a half hour drive up to Monteverde. Whereas Tico taxis are typically chatty, I always found shuttle drivers quiet. I assumed this was because of the larger group and assumption that the foreigners didn't speak Spanish.

Our driver did share one concern—carretera 606. The winding, northerly road that connects the Central Valley and coastal Puntarenas to elevated Monteverde had been under construction. If we arrived at the wrong time, we'd be stopped and have to wait as one-way traffic passed us by.

We lucked out on any road delays thanks to some heavy rain

that reminded me of the so-called green season back in Ciudad Colón. Nobody wanted to be working in that mess. But as we approached the final few kilometers to Monteverde, mud started to cover the road where construction workers had taken over the rare piece of flat land to keep unused equipment. Our driver paused as he observed the road ahead. A hole separated us from our final stretch into Monteverde.

One worker came running over in nothing more than jeans and a tee shirt, drenched from the downpour. At least he had boots on to deal with the mud.

I overheard him instruct our driver to go over onto the adjacent field and that would lead around the hole in the road. Of course, to get through the field we had to crawl over one small hill, a hill that would be insignificant in any other kind of weather but was far too slick with mud from the pouring rain. The shuttle simply couldn't get over the hump, metaphorically and literally. Instead we got ourselves stuck, the wheels spinning like a toy race car being held by a toddler, unable to gain traction. Two workers came over to help push the shuttle out of the way and we retreated back to the road, our driver appearing to think up a Plan B. No such plan materialized as we watched other vehicles more suited for this weather easily roll over the hill and onto the other side. I could sense concern from the driver, possibly because some Gringos can become incessantly impatient when things don't go perfectly their way. Thankfully this crowd appeared to feel more empathy than aggravation towards the driver.

Eventually one of the workers hopped into a nearby bobcat UTV and started scooping mud and filling the hole in the road. Another worker with a shovel flattened the dirt to smooth it all out. There was still a ditch to our left that our driver had to carefully navigate along the narrow pass. If a wheel slipped in, I'm not sure how we would have gotten out.

Our driver, however, handled the pass with ease, and gave a couple of friendly honks to the workers who helped us out as we sped into Monteverde.

On cue, the rain stopped by the time I got dropped off at the Arco Iris Lodge, a modest-sized lodge spreading out into different cabins connected by stone paths. The man who greeted me at the front counter in the main lodge appeared to be a Gringo, but I didn't want to assume. Even if he was, part of me wanted him to know that I wasn't one of those Gringos living in Costa Rica who couldn't speak a lick of Spanish.

Separating myself from the typical Gringo tourist was a constant battle and one in which I always engaged in by speaking Spanish first. More often than not, speaking Spanish proved successful in knocking down the assumption that I'm on my way to some gaudy resort. In Osa, a waitress who started recognizing me flatteringly called me, "Casi Tico" or "Almost a Tico." This felt like a huge win. But sometimes in the more touristy towns, I'd still get an English response.

Waitress: Good afternoon. Table for two?

Me: Sí, mesa para dos, por favor.

Waitress: Here you go. Something to drink?

Me: ¿Tienen frescas naturales?

Waitress: Yes. They're listed right here."

And so the impasse would continue until one of us broke.

"Buenas. Tengo una reservación," I said to the front desk.

"Buenas. ¿Como se llama?" he responded before another couple of tourists skipped ahead of me to ask a quick question in English. This appeared to fluster him as he attempted to switch his brain back to Spanish. But after taking one long look at me, he made the wild guess that I could speak English.

"Uh," he muttered, glancing down at his notes. "You speak English, right?"

"Yes," I admitted, but hoping his Tico colleague sitting next to him noticed that he stopped speaking Spanish first—not me!

One of the first things anyone asks someone who has been to Costa Rica is, "Did you go zip-lining?" Living there, folks back home assumed it was the mode of transportation.

Yet it admittedly isn't something I get all that excited about. I had previously done it twice, once in Puerto Rico and a second time in West Virginia. I enjoyed myself plenty, but I prefer hiking and taking in my surroundings as opposed to the quick thrill of zip-lining. Nevertheless, that's what you do in Monteverde, an ecotourism hotspot resting roughly 1,200 to 1,500 meters above sea level. You go zip-lining, and I was happy to give it a whirl with Sky Adventures.

My Monteverde group consisted of three American college girls, two Mexican women in their forties, and another American couple. One of the college girls had no intention to partake in the zip-lining, crippled by her fear of heights, but accompanied us nonetheless to take pictures for her friends. She did, however, endure the initial sky tram ride up to the top of the canopy course, giggling in anxiety the entire way as her eyes welled up in tears.

"Oh, you're so brave! You're doing good!" her friends offered encouragingly. Meanwhile, one of the Tico guides, a charismatic young man who knew his way around people, used it as an opportunity to chat her up.

"Don't worry. I've got you," he said as he stretched his arm around her, instructing the distraught girl's friends to snap a picture as he flashed a goofy smile. The gesture seemed to take her mind off what I'm sure she imagined was an imminent, crashing death from the tram.

Those of us not clinging for dear life were able to take in our surroundings. With the rain gone, we were treated to a remarkably clear sky that allowed us to catch Volcán Arenal out in the distance. Below, the dense forest swallowed everything that wasn't cleared out for the sky tram. The air was pleasantly cool with a bit of a mist, as one might expect in a cloud forest.

Stations were placed perfectly so that there was little hiking in between zip-lines along the canopy course. I generally prefer a bit of a hike, but others appeared thankful to avoid hiking with those adult-sized diapers they make you wear to latch onto the zip-lines. With a smaller group, we finished the eight-line course earlier than the expected two hours. Nobody was shy about hopping up for their turn once our heights-averse friend left the group to snap photos. It's an interesting process when you think about it. You're chatting, as one does with a new group, and in mid-conservation you pause to quickly slide down 750 meters of cable before picking up where you left off.

Me: Yeah, I moved to Costa Rica about nine months ago, and...

Guide: Ready to go, amigo?

Me: Sorry, one sec while I bullet across the forest.

The other highlight in town, perhaps even more popular than the zip-lines, is hiking in the Monteverde Cloud Forest Biological Reserve, founded in 1972 by scientists George Powell and the Quaker Wilford Guindon. That wasn't the first time Quakers got involved in Monteverde. In fact, U.S. Quakers whose pacifist values didn't mesh well with the draft effort during the Korean War founded present-day Monteverde. The dairyman Hubert Mendenhall led the group after first visiting Costa Rica in 1949. He was won over by the cool climate (hospitable to dairy farming) and the country's lack of a standing army.

My excitement for this hike tripled when I discovered my group was no more than a Tico guide and a Spanish couple. Doing tours exclusively in Spanish was as much a thrill for me as it was a challenge. It felt like an accomplishment if I could understand more technical Spanish, describing our surroundings and the biodiversity. I can order food in German, but I don't consider myself a German speaker (though I would if I could comprehend the language in the midst of a hiking tour that describes the local flora and fauna).

The Spanish couple were on their honeymoon. As we made introductions, I realized I had never spoken to a Spanish person in Spanish before. There were some Spanish students at UPEACE, but everyone mostly spoke English on campus unless surrounded by native Spanish speakers.

As I listened, I realized that I ironically had a more difficult time understanding Spain Spanish (*Spainish*, if you will) than I did the Latino variety. Most non-Spanish speakers think Latinos speak impossibly fast, but that title should be reserved for the Spanish. To the contrary, Ticos pride themselves in having what one might consider the most approachable form of Spanish. Many linguists agree. Ultimately I fared fine with my Spanish companions, even though I kept imagining flamenco music scoring the conversation.

National Geographic has called Monteverde "the jewel in cloud forest reserves." *Newsweek* wrote that it's one of the world's fourteen places to remember before it disappears. Perhaps this acclaim is why I was disappointed the hike didn't last longer. In the end, I'm not sure we walked any more than two miles and it wasn't especially difficult terrain. Maybe I would have enjoyed it more had I known going into the hike that our guide would be a birder. Few people impress me more than Costa Rican nature guides. They can diagnose the faintest squawk and point out the most distant creature rustling around in some bushes. Their knowledge is encyclopedic.

But, as we've already covered, I'm not a bird guy. A brilliant-colored scarlet macaw can only briefly hold my attention. The distant call and blur of a hunting hawk doesn't interest me. If I happen to cross paths with an interesting animal, great. I'm happy to pause and take it in. What kills me is waiting.

During our hike, rumor quickly spread among the guides that there was a quetzal afoot, which is a type of bird that's difficult to spot, I gathered. I was indifferent to learning more. Our good-natured guide insisted we hightail it back to the sighting. I stomached my groan as my eager feet wondered why we had to turn back.

It's in these moments that one might be prone to exaggeration, but we must have spent the better part of an hour staring at the visual cacophony of trees, branches, and leaves where the quetzal was said to be hiding. I was increasingly restless with every passing minute of anticipation. In my defense, I had made the assumption that this would be a short affair. We'd run back, see the stupid bird, and be able to continue our hike.

The quetzal, however, is apparently a rare find, which made it all the more exciting for the guides and hiking birders. A half an hour later, the damn quetzal had yet to come out and put on a show for its adoring audience. The birding crowd, however, persisted like a hoard of Apple fanatics camping out for the latest iteration of iPhones.

Our guide continued tiptoeing through the dense brush, staring intensely through the woods in hopes of spotting the quetzal. By now my Spanish companions had long lost their interest as well, meandering back and forth on the trail and snapping photos. Finally we were called over once the quetzal had been spotted again, perched on a faraway branch. I know I saw it, but my disinterest was so strong that the moment failed to even make its way into my short-term memory. By the end of this birding hunt, it was time for us to turn back for the colibríes (hummingbirds) fluttering around by the feeders placed near the reserve's entrance.

For as little as I care for birding, I do actually enjoy watching the colibríes dart around like avian jets, their rapidly flapping wings leaving something of a motorized sound in my ear. But having expected a hike along the lines of what I had done in Guatemala or El Salvador or even in the Orosi Valley, I was grouchy and ready to move on.

Oddly enough, I ended up being more entranced with the town of Santa Elena than anything else I had experienced in Monteverde. It was a walkable, picturesque little town that afforded its residents plenty of adventure opportunities a short jaunt away. I imagined myself living there, no longer at the mercy of guides, and getting lost in the cloud forests. For work I'd spend my days at Beso Espresso, even if only because a barista there made me feel important by noticing my camera and taking an interest in my travel videos. Melanie and I would then take in dinner at Tree House, a dimly lit, rustic establishment that features a giant higuerón tree growing from the center of the restaurant and stretching its limbs out and around the tables.

Then I snapped back to reality and realized I'd go crazy living in such a sleepy town, no matter how great it looks on a postcard. The peace and tranquility of Santa Elena would have the opposite effect on me. I need a city, a place with constant activity and a steady stream of people (even if I don't particularly enjoy many individual people, I do enjoy being around groups of people for the atmosphere). This all left me craving more than ever my upcoming weekend in San José—a city with actual people out and about enjoying life, culture and good food.

But first, I had a date with Tortuguero.

Hueveros and Tourism in Tortuguero

Tortuguero is the land of turtles, so it's convenient that "tortuguero" roughly translates to the land of turtles.

The Northeastern Caribbean village's national park is another Costa Rican specialty routinely included in lists proclaiming "Places you need to see before you die." It also fancies itself a bit of a romantic destination, especially popular with honeymooning couples, so of course I traveled stag.

Costa Rica's third-most visited national park covers 312 square kilometers of biological reserve in the Limon province. Its rich ecological diversity (harboring eleven different habitats, such as beaches, forests, lagoons, mangroves, rainforests and swamps) draws a good chunk of the country's annual two million-plus tourists. The twenty-mile coastline is a protected zone for sea turtles to come and lay their eggs, and is surrounded by a number of other reserves. There's only the tiny town of Tortuguero that serves as any substantial human presence, and it's all only accessible by boats navigating the coastline and canals. In other words, Tortuguero remains an especially remote and untouched corner of the globe. "Central America's Amazon," some even call it.

My route to Tortuguero was similar to Monteverde the week before. I bussed and dragged my bag over to the chain hotel in Santa Ana and waited for my pick up. This time the shuttle took myself and some other passengers to a seemingly random meeting point where we transferred over to another shuttle before again switching to a Greyhound-sized bus. This final bus was a traditional group tour bus, something I never imagined myself on. Even worse, it quickly became clear that most everyone was traveling with a significant other. Clearly I didn't belong here now that I was traveling solo with Melanie back in Cleveland. I wanted to sleep for the rest of the ride, but because it was a group tour, that meant we had an energetic host talking through a microphone the entire time. He alternated between history of the area and corny language lessons, Dora The Explorer style.

Host: Good afternoon, everyone! Or as we see, 'Buenas tardes.' Can you say that?

Bus: "Buen-nas tar-des!

The bus left us in a large dirt parking lot with one open-air restaurant and a port. Travelers, both those en route to and returning from Tortuguero, hustled to use the restaurant bathroom, dropping a hundred colón with the attendant for the privilege. Refreshed, we boarded a reasonably comfortable ferry for a ninety-minute ride into Tortuguero.

What began as a speedy excursion turned into something of a navigation course for the ferry's operator. You go to Tortuguero for the canals, and that's precisely what you get as you inch closer. Tight corners and occasionally shallow waters required steady maneuvering. Eager tourists clamored in excitement as we moved deeper into the jungle, making good use of their cameras. I watched wishing I could feel that excitement again for Costa Rica. They looked like I did when I first arrived with Melanie back in August. On the bright side, Costa Rica had taught me to be more selective with my photos, so I was able to relax a bit more than the other tourists who had never seen anything like Tortuguero.

The ferry left us at our hotel, the Pachira Lodge. Enthusiastic hotel staff greeted us with welcoming cocktails as we trudged along the docks and onto the property. There was just enough time for checking out the room and a quick lunch before we were all expected back at the docks to board a small speedboat that would take us to the town of Tortuguero.

The color of Tortuguero sticks out first. A welcome center covered in the interesting combination of a magenta exterior with a light blue roof sits just behind the docks. Inside there's the obligatory shopping of local art and products that tourists buy on the way out, but most just hit it up for the bathroom. Two tall statues of birds—one a scarlet macaw, the other a toucan stand like those gargantuan fast food signs off highways in the States. (This was obviously more appealing.) Though Costa Rica has no shortage of statues commemorating their historical heroes, I appreciated these unusual animal statues. It seems a bit cartoonish at first, like an amusement park or something. But it's Costa Rica; of course they should have statues of animals. That's their thing.

Back on land, we cut through the local school where children in matching uniforms were lining up and entering their classrooms. They paid us little attention, presumably accustomed to seeing large groups of fair-skinned tourists. Some in our group smiled and waved, receiving disinterested acknowledgement from the kids in return. I don't blame them. It must get old rather quickly to live in a town heavily trafficked by tourists, whether it's Venice in Italy or Tortuguero in Costa Rica. For tourists, it seems like part of the experience to see these kids. We immediately think of how we went to school and how we dressed in comparison. (Few walked to school at Dale R. Rice Elementary in Mentor, Ohio, nor did we have matching uniforms, which would have clashed greatly with my mid-'90s Cleveland baseball gear.) The kids probably gave two shits about us, and I again, I don't blame them.

A smattering of short green grass covered a mixture of dirt and sand surrounding the school buildings. It was hard to tell the difference with the beach in sight. Footpaths dictated where there was grass and where there wasn't. Two ragged bikes rested outside on one of the buildings, a popular form of transportation in car-free Tortuguero, I imagined. I could imagine how unpleasant getting around here might be for the students on a rainy day. It'd be mud city, folks.

The school was small and simple. Tin roofs and basic box construction with bars covering otherwise open windows that made it easy to overhear ongoing classes. Two of the school buildings were light blue, like the welcome center roof, with a mural of some Costa Rican wildlife painted on the side. It looked like something out of a pop-up book for kids, so the artist definitely knew his or her audience.

Continuing to the beach, our guide talked about the sea turtles that come to nest in this area between September and October. Four species use Tortuguero and its surrounding beaches for nesting, two of which are critically endangered. Working with the sea turtles is a popular form of non-profit work and volunteerism in Costa Rica. It sounds like a cute gig, but it's anything but. Take the story of Jairo Mora Sandoval for example. Jairo was a twenty-six-year-old Costa Rican environmental activist who gave his life protecting sea turtles. He worked for and lived at the Costa Rica Wildlife Sanctuary, patrolling beaches for the Wider Caribbean Sea Turtle Conservation Network. His target? *Hueveros* or poachers. Despite the danger, Jairo fearlessly snatched up the eggs himself to bring to the sanctuary out of harm's way. Once he even leapt from a moving truck to tackle a poacher, like something out of a Jason Statham film.

On May 30, 2013, Jario was volunteering with four women;

three from the United States and one from Spain. They were patrolling Moín Beach in the evening some fifty miles south of Tortuguero. A tree trunk blocked the way for their jeep, so Jairo hopped out to move it. Five masked and armed men ambushed him. The attackers threw Mora in the trunk of their car after beating him and drove off with the four female volunteers to an abandoned house. At least one woman was sexually assaulted before being tied up and robbed of their belongings, namely phones and money. The women eventually freed themselves and fled to the police, but Mora was taken to beach where he was stripped, beaten, and dragged in the sand by car. His naked body was found dead the next morning. Seven men were later arrested, four of whom eventually received guilty verdicts for the killing in March of 2016. I share this story not to frighten anyone away from visiting Tortuguero, but so you might better understand some of what goes on behind-the-scenes of conserving Costa Rica's tourism moneymaker. If you've ever been or plan to visit the natural wonders of Costa Rica, you have people like Jairo to thank.

Our hosts then left us with time to walk across town, the path being primarily one long stretch of dirt and concrete lined by restaurants, shops, businesses, homes and a park. I particularly enjoyed the park where painted murals offered universally applicable messages. There was one of a gray-skinned man with shaggy hair and a beard. His eyes were red with grey pupils looking off to the left. Behind his head were the flags of Costa Rica and Pan-Africa next to a peace symbol. The message read, "Mira hacia abajo a los caídos y dales la mano..." or "Look down to the fallen and give them a hand..."

Few Ticos live in Tortuguero. The best estimates say the population is between 1,200 and 1,500, yet it seemed livelier than towns I have visited in the States twenty or more times larger. I attributed this to the lack of cars, of course. An American might visit and think Tortuguero looks like a very poor village. Indeed, homes are very modest. I didn't step inside of any, but I had been in similar homes previously in Costa Rica. Basically it's one large open room with a busted-looking old wooden door separating everyone from the bathroom. Adults were almost universally dressed in tank tops, shorts and well-worn sandals. Kids not in school uniforms followed suit. I'm certain that it is a poor village, financially speaking, but I'm certain I'd find more enjoyment living in a place like this than in whatever's the latest boilerplate suburb to be included in a list of "Best Places To Live." (Ironically Mentor has twice made CNN's version.)

Now I realize I risk falling into heavily privileged territory with what I'm about to say. Many travel writers visit towns and villages far less fortunate than their own and mistake gratefulness for basic necessities with some kind of zen happiness. The Patron Saint of Canada back in Atenas comes to mind. They think this because they drop in for a quick visit before heading back to their air conditioned hotel room that's larger and nicer than anything most in said village can ever expect to experience and assume that folks back in the village wouldn't like to trade places. Maybe they wouldn't, but we often decide that for them without ever having a conversation. We project what we want out of someone who's just sitting on a bench. We don't know what it's like to eat the same rice-based meal every day or to work grueling hours in punishing heat and humidity for next to nothing pay. We see some people sitting outside in storybook surroundings and paint them as care-free simpletons who just have it "figured out" when in reality they'd probably love to try something different to eat and are likely a bit less entranced than we are with the beachfront view they see every goddamn day. So when I say I think I'd find more enjoyment in life living in a place like Tortuguero than what wins "best of" lists in the States, I'm counting the not-so-sexy stuff.

Tortuguero would still win, because everything is built to human scale and thus inviting to people. No parking lots, garages or car dealerships that take up entire city blocks. Footpaths connect homes to the main strip—again, just a simple concrete walkway—and everything from groceries to restaurants, shops, and even an artsy café were on the main path. In effect Tortuguero has everything that draws me to place, just a bit smaller. So I hope when people visit, they like it for what so many places around the world have developed away from—that is, making everything one could possibly need within a reasonable walk—and not because they saw some local smile and made the leaping assumption that they're happier with little.

Meals were rough on this trip. Not because of the quality, but because I could never eat alone. Though it'd be a stretch to call me a "people person," I'm certainly no hermit. However, my group was almost exclusively comprised of couples—several of which were on their honeymoon.

Everyone looked at me strangely as they nervously asked, "Are you here alone?"

"Yes," I'd reply with a mental sigh before explaining that I was a journalist writing about Tortuguero.

"Oh, okay!" they'd reply, seemingly relieved that I wasn't some crazy person going on a couple's retreat by myself.

I met perfectly interesting people. There was a Belgian couple on their honeymoon, preparing to build their first home, and a pair of Spanish couples and an Italian in the mix. But the dining was communal, making conversation obligatory or awkwardly silent. Not only were the meals rough for me, but I assumed also for the couples on their honeymoon having this silent stranger sitting across from them, taking up the third of four seats so another couple couldn't join to even out the numbers. They were stuck with me. Luckily it was more natural to ignore me when we went out on group outings, like a canal tour.

A canal tour is the thing to do in Tortuguero, but I'm sorry to say that I feel my description will do it no justice. A month earlier, Andrea told me herself that "you absolutely need to see Tortuguero before you die," confirming all those lists I had seen boasting about the national park. I wanted to see Tortuguero, but at this point I was checking off a list of places to see in Costa Rica before I moved home. That's not the way to travel. Plus I had done a similar tour in Palo Verde just a month or so earlier, spoiling Tortuguero to a certain degree. Sure it was a more intense and remote take on Palo Verde, but it was slow travel by boat through dense wildernesses and guides who pointed out different animals and bird calls. It's just not my thing, and remnants of those guilty traveler feelings I had first felt back on the beaches of Tamarindo started creeping up again. Why was I not enjoying this? Better yet, *how* could I not enjoy this? Am I spoiled? Am I crazy?

My best guess is that I had already been thoroughly spoiled by Costa Rica and that I would've enjoyed it infinitely more had Melanie been at my side. I wouldn't have had to constantly be the third wheel, for one, absorbing curious stares and answering sad questions.

I do enjoy traveling solo at times, but it's always nice to have someone to bounce comments and observations off of. Melanie and I are lucky in that we have similar traveling styles. We prefer cities, but love an outdoor excursion. I have more of a tolerance for the extreme side of things, say, an eighty-mile bike ride instead of twenty, but we generally agree on what to do and where to go next. Even better, she thinks I'm funny for some reason and laughs at my jokes. I can turn the name of a Swiss grocery store into a parody of "Zoot Suit Riot" by the one-hit-wonder Cherry Poppin' Daddies and she'd laugh. Not just laugh, but join in. A third party would objectively (and rightfully) find this strange and not get why it's funny.

Traveling solo works better for me when I have Melanie to come home to. Ciudad Colón didn't feel like home anymore once she left for Cleveland. It was just a place with my stuff. A glorified hotel room of sorts where I could hear too many of my own thoughts. Going back to Colón after these trips felt like an odd extension of the trip I was just on—a placeholder until the next one. Back in Cleveland I could leave Melanie for a week or so on an assignment overseas and remain mentally stable, like a normal adult, because I knew she'd be there when I got home. Without her there, it didn't feel like I was going home or ending the trip.

For the first time since arriving to Costa Rica, I felt like I might be ready to leave.

A Turk In Costa Rica

The bus had emptied, save two other passengers, by the time we reached my corner of San José. It was a long day of travel back from Tortuguero and I was ready for a shower.

I traced the bus driver using Google Maps on my phone, watching as our blue GPS dot started to crawl further from where I thought I should be dropped off. Eventually he pulled over on the side of a busy boulevard with heavy traffic and no pedestrians. The two passengers collected their bags and walked off. Standing outside, the driver shot me a confused look.

"Where are you going?" he asked in Spanish.

I named the hotel and pointed on my phone. "It's in Barrio Escalante."

"Oh, that's back there," he said, gesturing with his head.

There was a pause as I thought he might have something more to add. He finally filled the silence with a slight shrug so I knew there was a period to that sentence.

"Umm, how should I get there?"

"I can't go back there. I'd have to turn around the bus and there's no place for me to do that here."

Indeed there was no place for him to turn the bus around and the street had a median preventing left-hand turns. Still, this felt like a conversation that would have been better suited for thirty minutes earlier.

"It's just over there. You can walk it," he said.

Usually I appreciate the opportunity to walk to my destination, especially after long hours in a sedentary position when my hips start to forget that they are meant to extend and my knees begin to stiffen as if being turned to stone. But I had little idea where I was, and the jagged sidewalks of San José aren't entirely agreeable to rolling suitcases (I really need to get a messenger bag). Plus I was working with a tourism company, so I suppose I expected a little more assistance. It's not as if I waved down a stranger, asked for directions, and started to crawl into their vehicle to help me finish the job.

The half-mile walk to the hotel ended up being a non-issue. My trusty GPS dot led me to the hotel and I found a relatively safe section of the street to run across between speeding cars that led me to the more walkable, quiet section of the neighborhood.

Hotel 1492 sits just around the corner from the action of San José's Barrio Escalante. Its Spanish influences and terra-cotta tiled roof stuck out among its neighbors. Rafa, the owner, happily greeted me after buzzing me in through the gated fence, jumping right into the building's history.

"This was the home of Amalia Jiménez," he said, his eyes gleaming through his glasses. "She's a Costa Rican artist, and eighteen years ago, we turned it into a hotel."

To start, I went for a walk around the neighborhood. My epiphany in Monteverde was dead-on—I needed a city. For me, nothing beats traveling to a new city, especially when surrounded by a different culture, language and architecture— everything that makes a city a city. I try not to forsake or take for granted how fortunate I am to travel to some remote corners of the globe, and I hope I don't appear ungrateful now. I do love traveling deep into my natural surroundings, but I have realized over the years that I'm more likely to find stories talking to people in cities.

I had grown quite fond of San José over my time in Costa Rica. Barrio Escalante helped cement my appreciation for Chepe. It has all the ingredients of an urban neighborhood that I enjoyed back home. There's Kalu, the neighborhood coffee joint where I could go nod my head as if I understood the barista's passionate plea for this bean instead of that bean. There was fine dining, take out options, and even a brewery to satiate my need for beer beyond alcohol-infused water. To boot, it was all walkable over well-maintained sidewalks to save pedestrians from aggressive Josefino driving.

I could live here, I thought. Maybe not forever, but I could be happy for a time in Escalante.

The highlight of Escalante came with a visit to Restaurante Sofía Mediterráneo along Calle 33 or Calle Gastronómica. Lindsay, my new Outward Bound and travel writing friend, had finagled a reservation and meeting with Chef Mehmet Onuralp. After finishing our meals—Lindsay, with her plate of spiced vegetables and potatoes, and I with spinach and ricotta tortellini —Mehmet joined us tableside to share how exactly he ended up in San José from Istanbul.

Speaking Turkish-accented Spanish, Mehmet described his early years of being raised in Istanbul before moving to Germany as a young adult. It was during his time in Germany that he gained an itch for travel, making his way to the mediterranean trifecta of Greece, Italy and Spain. It was in those countries that he learned the various recipes and stylings of the respective kitchens that would go on to inspire his own cooking.

Eventually Mehmet grew tired of what he saw as a rigid lifestyle in Germany. Indeed, the Germanic style of life is a tad more punctual and uniform than those other nations where he found culinary inspiration. So on a bit of a whim, he traveled to Costa Rica in 1991.

"I didn't know anything about Costa Rica except that it was famous for its environment," he said. "I liked it because it is a small country, but very diverse."

Mehmet, as most do, fell in love with Costa Rica. Following his return to Germany, he left his job and moved to Costa Rica with no Spanish in his linguistic repertoire. He landed a gig in tourism and started cooking for friends to sharpen his skills. Pointing across the street, Mehmet noted the building where he learned Spanish.

Several years ago, with the encouragement of friends, Mehmet pursued his passion for cooking and opened a small sandwich bistro where Sofía is situated today. The word quickly got out and Mehmet found himself serving lines that went out the door. They expanded, doubling the space, but still not quite meeting demand. Finally they moved forward on a table service concept for Sofía, named after the Santa Sofia temple (or Hagia Sophia) in Istanbul. "Santa" got dropped when Mehmet decided to broaden his menu to include additional Mediterranean culture.

Mehmet brings an altruistic, universal approach to his cooking.

"Food," he said, "is a relation between world countries." To him, it's like music. "There are no borders. You cannot say 'this is my recipe.' No. Recipes do not belong to an individual, they belong to humanity."

Mehmet hardly paused to take a breath. The man's eyes beamed with pride, his hands and arms swirling with the passion of someone who's doing precisely what they're on this planet to do.

In line with his philosophy, Mehmet is also playing a leading role in promoting Barrio Escalante as a culinary destination.

Sofía is one of six restaurants that belong to a recently developed culinary association dedicated to improving and promoting the neighborhood. The association is the one responsible for new lighting placed along Calle 33, giving it the moniker *Calle de la Luz* or Street of Light.

Our conversation ended with Mehmet running back to the kitchen and returning with a plate of baklava.

"Is baklava from Turkey?" Lindsay asked, knowing many nations and cultures hold a claim to the popular pastry.

"Baklava is generally seen as Turkish," he said, but he suggested that it comes from Syria. Independent research shows nobody really knows for certain where it comes from. Most answers appear to be educated guesses. Ultimately the mystery behind baklava's origins helped Mehmet cement his point.

"Food doesn't ever come from one place," he said. "It is a fusion. Recipes are always a synthesis."

After saying our goodbyes, he returned to his dash between tables, ensuring the satisfaction of his guests, flashing a wide smile, and nodding his head.

Target Practice and the Dutchman of San Marcos

I was ready for conflict field training to begin for one simple reason—the bathroom bug had returned.

Before Melanie's early April departure, I was awoken in the middle of the night on a few occasions by her shrieks.

"There's a cockroach in the bathroom!" she said as I slipped between slumber and consciousness. Yet every time I went for a follow up investigation, nothing. She started calling it "the bathroom bug," which struck her as easier to stomach than calling it what it was—an enormous, gnarly cockroach.

I began to tease her when I'd search more thoroughly the morning after alleged sightings.

"My stars and stripes!" I shuddered in a mock southern woman's accent. "The bathroom bug has escaped again!"

Then, one night, natured called. I rolled out of bed, stepped onto the hardwood floor, walked out of the room, and flipped on the bathroom light. And there it was, grimacing at me as if to say, *Surprise!*

My sleepy haze immediately shot to full alert, all hands on deck. Then, after a brief moment of deliberation, I decided I didn't want to touch it, trap it or squash it. This was my first sighting and Melanie had never seen it in the morning. This wasn't an emergency bathroom situation, so I closed the door, and told my bladder it would have to wait.

As planned, it was gone the next morning. But it returned, night after night, seemingly after nine at night for some reason. I changed my schedule accordingly, brushing my teeth early and limiting water consumption after my final visit to the bathroom for the night. Conflict field training was approaching and I'd be out of the apartment soon enough.

Nobody knew what to expect in conflict field training. All we had received was a sheet of paper telling us what to pack and spelling out the fictional scenario that would guide our simulation. It was a mishmash of Guatemalan and Salvadoran Civil War history taking place in the fictional Central American country of San Marcos. I was assigned to a group playing the role of AP journalists who would be staying in an international compound alongside a variety of representatives from international NGOs and a national newspaper. It was admittedly a bit of a stretch that we would all be staying together in a real-life scenario, but the professors were working off a bare bones budget.

Students were instructed to meet at the Super Mora parking lot in Ciudad Colón with bags pack and ready to board the bus to "San Marcos." We still didn't know where we were going, but it was stressed that everyone needed to board the bus in order to start the simulation. This led many of us to believe we would be getting stopped by "authorities" to kick things off. Sure enough, as the same shuttle we used for UPEACE commutes worked its way up the twists and turns to El Rodeo, flashing lights had the bus come to a halt. Some started to snicker as the story began. Even though we knew it was a simulation, it was impossible to suppress the human reaction to want to know what the hell was going on.

A group of harmless looking men dressed in polos boarded the bus and demanded that we get off with our passports in hand. The group of us, twenty or so, stood out in the black as the confusion continued. Only the headlights of the vehicles gave us anything to look at.

It started to become clear why they asked us to bring our passports. They were looking for someone in particular, like, me.

Of course it was me, I thought. I chatted with Andrea about her own experience in a similar simulation for her work with Doctors Without Borders. She shared how she was "kidnapped" on several occasions, making me certain that I would share her fate.

"You'll have to come with us," one of the men told me as he put a blindfold over my eyes. "Stay calm, but you need to get in the car."

That's all it took to hook everyone into the simulation. People started calling out after me as I was taken into the vehicle with a fellow captive.

"Where are you taking them?"

"Who are you?"

"What did they do wrong?"

It didn't matter. We were already driving away.

Riding in the back of a car with a blindfold on was an interesting experience. I started to think more about my other senses since my sight had been taken for me. I was trying to mentally piece together where we were going. It all seems perfectly ridiculous to recount in retrospect, writing as if I were in any danger when I clearly never was, but such was getting absorbed into the simulation.

Eventually we were stopped and taken into some room for questioning, our blindfolds still tied tight. The gist of their suspicion stuck with the script of the simulation. We were the first foreigners coming into the country since everyone had been kicked out following a coup. Drug trafficking was allegedly on the rise, and these guys wanted to make sure we weren't part of the trade.

"No drugs, right? No drugs?" one man asked repeatedly, raising his voice each time before switching tones. "Tranquilo, amigos. Tranquilo."

Before long, they seemed to buy our story, escorting us back to the vehicle, and taking us to our compound. (I later learned that where we were taken for questioning was the UPEACE security booth. I walked by it every morning before class.)

The compound, we now knew, was UPEACE property. I was initially disappointed that we couldn't be some place truly unknown to help fuel the scenario, but I was too busy recounting the experience to my colleagues already laying out their sleeping bags over the tile floor.

"I recorded it all on my iPhone," I whispered to my partner. "They searched my pockets, but missed it." It was a bold move I'm certain I would never try in real life.

The simulation was planned to last a week. Every group had a set of responsibilities they needed to cover each and every day, but they were all generally the same: talk to locals, figure out what's going on. We learned early on that there wouldn't be much time to carry out our assignments as the first of many threats from local "narcos" came our first morning.

We had been out in the woods with Carl, a Dutch military man working as a visiting professor. His job was to equip us with survival skills over the week, such as starting a fire, building a shelter, and how to stay in shape. When we returned from our first session, there was a message on the bathroom windows written in "blood," demanding that we leave immediately. Such threats would continue throughout the scenario until the narcos attacked one morning an hour or so before sunrise.

I snapped out of deep sleep as explosives started going off

outside our compound. We had previously wasted hours debating whether or not we should have a rotating night watch should nefarious individuals come in the middle of the night. Narcos were already threatening us and drunken locals looking to party visited us, leaving unhappily when we refused to join them. After showing they were heavily armed, the leader threatened a particularly divisive member of our compound (the Frenchman crazy about Occupy Wall Street hand signals, coincidentally) and sped off on his motorcycle. Suffice it to say, we had reason to want around-the-clock security.

We were working with an incredibly indecisive group, though, many of whom refused to work in traditional power structures with leaders making decisions. Anyone with so much as the smallest objection could send our discussions back to the drawing board. It was as ineffectual a process as it sounds, and we could see our professors rolling their eyes in frustration, trying to remain silent. With this attack from our new narco friends, a new appreciation for decision making grew.

The biggest surprise came in their entrance. They actually did break a window and climbed through, bringing a sense of reality and shock to some who had struggled to accept the scenario.

"Get on the floor! Stomachs on the ground! Hands behind your back!" they yelled in Spanish. Silent murmurs started to fill the room as students translated for one another, something the invaders didn't appreciate.

"Shut up, bitch!" one of the female assailants yelled. "Look at this whore!" she said, laughing as she pulled someone's head up by her hair, another assailant laughing along.

Indeed, shit got real.

Over in my corner, a gunman appeared and started questioning my partner.

"Who are you? What're you doing here?"

I started translating for her at which point the gunman shoved his weapon into my temple.

"Otra palabra y voy a matarte!" he yelled. "Another word and I'll kill you!"

Duly noted, I thought.

After questioning a non-Spanish speaker went nowhere, he turned his attention to me.

"Are you married?" he asked.

"Yes," I responded, immediately realizing I probably should have lied.

"What's her name?"

"Karen," I said, thinking I could at least lie about the name.

"I thought her name was Melanie?" he responded.

Shit, I thought. "Oh, uh, yeah. Sorry. I didn't understand." For this, they pulled my head up by my hair as well and let it drop to the hard floor below.

The scenario continued with the narcos taking out hostages, who we thought for sure were goners. As soon as they left, I freed my hands and helped a couple of others before wondering if we should make a run for it. A small group of us decided it was a good idea, so we set off running through the backdoor where we had previously seen some brush to hide behind. Unfortunately for me, in the black of the early morning, I missed the ledge that dropped a good six feet to a dry ravine and went tumbling over. Another fell alongside me and we held our positions for over thirty minutes of quiet until we started hearing distant screams.

"Ayúdame! Ayúdame!" or "Help me! Help me!"

We wondered if this was a trap or if running out toward screaming people would get us all killed. Someone from our compound came out a little later to let us know it was safe to come up, and so we returned to a room of bloodied men lying on the floor as some people tried to give them aid.

"It was the narcos... the narcos," they cried.

"They're hurt, we're not medical, and they say it was the

narcos. We should split," I said to my fellow media representatives.

This is where it was subconsciously difficult to keep to the scenario. Even though we were in "San Marcos," I really did know my surroundings. I knew where it was safe and I knew paths around the nearby UPEACE park where we could run and hide. Yes, one of the actors gave a line saying that area was dangerous and owned by the narcos, but I didn't buy it. I ran those trails countless times between class and lunch back when it was "Costa Rica." So whenever the question of fleeing came up, I always voted in the affirmative and almost certainly flummoxed how the professors saw things playing out.

By the end of this scenario, a good number of us had gone hiding behind the front wall of a local's home (one of the student's in reality). Carl came running down, calling the scenario off. Apparently there was concern that we'd run into some poisonous snakes given the early hour and our rustling around the woods.

Back at the compound, we learned that two of our colleagues were not actually goners. In fact, we were expected to stay and negotiate. None of this came through to us in the midst of the fireworks.

We then sat for a brief discussion with the actors, many of whom were UPEACE employees, to talk about our reactions and how we did both individually and as a group. It also gave me the opportunity to figure out how this random narco knew my wife's real name.

"Hey, Joe!" said Enrique with his disguise revealed. He was smiling that "I know something you don't know" smile. "Why did you lie about Melanie?" he asked.

"That was you?"

"Yep! Sorry if I pushed the gun too hard into your head." I did notice a bruise there.

Enrique, besides proudly serving as a fictional narco, was the school nurse at UPEACE. Melanie had met him not long before leaving, mentioning that she was my wife.

"I'll let Melanie know you almost killed me," I offered.

While I enjoyed the simulation plenty, there was a fair amount of frustration in dealing with the indecisiveness of the group. Toward the end I started to mentally tap out, agreeing to go with the group even if I disagreed just for the sake of moving along on a decision.

What I consistently appreciated were the training sessions with Carl and other visiting instructors. After the narcos scare, we were instructed by Costa Rican officers (who participated as narcos) on medic situations and how to pull an injured comrade from a dangerous situation without putting yourself in danger. We were on our stomachs, crawling across gravel and dragging a gurney with our instructors yelling at us to "keep your head down!" A volunteer fire department came out to start a fire then show us, hands on, how to put it out safely. Then there was the firing range in Escazú.

Yes, the firing range. The University For Peace shuttled us to a firing range in the middle of the simulation. I had heard rumors of previous classes going, but they were always unconfirmed. The American in me couldn't imagine a university taking students to a firing range without so much as signing a waiver, but such was the Tico way. In the States, we have to sign waivers for damn near everything.

Borrowing skis at a resort? Sign here stating you won't sue after crashing into a tree.

Going whitewater rafting? Jot your initials here, here, and here stating we get off scot free should you hurl yourself idiotically at some rocks we told you to avoid.

Signed up for surf lessons? Kindly supply your John Hancock

on the bottom line, agreeing that you're Poseidon's property now.

I don't think I had ever signed anything before in Costa Rica declaring I would not sue if I did something stupid to myself. A litigious coffee drinker ordering a hot brew would not fair well here, so I suppose it shouldn't be surprising to know I could get to a firing range without too much trouble.

Though Escazú is home to the largest North American population in Costa Rica, I had never been before. I thought I'd at least make it out of morbid curiosity to see what a purely Gringo town in Costa Rica looked like, but I never made much of an effort. So why not a trip to go fire some weapons sans training or experience?

My first and only visit came with a shuttle drop-off on the side of a derelict street that reminded me of industrial Cleveland. The building, Poligono Centro de Defensa Civil, was nothing more than a giant concrete block. But what more does one need for a place where you fire weapons?

Inside there were tables for waiting parties to sit and one man behind the counter where we filled out forms if we were interested in firing a few rounds. To my surprise, we were presented with something to sign before being given a loaded weapon.

Before getting sent off to the range, we were escorted upstairs to the classroom to discuss the firearms we would be working with and their presence in conflict zones. Our teacher was a man named Jorge, who started by sharing his reasoning for owning a gun. A few years ago, he was robbed of his personal possessions and car on his way home from work. This was enough to convince him that he needed a gun. From there, he began firearms training. He realized he liked it and continued all the way to working at the firing range where he gives lessons and even proctors the exams anyone has to take in order to get a license for a weapon. Shaking his head, he admitted that the exam is far too easy, allowing for too many wrong answers.

"You all could probably pass it right now, your first try," he said. But he doesn't feel he's ever sold guns to anyone interested in anything other than self-defense. Only once did he feel suspicious of someone calling in for an order of tens of thousands of dollars. Rather than anger someone with lots of money and a clear interest in weaponry, he fibbed, and said they didn't and wouldn't have the requested weapons in stock. That was that.

By all accounts, Jorge was a knowledgeable, friendly, and a pleasant enough man. He was familiar with international law and easily recounted examples of gun law from around the globe. There was no question that this guy loved guns, sincerely believing that anyone who doesn't own a gun for personal protection is foolish.

I'm a left-leaning American. The American part means I understand guns in the context that there's a mass shooting in the United States every day. The left-leaning part means I think they're largely unnecessary and far too readily available. I don't know the explicit answer for my country's weapon woes, but I do know that an instrument of death should be more difficult to procure than Sudafed. Without hesitation, I can say I fully loathe and despise guns in the same way I loathe anything else that kills around 40,000 of my countrymen and women annually.

That said, I'm also all for hearing new perspectives. I appreciated Jorge's expertise and willingness to engage with a classroom of students who he wasn't about to win over to gun ownership anytime soon.

To my surprise, everyone without exception was willing to experience firing a gun at the range. There were no protests, no blanket condemnation. Even our Occupy Wall Street hand waving friend appeared giddy for the opportunity despite having argued with Jorge until our professor politely told him to shut his trap.

I was one of the first to step into the firing range, following the instructions of both Jorge and Carl, who was asked to assist given his own passion for firearms and background in weapons training. With my protective glasses and shooting earmuffs on, I watched as Jorge instructed the first student on the proper grip, stance and how to line up the shot. The sound was even louder than I imagined. How do criminals and warlords, none of whom appear to additionally arm themselves with earmuffs, not suffer from loss of hearing?

Then it was my turn, shooting from two weapons that I was most likely to find in the field should I pursue working in conflict zones: the AR-15 that NATO uses and a common handgun. Jorge had previously shown us how to disarm them in the classroom— a piece of knowledge I wish stuck with me but was quickly lost in the flurry of adrenaline, nerves and excitement.

I lined up in my stance, feet slightly wider than shoulder-width and squared up with the target. I slowly raised my weapon with Jorge standing at my side. He always stayed at the student's side, I assumed to prevent them from stupidly turning around to ask a question with a loaded weapon in their hands.

From there, I lifted the gun and aimed at my target using the sight as instructed.

"Don't just pull the trigger," Jorge instructed. "Take a deep breath and let your finger do it naturally."

It felt like a minute had passed between my breath and when my finger finally applied enough pressure to the trigger to fire. The recoil was surprising. I had heard about the recoil from my father, who worked as a probation officer before I was born. He, too, detested guns, (smartly) never letting us so much as own a toy gun during our childhood. With children on the way, he quit his job as a probation officer because he didn't want a gun in the house. Despite all that, he had imparted some gun knowledge onto me years ago, noting that the proper gun stance is what it is in order to handle the powerful recoil.

Still, the recoil was a shock to the system. I felt as if the gun was literally trying to leap from my hands. My nerves never entirely cooled for the remainder of my rounds. Yet when Jorge pressed the button to bring my target in for examination, all of my shots hit.

"You could be a Costa Rican police officer," he joked.

Conflict field training ended early after our decisions appeared to exhaust all options in the scenario. One morning we were approached by one of the players, saying the leader of the area's Autodefensa requested our presence at his compound early that afternoon. Everyone was expected to attend without exception. Of course none of us thought that was an entirely good idea, so a handful did stay behind.

We marched for about twenty minutes down the familiar El Rodeo road that we were imagining was a war-torn street of San Marcos. His compound, it turned out, was the old home of UPEACE radio. After years of neglect, the building did mesh quite well with my Hollywood image for sketchy warlord headquarters.

Two guards (evil henchmen) greeted us at the metal gate, which we had to squeeze through in order to enter. We were lined up, searched, relieved of our phones, and escorted into the compound over gravel, broken glass and concrete. One person from each group was instructed to sit at the front while the others moved to the back. I was one. Moments later, a bald white man with a goatee dressed in shades and a suit walked in yelling Dutch into a cell phone. It was Carl taking on the role of Autodefensa commander.

I admit seeing Carl took me out of the scenario for a moment, though it wasn't entirely farfetched. A Dutch woman by the name of Tanja Nijmeijer studied at the University of Groningen before moving to Colombia in 1998 to teach English. In 2002, she made a second trip to Colombia to join the Revolutionary Armed Forces of Colombia better known by its acronym, FARC. Ms. Nijmeijer has since moved up the ranks to become one of the more prominent leaders of FARC, even playing a role in negotiations with the government. She's also been indicted by a U.S. court on kidnapping charges and could face up to sixty years if extradited and convicted.

So evil Dutch leader in Latin America wasn't complete fantasy.

Carl, in character, trotted out one of our own who had been captured and turned to the side of Autodefensa.

"He's happy here! Right, Steve?" To which our fellow student nodded like a good puppet.

From there he asked how we could help him in his cause to rid San Marcos of its government and narcos. He even offered us a toast of vodka, something I assumed we weren't actually supposed to drink, but I saw little way around it.

As expected, his tone turned heated. He had his comrades escort a select few out back for one reason or another before turning his sights back to the group leaders. It was eventually decided that we were all useless to his cause.

"There will be a bus sent to pick you up in one hour. You will all be on that bus. Anyone I find left behind will be mine."

Silence.

"Well, go already!" he shouted, sending everyone to their feet. "Except you," he said, pointing to me.

The group sprinted ahead as I was left behind.

"Useless," he repeated as he walked in circles. "Stand up against the wall," he demanded. "See how quickly they left you? They don't care about you. Join my cause and you can help me."

I went through the best script I could come up with,

something about how, "I'm media and could best serve your cause telling your story to an international public." Of course this did nothing to satisfy him and I was instructed to flee as well. By now I had less time, and was forced to sprint back to our compound with a shot of vodka sloshing around in my stomach.

"After vodka? Seriously?" I jokingly shouted at Kevin, one of the instructors I passed on the way in a brief, light-hearted moment.

Back at the compound, there was the usual cocktail of confusion, indecisiveness and panic. Nobody wanted to board the bus when it arrived. Some of us, myself included, weren't even sure if we were included on his list of people to board the bus. So we did as we had been doing all along and fled to the familiar grounds of UPEACE Park even though the scenario said it was dangerous. A Tico not involved in the scenario approached me slowly as I hid behind an empty bus on my way to the park.

"What's going on?" he asked, noticing packs of students running around with suitcases.

"It's just a simulation. We're pretending," I said, stepping out of character for a moment. Because we never knew the extent of the simulation, we had to pretend everyone was involved, making for some awkward conversations with locals who clearly weren't. There was the Tico in his truck late at night who we thought was a spy of sorts. Turned out he was just using the university's WiFi to check Facebook. Then there was Nelson, the adored naturalist resident of El Rodeo who played the fitting role of a naturalist in San Marcos. Instead of leaving the compound after his scenario was complete, he completely dropped character.

"That was fun! You guys did a good job," he exclaimed. Only in San Marcos, I suppose.

Carl eventually found us hiding in the park, but he was wearing his street clothes, indicating that he was back in "ghost mode" and not in his role. After ten or so minutes of standing around, crouched behind a wooden sign with our belongings in tow, the professors called the scenario and asked us to return to base where we were informed that the simulation was over. As unrealistic as many aspects of the simulation were, for the sake of experiencing as much as possible, the professors said there was no way any of us would stay in a country like San Marcos after the week we had.

"You've been threatened, attacked, and told to leave the country or be killed," our head instructor said. "All of you would enact your emergency evacuation plans at this point and be gone."

Although the end of the simulation got me out of night watch duty at two in the morning, I was sad to have it end. I had gotten used to sleeping on the ground in my hiking clothes and boots, prepared to wake up in less than thirty seconds if necessary. Besides, we ended the simulation earlier than originally anticipated. Was less than a week really enough? At the beginning, Carl had pointed out that we needed at least two weeks for the simulation to prove truly effective. I wanted to continue, dammit! Then I got home and had my first hot shower in over five days. All was forgiven.

Still, I felt like I did walk away with skills and knowledge that will stick with me. Conflict field training had inarguably been one of the most, if not the most, beneficial courses in my life. While I had no aspirations to embed myself in the frontline of a military unit, wearing a bulletproof vest that read "PRESS" across my chest, I realized many of the skills I learned in that brief time would prepare me for following my ambitions. I envisioned myself traveling to more countries, like El Salvador, that are technically out of conflict but are still feeling the ramifications of war. Too many journalists pack up and leave as soon as the peace treaty is signed. There's little to no follow up with the citizens of that country. I saw myself traveling to those countries and telling their story, and maybe even enticing others to visit for themselves. After all, there's no better testament to what's going on in the world than seeing it for yourself.

That night, I went to sleep feeling more justified than ever before in my decision to study abroad at UPEACE. I had traveled extensively through Costa Rica, El Salvador, Guatemala and Panama. I learned a new language, experienced different cultures, and learned more about my own country and what I want out of life in the process. What more could I ask for?

The glow lasted all through the night. That is, until nature called and I trudged into the bathroom to see my old friend had returned.

"Dammit!" I shrieked. "I forgot about the bathroom bug."

¡upe! (*oo*·pe)
exclamation

1. A verbal knock, because many Costa Rican homes have fences surrounding the property. You couldn't physically knock even if you wanted.

Example: "¡Upe! Anyone home?"

Despedida

It was a strange feeling to wake up to a nearly empty apartment on my final morning, June 1, 2014. It should have looked the same as it did when I first arrived with Melanie back in August, yct it felt hollowed out. I refused to dwell on it too long, lest those pesky feelings and emotions rear their ugly head and force this stereotypical Midwesterner to deal with them.

Back under the rug, I say!

Instead, I kept myself busy, finishing any last minute packing, watching something on my laptop, and exchanging texts with Melanie. I did keep an eye out for Esteban to make sure I'd have a chance to say goodbye. As soon as I heard the clang of Carolina sliding the front gate open to let the dogs out, I ran downstairs to offer my final "Buenos días" and let her know to call me down when Esteban was leaving.

Fifteen minutes or so later, I caught Esteban on his way out. He pulled up his car up to the gate, parked and stepped out to give me one last hug and slap on the back.

"Keep in touch and I hope the best for you and Melanie," he offered. This was the first goodbye of someone I knew I wouldn't be seeing again for a long time that I actually cared about. I can't overstate how cool Esteban is. The man just drips awesomeness. I just think of his thunderous laugh anytime I need a pick-me-up. He always made Melanie and I laugh and really did feel like a father of sorts during our short time in Costa Rica. The same goes for Carolina. Both couldn't have been more welcoming to a couple of linguistically-challenged Gringos. We still talk about how lucky we were to live above them, especially after hearing horror stories from other students.

At Juan Santamaría, I stepped out of Ramiro's car the last time. He gave me a hug, just as he did with Melanie two months ago after her final ride. Considering the amount of business we gave him with all our airport runs, I suspect he was sad to see us go, too.

Costa Rica has its issues, including increasing violent crime, sex trade with minors, and a growing role in the international drug trade—pretty much everything you don't want to see go up. I'll never forget my surprise when I first saw the macabre commonly displayed in Costa Rican newspapers: mangled corpses of the victims of traffic crashes or those gunned down in some crime. Even more interesting was sometimes catching a live drug raid on television in the early morning hours on Canal 7.

There are stories that are antithetical to the pura vida narrative. One in particularly has burrowed its way into my memory.

Twenty-two-year-old Gerardo Cruz Barquero was celebrated after uploading a video that went viral in which he caught an employee of the Ministry of Finance filming up a woman's dress in San José. Gerardo can be heard confronting the man in the video that went on to receive millions of views. His actions started a movement to criminalize street harassment. Sadly, on his way to a media interview, assailants stabbed Gerardo twice. Most assumed it was retaliation, but police say the two events were unrelated. Nevertheless, Gerardo died six weeks later.

It's not all tragedy. There are the mundanities of everyday life in Costa Rica, too, of course. Weather, traffic, weather and traffic again. Ticos are very much like North Americans in this regard, except instead of complaining about the snow in the winter, they complain about the strong gusts of wind in December that smacks you across the face without warning. Nature's sucker punch, if you will.

We also learned what it's like to cycle in San José with ChepeCletas, a non-profit organization pushing for a cultural change away from cars and toward "active mobility." A young Tico named José from Alajuela met us early one Saturday morning near their office headquarters in Barrio Amón. He was in his early twenties and I saw a lot of myself in him when I was that age. José shared that he was excited to move into downtown San José the first chance he got, realizing he hates long commutes and vehicular transportation much in the same way I started to at that stage in my life.

Curious, I asked him about the relationship between cyclists and cars.

"Not good," he said. "There are a lot of problems."

It was easy for me to empathize. As a fellow cyclist, I knew too well of how reckless drivers could be around cyclists. The number of times I've been honked at, yelled at and given close calls by over-eager motorists are countless.

Frankly it was this carelessness that had me slightly concerned about cycling in San José. I had seen cyclists and motorists share the road peaceably in Costa Rica before, but read stories across the country of drivers mowing over everyone from pedestrians to my two-wheeled brethren. But I didn't let cars keep me off the road in the States, so I wasn't going to in Costa Rica. We also had the added benefit of cycling relatively early in the morning on a Saturday, well before much vehicular traffic took over the streets.

Though José's English appeared to be superior to our Spanish, he humored us nonetheless and spoke mostly in Spanish, as so many other obliging Ticos had done before. We cruised for something around a brisk seven kilometers that mostly wrapped around Barrio Escalante, stopping only a couple of times—first early on outside an old entrance to the Simón Bolivar Zoo.

"It's a pretty disgusting place," José said, confirming what we had heard from other Ticos.

I was frankly surprised a zoo even existed. Cramming wild animals into small cages hardly seemed the Tico way, hence my earlier objection to the jaguar at La Paz Waterfall Gardens. I later learned environmentalists had come close to shutting the zoo down in recent years, but the zoo fought back and came to an agreement with the government to remain open for at least another ten years.

Our only other memorable stop came at the Fería Verde organic market, coincidentally ending our final visit to San José together at one of our first stops back in August. We torpedoed down Calle 15 on our beater bikes until running into parked cars trying to navigate a congested parking lot.

"See?" José said looking back. "Much better on a bike."

I'll remember hearing someone yell, "Upe!" outside of our apartment. It was always someone selling something. Each time we heard it, Melanie and I would lock eyes and go into a quiet, power-saving mode until the solicitor left. Once I engaged with an "Upe!" thinking it might be a friend of Esteban and Carolina's. She seemed young and was holding a small child instead of carrying bags of fruit or vegetables to sell like all the others.

"Hola! ¿Como estás?" I called out over our balcony. "Are you looking for Esteban or Carolina?" She seemed confused before responding.

"I'm walking around the neighborhood to collect money so I

can buy diapers for my daughter," she said as she rocked the little girl in her arms.

My heart immediately broke. We're trained in the States to be cautious about giving money directly to solicitors rather than donating to a charity. By donating to a charity, you supposedly know the money is going where it needs to go. The only time I had given money in Costa Rica was when a man in maybe his forties boarded a bus, asking for any spare change after he shared his sad story in the form of a sales pitch. I had read about these bus speeches in the past. You either give or don't. There's no aggressiveness on the part of the solicitor and no expectation. Most Ticos, it appeared, do give, and so I obliged with one of my colón coins. Having it happen at my home hit me differently and caught me off guard for some reason.

"Oh, I'm sorry. I really don't have any change. I'm sorry." I kept repeating as she continued in her plea for help.

"Please. Anything will help."

"I'm sorry. I really don't have anything." I said once more as I sheepishly ducked back into the apartment and out of sight until she moved onto the next house.

I've grown to hate the inherent distrust of those less fortunate we learn at an early age. See a homeless person on the street? Leave them alone. Somebody asks you for change? Ignore them.

That said, I really don't know what the answer is. All I know is that "upe" lost its charm for me.

Like Cleveland, I eventually found things to be annoyed with, such as the sound of motorists speeding up the hill outside of the apartment, their engines drilling into my ears no matter how late the hour. I couldn't stand how drivers blew through stop signs or even red lights, a frustration of Ticos, too, evidenced by a petition drive in Ciudad Colón to enforce safe driving.

There was the comical, too, like when after a Sunday morning of playing volleyball I noticed I had stepped into something on the way back. I took my sandal off to observe. There was a light brown blob, and it wasn't mud, folks.

"Haha!" went Esteban's booming laugh. "Caca en tu sandalia" or "Shit on your sandal!" he shouted, unable to contain his laughter. "Huele feo" or "Smells bad," he told me as I passed the apartment gate, plugging his nose with one hand and waving the other.

I'll also remember Costa Rica for more than the experiences recounted in this book, experiences that when recalled bring an image to my mind and spark a smile or brief memory, like Thanksgiving with a mixture of expatriates, traveling Gringos and Ticos at the B&B in Brasil de Mora where both Melanie's parents and my aunt stayed while visiting. There was the "gender bender party" thrown by a group of UPEACE students. Melanie looked convincing in my tee shirt, jeans and baseball cap, but if I may be so bold, I surely stole the show in my flowery white dress and healthy helping of eyeshadow.

I'll remember the good fortune we had to experience some of the best hotels we had ever seen, like Finca Rosa Blanca in Heredia province where we stayed on a coffee farm just outside of San José and a short drive from Parque Nacional Braulio Carrillo. In fact, that weekend, toward the end of our time in Costa Rica, was probably one of our most memorable weekends yet it hardly felt eventful enough to recount in greater detail. It was the good kind of uneventful where one recharges their batteries and breathes fresh air.

The scenery was exquisite. It felt remote, yet we could still walk to the nearby town of Santa Barbara if so inclined. Nearby Braulio Carrillo, too, was one of our favorite national parks. Tourism is for all intents and purposes non-existent in the area, explaining why it remains a rarity in travel itineraries compared to some of Costa Rica's more traveled national parks.

Indeed, what led us to Finca Rosa Blanca in the first place was the fact that it was one of the few places that advertised transportation to Braulio Carrillo. Unfortunately our time was limited there. What reading there is on the park says it's a fantastic camping ground for a multi-day excursion, but we still enjoyed ourselves immensely hiking up to the view of the Volcán Barva crater lake, quiet now for over 8,000 years. Naturally there are powers hoping to bring more tourism to the area, but considering its creation story—an agreement achieved by lobbying environmentalists following the construction of Ruta 32 through the park—I can't help but hope they continue leaving it alone.

At the end of the day, what I'll appreciate most about Costa Rica are the Ticos and their lifestyle. While I generally disdain broadly characterizing a group of people, it feels safe to say that Ticos really do have a *pura vida* mentally, a genuine belief that everything will be okay in the end. They very much believe that you work to live, not live to work. Some might read that as a pledge of laziness, but I'd put up the average Tico's work ethic against a North American any day of the week. Esteban always impressed me with his ability to keep a smile on his face despite nearly twelve-hour days that started with his morning commute around a quarter past six. Even after that, he'd return to working household chores into the late hour, but was always willing to take a break and split a couple of beers and share a laugh. I never saw the man asleep or tired. The man is a machine. Seriously, Esteban rules!

And who doesn't love the pacifism embedded in Costa Rican culture? Yes, their police force in many ways can act like a standing military (we saw a hint of that at El Clásico), but visit the national museum in San José and you'll notice a distinct lack of wars along their chronological timeline. It's a stark contrast for any U.S. American who can mark periods of time by what war we were in or who we were bombing.

This doesn't mean Costa Rica's government is perfect. Far from, and you'll hear Ticos complain about corruption and incompetence across the country. But I never heard the calls to radicalism that I've seen in the U.S. or even parts of Europe. I'm always amazed to see some Americans fretting over the loss of freedom, to which I always wonder, "What am I not allowed to do now that I was before?" Ticos, for the most part, seemed to remain generally optimistic—even through that soul crushing rainy season. (Truth be told, I was giddy when the first, far shorter and more tolerable storms started to return in May.)

My goal in writing this was in part to fill a hole. When I first thought of visiting (much less living in Costa Rica) I wanted to read about someone else's experiences, and learn a thing or two about the history and what's going on today. There wasn't much out there, save name brand guidebooks—some of which did prove useful in offering suggestions on places to visit and their history.

I hope those unfamiliar with Costa Rica and Central America got something out of this much in the same way I did when I first read Bill Bryson's *A Walk in the Woods* or *Swiss Watching* by Diccon Bewes. I'm also well aware that this account hardly covers everything worthy of being discussed in Costa Rica. Missing Carnival in Limón immediately comes to mind, as does cave-diving in Parque Nacional Barra Honda, and the cyclist in me regrets not finding my way to the three-day La Ruta de los Conquistadores, "the toughest mountain bike race on the planet" that retraces the conquistadors by my favorite mode of transportation.

I wish we had made more friends, something living in tiny Ciudad Colón made difficult. We talked about moving to Barrio Amón or Barrio Escalante in San José and getting more involved with ChepeCletas had we stayed another year. And of course, as we had terrific experiences in Panama, Guatemala and El Salvador—the latter proving truly impactful—we wish we had finished the isthmus by traveling to Nicaragua, Honduras (beyond our terrifying landing in Tegucigalpa on our return from Guatemala) and Belize.

If you expected an all-encompassing approach going in, I apologize. But I also started by saying this ten-month stay would be a year-long venture, so I suppose my words can be rather meaningless at times. Ultimately I tried to share what I found most interesting during my experience and upon reflection. I could have talked about the visit to the jade museum in San José or I could have really brought your imagination to life by offering an image of myself, shirtless and in athletic shorts, sitting on our couch with my arms spread out and my head dangling backward as I groaned, unable to rid our apartment of the humidity and heat. But I wanted to spare you those moments, dear Reader, only mentioning them now for the possibility of a cheap laugh at my expense and your understanding for why I wrote this the way I did.

I must admit I had a higher purpose, if you can stomach that, for moving to Costa Rica. I wanted to figure some shit out, in layman's terms. What am I doing with my life? Considering the cosmos is estimated to be nearly 13.8 billion years old, I've long since given up on achieving some sort of historic immortality, and childhood dreams of being cast in a remake of *Indiana Jones* have begun to fade. Still, I've known for a long time that I want to do something impactful during my brief time around this planet. I've also learned that I need to keep it realistic, unlike my younger aspirations to be a three-sport first round draft pick. My brother Dave quickly lassoed those dreams out from the Heavens and gave them a swift, merciful death.

"You're not going to play professional basketball," he once put it bluntly during a time of my childhood when my father was still trying to convince me I could do anything I put my mind to.

Needing to stay realistic, I searched for opportunities to do good deeds within my areas of interest. Since maturing through my twenties, travel has without question become my passion in life. But not just travel, rather the possibilities of travel. Travel changes minds, exchanges ideas and generally makes people around the world hate each other a little less. I'm a firm believer in what Alexander von Humboldt once said: "The most dangerous worldview is the worldview of those who have not viewed the world." I've been exceptionally fortuitous to see some of the world. So what can I do with that?

Traveling to El Salvador especially showed me that something in me gets indescribably excited in telling stories people don't expect to hear. It continues to bother me when people flatly dismiss an entire region and its people as "too dangerous."

Now for as much as I admittedly brushed off UPEACE at times, I genuinely did enjoy conflict field training. Something about that experience resonated with me. Again, I sincerely doubt I'd have the stones to embed myself in a military unit.

I do enjoy venturing to places that are underrepresented in the world of tourism and travel writing. Perhaps that's my thing then; traveling to destinations smacked with an unflattering or unfamiliar image, and telling a different story based on the people living there and showcasing that to anyone who will pay attention. Sure, it's hardly a life of fortune, but money doesn't follow you to the grave. It's something that at least gets me excited, and for that I have Costa Rica to thank.

If nothing else, that's a start.

Acknowledgements

Oh, boy! We're at the part where I thank people. That must mean I'm really going through with publishing this thing one way or another. Who would've thought that'd happen?

Anyway, let the thanking begin!

My family can go at the top of this list. Nobody has been more supportive of my career or just, y'know, me in general than my parents, Rodger and Jan, my brother, Dave, his wife (my *cuñada*) Holly, my Aunt Barb, and of course my beautiful, glowing, *complimentary adjective* wife, Melanie, who has the patience of a saint and the most forgiving heart to put up with a meandering and flawed buffoon, such as myself, cursed with constantly itchy feet and the attention span of a drug-addled hyena. I could ramble on for hours on how thankful and indebted to her I am for not only following me along to Costa Rica, but for sticking with me and supporting me endlessly through thick and thin.

Now I can move onto thanking my new family, *mi mama y papa Ticos*. Not only did they give us a home (sure, we compensated with rent), but they treated Melanie and myself like family. They made our little apartment actually feel like home.

Jess Simms gets exceptional thanks for editing this project. Her notes often saved me from myself, encouraging me to get to the point and scrap "the shoe leather." I'm emboldened to write another book if only because she definitely deserves more money. If you write a book, you should have her edit it. You can contact her at drunkenjester.wordpress.com.

Sarah Hinnenkamp offered invaluable initial edits and can be reached at mccurdywriting.com. I owe a considerable amount of gratitude to Alicia Underlee Nelson who has proven to be an invaluable writing partner and critic, constantly insisting that I share how certain things made me feel despite my own insistence that I felt nothing. Find her at prairiestylefile.com. I'm also grateful to Rob Williams, who with vague instructions quickly designed a book cover that I quite like.

Everyone I worked with at *The Tico Times*, specifically their managing editor who thought it worthwhile to contact me when they had some room for another writer. Katherine Stanley's "Maeology" column was especially useful in learning more of the background behind some of Costa Rica's unique vocabulary. I'm also thankful for the opportunity to work with *The Tico Times* where small portions of this book were originally printed in some form.

Florence Quesada Avendaño was kind enough to look for historical inaccuracies and to offer corrections or clarifications. Still, it's possible I misinterpreted or included something on my own after the fact that she didn't get a chance to check, so it goes without saying that any misinformation currently in the book is my own dumb fault.

I'm additionally grateful to the fine folks at the University For Peace, most notably a certain Canadian and Austrian professor whom I especially enjoyed throughout my program.

Then there's you, dear Reader, who took a chance on a self-published venture. I truly hope you enjoyed this peek in and around Costa Rica.

About The Author

Joe Baur is a travel writer, filmmaker and author. This is his fourth book. He's also the creator of Without A Path, the host of The Germany Travel Show, and has contributed to a variety of international travel publications. He loves a fried egg on a variety of meats, but hates pretending someone else wrote this bio. Now he lives and works out of Düsseldorf, Germany.

Find more of Joe's work at joebaur.com.

Printed in Great Britain
by Amazon

44075162R00198